D1198632

THE LIVING THOUGHT OF SAINT PAUL

THE LIVING THOUGHT OF SAINT PAUL

An Introduction to Pauline Theology Through Intensive Study of Key Texts

Second Edition

GEORGE T. MONTAGUE, S.M.

*Professor in Biblical Studies
of the Faculty of Theology
University of St. Michael's College
and
The Toronto School of Theology*

Benziger
A division of Glencoe Publishing Co., Inc.
Encino, California

NIHIL OBSTAT:
J. Terence Forestall, C.S.B.
Censor Deputatus

IMPRIMATUR:
† Philip F. Pocock
Archbishop of Toronto
April 22, 1976

The nihil obstat and The nihil obstat and imprimatur are official declarations that a book or pamphlet is free of doctrinal or moral error. No implication is contained therein that those who have granted the nihil obstat and imprimatur agree with the contents, opinions or statements expressed.

Copyright © 1976 by Benziger Bruce & Glencoe, Inc.

All rights reserved. No part of this book may be reproduced or transmitted in any form or by any means, electronic or mechanical, including photocopying, recording or by any information storage and retrieval system, without permission in writing from the Publisher.

Printed in the United States of America

Benziger
A division of Glencoe Publishing Co., Inc.
Glencoe Publishing Co., Inc.
17337 Ventura Boulevard
Encino, California 91316
Collier Macmillan Canada, Ltd.

ISBN 0-02-659680-6

2 3 4 5   84 83 82 81 80

Foreword

Saint Paul is one of the first and the greatest Christian thinkers and writers. Through his fascinating letters, the Church of the apostolic age takes its rightful place in the field of religious literature. Through these letters we of the twentieth century are able to glimpse the problems and difficulties, the triumphs and failures, of second generation Christians. Through these same letters—and this is by far most significant—the Church of subsequent generations was provided with a rich store of theological thought upon which she has continued to live right to our own day of the Second Vatican Council. It is no accident that the letters of Saint Paul continue to provide a major item for the spiritual diet which the Church in her liturgy offers to her children. There is no evangelist whose book is proclaimed at Mass quite as frequently as are the Pauline letters.

Vital is perhaps the term which best characterizes the thought of Saint Paul; and Father Montague has happily drawn attention to this vitality by entitling this splendid book *The Living Thought of Saint Paul*. Someone has said that any genuine piece of literature is the fruit of a dialogue between the author and his contemporary society. This is particularly true of Paul's correspondence with the various Christian communities of the first century Mediterranean world. This very vital personality constantly maintained contact with various sectors of the nascent Christian Church of his day; and as a consequence he stands as a specially privileged witness to the depth of their faith and the high quality of their spirituality. Moreover, through the letters of Paul, we can span the gap of twenty centuries separating us from these early Christians, our brothers in a common faith, and learn how to make that faith relevant to our contemporary society and its problems.

Father Montague has, in the present book, presented us with an anthology of this "living thought" of Saint Paul. He has of necessity restricted himself to certain "key passages." Even a rapid survey of these selections, however, reveals Father Montague's expertise and sure instinct for selecting those readings which best exemplify the vitality of Pauline thought. Can we briefly present the reader with some of Father Montague's reasons for characterizing the thought of Saint Paul as "living"?

Pauline thought is "living," in the first place, because it is *traditional*, that is, it has been fed fully upon the authentic evangelical traditions stemming from Jesus himself and from the apostolic preaching of Jerusalem. In writing to Thessalonica Paul draws upon the same sources for his presentation of the Christian eschatological hope which the Synoptic evangelists made use of. He cites for the Philippians some strophes of an ancient liturgical hymn, deriving probably from Palestinian Christianity. He recalls for the Corinthians the venerable traditions regarding the celebration of the Lord's Supper, the form of the primitive kerygma or gospel and the genuine apostolic faith in the resurrection of the just. Paul will remind the Church of Rome that "the Scriptures" of Israel constitute part of the authentic "gospel of God"; and he will review for this community, as yet unknown to himself, their common heritage of faith from the apostles.

The thought of Saint Paul is "living," in the second place, because it is *creative*. Paul is well aware of the inestimable value of the sayings of Jesus preserved in the living memory of the Church. Yet he does not hesitate to speak in his own name with apostolic freedom and authority. He can order his letters to be read at public worship. For Paul knows that he possesses "the mind of Christ," that he is a man endowed with the Spirit of Christ. Hence he does not hesitate to correct the erroneous ideas concerning the Parousia entertained by some Thessalonians, or to formulate his own arguments against sexual impurity or to point out the significance of Christian virginity for the Corinthian community.

It is perhaps Paul's theology of the redemption which best exemplifies his originality and creativity. He presents the risen Christ as "the last Adam," who through his salutary obedience has reconciled rebellious humanity with God his Father. God's Son entered the world "in the likeness of sinful flesh," and became—as far as was possible for one who was sinless—a member of the sinful family of the first Adam. By his redemptive death Jesus destroyed this ancient, corrupt solidarity: by his resurrection he created the new supernatural family of grace. Yet by dying and rising for mankind, Christ did not intend to excuse or exclude mankind from these two redemptive experiences. Rather, he opened up for men the possibility of the utterly new experience of Christian death, and, ultimately, of rising with Christ to the new life in God. This redemptive process is inaugurated for each Christian by the sacramental experience of dying and rising with Christ in baptism. It is sustained and developed by participation in the Eucharist. In all this, the role of the Holy Spirit is of paramount importance, since it is the Spirit who fosters and develops in the heart of the Christian the consciousness that he is truly one of God's children.

Father Montague has, with the publication of *The Living Thought of Saint Paul*, provided the student of college theology with an effective tool by which he can be introduced to one of the great theologians of the early Church. May this book receive a warm welcome among all who wish to acquire a solid, basic knowledge of the thought of Saint Paul.

DAVID M. STANLEY, S.J.

Regis College
Willowdale, Ontario

ABOUT THE AUTHOR

George T. Montague, S.M., a Marianist priest, did his doctoral dissertation in Pauline theology at the University of Fribourg, Switzerland, in 1960. Since then he taught Scripture at St. Mary's University in San Antonio, Texas, where he was for ten years director of the graduate program in theology. Appointed rector of the Marianist Theologate in St. Louis in 1972, he taught Scripture at the St. Louis University School of Divinity, and when the Theologate was transferred to Toronto in 1974 he was appointed to the Faculty of Theology of the University of St. Michael's College. A popular and internationally known lecturer, he has written widely on scriptural topics and since 1968 has been on the editorial board of *The Catholic Biblical Quarterly*, serving as General Editor 1973–1975.

Author's Introduction

The aim of this book is to give the student an appreciation of Christ as seen through the eyes of the first great theologian of the Church, Paul the Apostle. An attentive study of the Synoptic Gospels reveals that the early Christian community meditated on the significance of the events that had been experienced by eyewitnesses in her midst. These gospel accounts are not just facts but facts with meaning, as this meaning was seen and recorded in the apostolic tradition. The Christian community theologized, and it used as the basic framework its own vivid souvenirs of the Master.

For Saint Paul it was different. Not that he was ignorant of the basic facts of the life, ministry, death, and resurrection of Jesus. These formed the core of the original tradition which Paul transmitted in his preaching. But when it came to theologizing, Paul had different tools to work with. Like the other Apostles, his basic starting point was the resurrection of Christ—no one more than Paul was fired with the conviction of the reality of the risen Lord. But unlike those who took the road of personal memories back to the public life of Jesus, Paul preferred the road he knew better—Scripture and the rabbinical formation of his youth, and his knowledge of the gentile world. He sought, therefore, to understand and explain the risen Lord in relation to: (1) the basic quest of the Israelite for salvation, which he knew, better than any other, had become tied to the observance of the Torah; and (2) to the basic preoccupations of the Gentiles to whom Paul was presenting Christ.

It is in the Apostle of Tarsus above all that we get a real introduction to theology, for we see how Paul, penetrating the Roman Empire with the message of Christ, is faced with questions of doctrine and moral from Jew and Gentile, from persecutor and magistrate and convert. In answer, he not only recalls the basic truths of the kerygma, but deepens his own understanding of them and finds in them ever new depths. For Paul, above all, Christ is the living, risen Lord coming at the end of time but likewise present and active in the Church, transforming and giving meaning to all it experiences.

The riches of Paul's insight lie for us today in his epistles. Yet it must be confessed that many Christians who listen to passages read from those epistles in worship, if asked what they were hearing, would have to reply with Hamlet, "Words, words, words!" One of the chief fruits to be derived from this study of Saint Paul will be an ability to understand better and appreciate more deeply the word of God that comes to us weekly through the Apostle Paul.

There are many ways of approaching the versatile personality and thought of Saint Paul. The many books written on his life naturally have as their chief concern factual material, the events of his journeys, dates, geography, links with events and personages in contemporary history. But there still remains the *thought* of the Apostle, which can never be adequately appreciated by the mere whodunit of his tumultuous career. And if Paul is to be understood at all, he must be understood first as a theologian. At the other end of the spectrum a number of theologies of Saint Paul have appeared, notably the volumes by Father Prat and Canon Cerfaux. These have been attempts to synthesize the Apostle's theology, and their success has made them classical.

However, for the beginning student, they present the difficulty of a ready-made synthesis, leaving the student little of the joy of discovering for himself the progressive heights to which Paul's own developing thought rises. Thus there is a gap between the life story of Paul and the final synthesis of his thought. The present text is an attempt to bridge that gap by setting each epistle in its chronological sequence in Paul's life and then studying intensively those passages most characteristic of the letter, passages which are the pillars on which any final theological synthesis will rest. Obviously the mere limits of space imposed a choice, which rarely will coincide in every instance with the personal preferences of the professor using the text. (The author himself would like to have discussed several other passages, but was forced to tailor his desires to reasonable limits.) But the text calls for a reading of the intervening passages and provides an outline of each epistle for this purpose, and the professor may give any of these the attention he wishes through the use of available commentaries (see the bibliography).

As the student moves through this text, he should first become thoroughly acquainted with the life of Saint Paul; and for this reason it is suggested that during the first half of the semester the student read at least one of the biographies listed in the bibliography. At the same time, he may be directed by the professor or by his own interest to pursue some of the suggested readings occasionally indicated in the text. These have been chosen with some thought as to their availability to English-speaking students in Catholic colleges and universities. In the second half of the semester, after some experience in the analysis of texts, the student is encouraged to begin his own study of some chosen Pauline theme, using the method suggested on p. 230, organizing the results of his study in a paper due toward the end of the semester. The index at the end of the book will also prove helpful here. This method, the author has found from experience, is excellent for leading the student to a personal synthesis, however partial, of the thought of Saint Paul, and frequently to a sustained enthusiasm for Pauline study. Only by this personal involvement can the student prepare himself to appreciate how pertinent for his own life and for the modern world is the living thought of Saint Paul.

THE SECOND EDITION

The second edition has been revised to update bibliography and content not only in the light of important studies made in the years since the first edition but also in the light of emerging concerns in the contemporary Church, light for which is sought in the texts of Paul. The author was not able to make all the revisions he would have liked, but this second edition has incorporated, among other things, some new insights about the mysterious "restrainer" in 2 Thessalonians, about the charisms and charity in 1 Cor 12–14, about marriage in 1 Cor 7, additional background on the resurrection in 1 Cor 15 and the future life in 2 Cor 5, and important considerations about the "wrath of God" in its relation to the saving justice of God in Romans. The success of the first edition and the several printings it went through has confirmed the author's conviction that the best way to study Scripture is through an intensive study of key texts. This method of the "biopsy" offers the student an access to the rest of a given author's work and a method for further personal study, and leaves the teacher free to develop any other texts desired.

GEORGE T. MONTAGUE, S.M.
March 15, 1976

CHRONOLOGY OF PAUL'S LIFE AND LETTERS

(For some of the dates only an approximation is possible.)

(A.D.) Dates	Events in Paul's Life	Documents	Paul's Letters	Contemporary Events
10	Birth of Paul	Acts 7:58; Phm 9		
14–23 (?)	Arrival in Jerusalem; beginning of studies	Acts 22:3; 26:4		Death of Augustus; accession of Tiberius, August 19, A.D. 14. Pilate is procurator 26–36; death of Jesus: 30
34	Stoning of Stephen, Conversion of Paul	Acts 7:58; 9:1–19; 22:4–20; Gal 1:13–16		
34–36	Sojourn in Damascus, in Arabia, and again in Damascus	Acts 9:20–22, 23–25; Gal 1:17		
36	First journey to Jerusalem, fifteen-day stay there	Acts 9:26–28; Gal 1:18–20		
36–44	Sojourn in Tarsus	Acts 9:29–30; Gal 1:21–24		Death of Tiberius, accession of Caligula, March 16, 37. Death of Caligula, accession of Claudius, January 24, 41. Death of Agrippa I, 44.
45–46	Sojourn in Antioch	Acts 11:25–26		
47–48	FIRST MISSIONARY JOURNEY (Cyprus and Asia Minor)	Acts 13–14; 2 Tim 3:11		
49	Famine and second journey to Jerusalem (to bring contributions)	Acts 11:27–30; 12:25		Claudius expels the Jews from Rome, 49. (cf. Acts 18:2)
49	Apostolic Council in Jerusalem	Acts 15:1–35; Gal 2:1–10		
49	Dispute with Cephas in Antioch	Gal 2:11 ff.		
50	SECOND MISSIONARY JOURNEY begins	Acts 15:36–18:22 (cf. Gal 4:13–15)		
50	Philippi, Thessalonica, Athens	Acts 16:11 ff. Acts 17:1 ff.		
50–52	Corinth	Acts 18:1 ff.	1 Thessalonians 2 Thessalonians	Gallio proconsul in Achaia, 52—53
53	THIRD MISSIONARY JOURNEY begins	Acts 18:23–21:17		

(A.D.) Dates	Events in Paul's Life	Documents	Paul's Letters	Contemporary Events
53	Galatia-Phrygia			
54–57	Ephesus	Acts 19:1 ff.	*Philippians* *1 Corinthians*	Death of Claudius; Nero elected emperor, October 13, 54
57	Departure from Ephesus Sojourn in Macedonia Journey to Illyria (Rom 15:19)?	Acts 20:1–6	*2 Corinthians*	
57–58	Corinth (three winter months)	Acts 20:3	*Galatians* *Romans*	
58	Journey to Macedonia, Philippi, then to Jerusalem, arrest	Acts 20:3–23:25		
58–60	IMPRISONMENT IN CAESAREA	Acts 24–26		
60–61	Sea voyage, shipwreck at Malta. Arrival in Rome	Acts 27–28:16		Porcius Festus, procurator, 60–62
61–63	FIRST IMPRISONMENT IN ROME	Acts 28:17–31	*Colossians, Ephesians, Philemon*	
63–65	Journey in the Orient (Ephesus, Crete, etc.), Macedonia, Nicopolis Return to Rome	1 Tim 1:3; Tit 1:5; 3:12		Burning of Rome, July, 64
65	Journey in Spain (?)		*1 Timothy* *Titus*	
66–67	SECOND IMPRISONMENT IN ROME	2 Tim 1:15–18; 4:9–21	*2 Timothy*	Revolt of Judea, 66–70.
67	Martyrdom			Death of Nero, June 6, 68

ABBREVIATIONS

CBQ *The Catholic Biblical Quarterly*
EDB *Encyclopedic Dictionary of the Bible* (ed. L. Hartman, New York: McGraw-Hill, 1963).
JBC *Jerome Biblical Commentary* (Englewood Cliffs, N.J.: Prentice-Hall, 1968)
NTS *New Testament Studies*
P.G. *Patrologia Graeca* (Migne)
P.L. *Patrologia Latina* (Migne)
TBT *The Bible Today*
TD *Theology Digest*
TDNT *Theological Dictionary of the New Testament* (Kittel, English)
TS *Theological Studies*

BOOKS OF THE BIBLE

OLD TESTAMENT

Gen	Genesis	Ca	Song of Solomon
Ex	Exodus	Wis	Wisdom of Solomon
Lev	Leviticus	Sir	Sirach
Nm	Numbers	Is	Isaiah
Dt	Deuteronomy	Jer	Jeremiah
Jos	Joshua	Lam	Lamentations
Jg	Judges	Bar	Baruch
Ru	Ruth	Ezek	Ezekiel
1 Sam	1 Samuel	Dan	Daniel
2 Sam	2 Samuel	Hos	Hosea
1 Kg	1 Kings	Jl	Joel
2 Kg	2 Kings	Am	Amos
1 Chr	1 Chronicles	Ob	Obadiah
2 Chr	2 Chronicles	Jon	Jonah
Ezr	Ezra	Mic	Micah
Neh	Nehemiah	Nah	Nahum
Tob	Tobit	Hab	Habakkuk
Jdt	Judith	Zeph	Zephaniah
Est	Esther	Hag	Haggai
Job	Job	Zech	Zechariah
Ps	Psalms	Mal	Malachi
Prov	Proverbs	1 Mac	1 Maccabees
Ec	Ecclesiastes	2 Mac	2 Maccabees

NEW TESTAMENT

Mt	Matthew	1 Tim	1 Timothy
Mk	Mark	2 Tim	2 Timothy
Lk	Luke	Tit	Titus
Jn	John	Phm	Philemon
Acts	Acts of the Apostles	Heb	Hebrews
Rom	Romans	Jas	James
1 Cor	1 Corinthians	1 Pet	1 Peter
2 Cor	2 Corinthians	2 Pet	2 Peter
Gal	Galatians	1 Jn	1 John
Eph	Ephesians	2 Jn	2 John
Phil	Philippians	3 Jn	3 John
Col	Colossians	Jude	Jude
1 Th	1 Thessalonians	Apoc	Revelation (Apocalypse)
2 Th	2 Thessalonians		

Contents

Paul's Life Up to the Writing of
1 Thessalonians

Assigned reading: Gal 1–2; Phil 3; Acts 9:1–18; 22:5–16; 26:12–20. A chronological table and maps are provided on pages xii, xiii, 7, 9, 48, 189.
   Suggested reading: See the biographies of Paul in the bibliography. Also J. A. Fitzmyer, "A Life of Paul," *JBC* 46:1–45; E. May, "The Life of St. Paul," *TBT* 10 (February 1964), 623–629.

EARLY LIFE

What we know of Paul's life comes from two sources, his letters and the Acts of the Apostles. Of these, the letters are the primary and more valuable historical source because they come directly from the time and life-situations of the Apostle. The book of Acts is the work of a reporter-interpreter who uses historical souvenirs about Paul as pieces of a vast mosaic in which he interprets the meaning of early Church history for a later generation. Consequently, while the author of Acts no doubt gives us a wealth of reliable tradition about his hero, we must always assess it in the light both of his theological intention and the events reported in the Pauline letters.

Paul was born in Tarsus of Cilicia (Acts 21:39; 22:3), "no insignificant city" (Acts 21:39). Situated in a fertile area twelve miles up the river Cydnus from the Mediterranean, it flourished not only in trade but also in the sciences and the arts. Stoic and Epicurean philosophers settled and taught there. There was a Jewish colony originally settled there, it is said, by Antiochus IV (the Illustrious) around 170 B.C.

Paul was thus a Hellenistic Jew. Though named Saul after the great first king from the tribe of Benjamin, he was also given, probably from childhood, the Roman name Paulus, in keeping with a common practice among first-century Jews to take such double names (compare, for example "John Mark" in Acts). Bearing a Latin name was especially appropriate inasmuch as Paul enjoyed Roman citizenship (Acts 22:22–25). He learned Greek at an early age and used the Greek Old Testament as a diaspora Jew would. Did he frequent the Hellenistic schools of rhetoric? The evidence is not compelling that he did. He does use a number of the Stoic categories to elaborate his theology—freedom, nature, reason, conscience. And he uses the diatribe (a debate carried on with an imaginary opponent) as a tool for elaborating his thought. But the Stoic concepts had become part of popular language just as many terms of psychology have become commonplace today, and the diatribe was used by itinerant preachers in the Greek-speaking synagogues of the day. Similarly, Paul's occasional citation of Greek authors (Menander in 1 Cor 15:23; cf. Aratus in Acts 17:28; Epimenides in Tit 1:1) simply means that he was familiar with popular quotations and thought patterns of the Greek world.

But in heart and soul Paul was a Jew (Phil 3:5) and, despite the liberalism of Hellenistic Judaism, he was reared in the strictest observances of the Pharisees (Phil 3:5; Acts 23:6). This meant learning to read the Hebrew Scriptures at an early age and, from about the age of ten, beginning to learn the long oral commentaries on the Law called the "traditions of the Fathers" (Gal 1:14). An interpretation of Acts 22:3 and 26:4 f. would have Paul coming to Jerusalem at an early age ("brought up at my mother's knee in this city"). According to Acts 22:3 he studied these under the famous rabbi Gamaliel the Elder, who flourished 20–50 A.D. Though it does not follow from this that he actually became a rabbi (cf. *JBC* 46:14), he did become a proponent of the strict Pharisaic observance (Gal 1:14, Acts 22:3), and he was so imbued with rabbinical thought patterns that he would often use them later in developing his Christian theology. Thus, for example, despite all that Paul says in his letters about his rejection of the old Law, he applies to Christ many of the ideas which Jewish and rabbinical tradition had elaborated about the Law as God's wisdom and light, and its role in creation (cf. W. D. Davies, *Paul and Rabbinic Judaism*). As a Pharisee Paul shared the belief that the resurrection of the dead would surely come and that it would mark the threshold of "the age to come," the dramatic inbreaking of God's direct rule in the world, radically different from "the present age."

The Acts and Paul's letters agree that he became a persecutor of the Church. Why? There is no evidence Paul had known Jesus during the public ministry. The statement of 2 Cor 5:16 that "even if we once knew Christ according to the flesh" simply means that prior to Paul's conversion he knew of Jesus only in a human and materialistic way. What led Saul the Pharisee to become Saul the persecutor was not the public life Jesus had led, and probably not even what Jesus had taught. Nor was it the kind of observance of the Law continued by the Jewish wing of the Church. Nor could it have been the belief in a Messiah, for this was an honored Jewish and Pharisaic belief. What he could not accept was that the dead Jesus was being preached as now reigning, and his enthronement as Messiah as an incredible resurrection from the dead. This was unacceptable because it broke down the radical distinction between this age and the age to come. More than that, the Christians were interpreting this resurrection as a glorification revealing Jesus as *Lord*, a title reserved to Yahweh alone in the Old Testament. And in the Hellenistic communities this would soon become "Son of God," a title laden with evident divine connotations. But even more existentially nettling than that, the Christian communities, especially the Hellenistic ones, showed an openness regarding membership that left no room for the kind of elite-consciousness that had become hardened in Saul the Pharisee. Not only were the "God-fearing gentiles" admitted into the Hellenistic communities without requirement of circumcision, but among the Jewish Christians table-fellowship was extended to the common and the unlearned persons the Pharisees had come to label "sinners" because it could be assumed that since they were unlearned in the Law they transgressed it frequently. Free association with them would put the Pharisee in proximate danger of legal defilement, an accusation already made against Jesus: "He eats with publicans and sinners" (Mk 2:16). It thus became a matter of life and death, a defense of God himself (Acts

26:9) for Saul to get the intervention of Jewish authorities to exclude these heretics from the synagogue or to inflict upon them premature scourgings. Saul's approbation of the stoning of Stephen fits this picture (Acts 8:1).

CONVERSION

Luke considers the conversion of Saul so important that he relates it three times in Acts, once as his own narration (9:1–19), twice on the lips of Paul (22:1–21; 26:1–23). Concerned to show that the polarities and diversities obvious in the early Church were only part of a much vaster plan of continuity in a divinely led sacred history, Luke faced the greatest challenge in explaining how the gentile mission was not *really* in discontinuity with the best of Judaism and how the irruption of Paul into the early Church was not really as much a breach as it may have seemed to many of Paul's contemporaries. To this end it was important to show that while Paul could not qualify to be one of the twelve witnesses of Jesus since the time of John the Baptist (1:22), he really had *seen* the risen Christ (first account) and indeed in the *light of glory* (second account)—a detail significantly absent in Christ's appearances to the twelve. Moreover Paul's calling was a prophetic one like those of Ezekiel, Jeremiah and Second Isaiah. Through him the prophecies spoken of the Servant of the Lord who would bring the good news to the Gentiles through a ministry of preaching and suffering, were actually fulfilled (the third account).[1] Thus what Paul lacked in witness concerning the public ministry of Jesus was amply compensated by the kind of witness he was called to give in his worldwide mission.

How did Paul himself view his conversion? It had something of the violent about it. This arch-enemy of the Church had suddenly been captured by Christ (Phil 3:12), and his entry into the apostolic college was like a birth out of due time (literally, a "miscarriage," 1 Cor 15:8). It was a calling not from man but from God (Gal 1:11), akin to that of Jeremiah and Second Isaiah (Gal 1:15; Jer 1:5; Is 49:1). Twice Paul describes it as a *revelation* (Gal 1:12, 16), hence a new kind of knowledge. Whereas his ideal as a Pharisee had been to know the Law (Rom 2:17–21), it is now to know Christ in an experiential way (Phil 3:8, 10), a radical shift from code to person, from performance-expectations to living in the gift of God and the love God gives in it (Gal 1:14; 2:20–21; Rom 5:5; 8:39). This was a revelation not only to Paul but *in* him for the Church, especially for the Gentiles (Gal 1:16). That is, he was

---

[1]Cf. D. M. Stanley, "Paul's Conversion in Acts: Why the Three Accounts?" *CBQ* 15 (1953), 315–338.

called not only to preach but to live out the message in his life. The vision of the face of Christ in glory must have made a profound impact on Paul, for he alludes to it to describe not only the glory of the new revelation (2 Cor 4:6) but the goal of the whole Christian life (2 Th 1:10; 1 Cor 13:12).

PAUL'S FIRST YEARS AS A CHRISTIAN

After his baptism in Damascus, Paul withdrew into Arabia (Gal 1:16 f.), no doubt the region near Damascus that belonged to the Nabatean kingdom. The motive for this retreat is not clear, but we can well imagine he needed to assimilate the experience he had had and to see how all his previous values were reversed or transferred to Christ (Phil 3:7–12). In this area Essenes were still living, and he may have had occasion to interact with them. Some scholars think this likely since Paul shares with them certain concepts: dualism, angelology, the notion of "mystery" as God's plan for the world, and especially righteousness as a gift of God.

Returning to Damascus he preached Jesus as the Son of God (Acts 9:20). He spent considerable time there (Acts 9:23), specified in Gal 1:18 as three years (according to Jewish calculations, a little more than one full year would suffice to reckon it as three). His influence eventually antagonized the Jews, who sought to kill him (Acts 9:23). Escaping in a basket, he went to Jerusalem, where he was received with suspicion by the Christians, but Barnabas, a man of great breadth, who played a prodigious role of diplomacy in the early Church, received him and introduced him to the Apostles (9:26 f.). Again beginning to preach in Jerusalem, he incurred the anger of the Greek-speaking Jews there, and it was thought best for him to leave for Caesarea, where he sailed back to his native Tarsus. He must have made this the headquarters for apostolic activity, for Acts (15:23, 41) speaks of flourishing communities in Cilicia and Syria at the time of the Council in Jerusalem, and these may well be due to Paul's evangelizing those regions after leaving Jerusalem (Gal 1:21).

Meantime, some of the other Greek-speaking Christians who had been driven out of Jerusalem brought the gospel to Antioch and established a flourishing community there (Acts 11:19 f.). When sometime later, Barnabas arrived from Jerusalem to see how things were going, he was impressed with the great opportunity this center offered, and went to Tarsus to fetch Paul (A.D. 44). Paul subsequently spent at least a year laboring in the community of Antioch. It is at this time that many scholars have traditionally placed the account of Agabus and the famine which led to a mission of relief to the poor in Jerusalem, since the account follows immediately in Acts 11:27–30. Modern scholarship, however, is tending more and more to identify this journey with that whose major purpose was the apostolic council in Jerusalem related later in Acts 15:1–35 and Gal 2:1–10.[2]

During these more than ten years which now separated Paul from his anti-Christian past, he had time to assimilate thoroughly the tradition of the Christian communities regarding Jesus the Messiah. He had learned the major facts of Jesus' life and above all his teaching, in the repeated accounts of eyewitnesses and in the *logia*, the sayings and sermons of Jesus, which no doubt were soon collected in written form in the various communities. (We shall see how he refers to these in his letters.) Likewise he learned the early credal formulas repeated in the churches (as 1 Cor 15:3 reveals, for example), and the liturgical hymns which soon began to take shape (e.g., Phil 2:6–11; 1 Tim 3:16). Paul will bring his own genius to bear in the theological penetration of the Christian message, no doubt, but he was aware of the importance of making sure his doctrine did not differ essentially from that of the apostles in Jerusalem (Gal 2:2).

FIRST MISSIONARY JOURNEY

The community at Antioch solemnly commissioned Paul and Barnabas to undertake a missionary journey. Taking along John Mark, they crossed first to Cyprus, Barnabas' native country, where, at Paphos, the proconsul Sergius Paulus was won to the faith (Acts 13:4–12). From Paphos the band of missionaries, with Paul now in charge, crossed the sea to Perga in Pamphylia, and from there to Antioch in Pisidia. Paul's sermon given here (Acts 13:16–41) in the synagogue is Luke's thumbnail sketch of sacred history, the promise to David, the Jews' unconscious fulfillment of the prophecies in sentencing Jesus to death, the resurrection as the promised Davidic enthronement and preservation of the "Holy One" from decay—and the call to faith, which gives what the Law could not give—forgiveness of sins.

What happened at Antioch was typical of the rest of the journey: failure to win any appreciable number of the Jews, to whom the

---

[2]The reasons for this view are too involved to detail here. They derive mainly from a consideration of the literary form Luke is following in chapters 10–12 of Acts, which led him to complete his diptych of the Antioch-Jerusalem communities by an incident which chronologically may have occurred much later, as indeed seems to be demanded by Gal 2:1, which places fourteen years between Paul's first visit to Jerusalem (A.D. 36) and his second (A.D. 49). See B. Rigaux, *Saint Paul et ses Lettres*, 103–122; J. M. Gonzalez-Ruiz, *Epístola de San Pablo a los Gálatas,* Madrid, 1964, 30–36; and the review of this work by G. T. Montague in *CBQ* 27 (1965) 75–76.

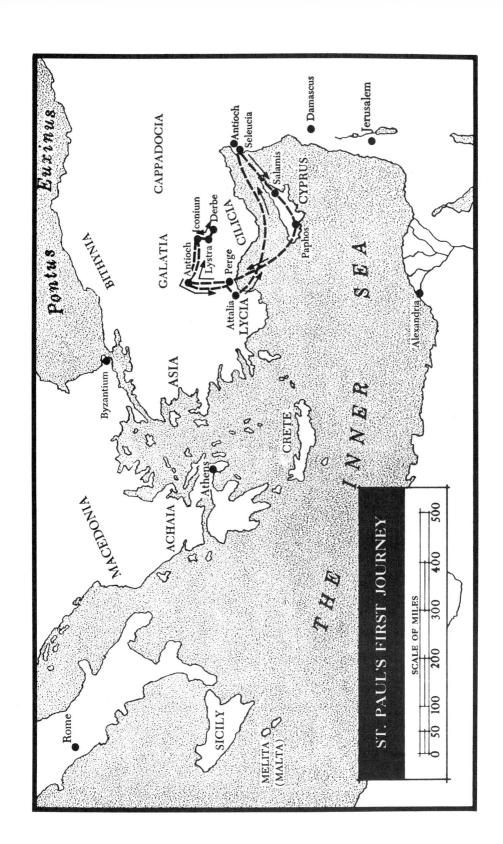

ST. PAUL'S FIRST JOURNEY

SCALE OF MILES

0 50 100   200   300   400   500

missionary band preached first, but remarkable success among the Gentiles, beginning with those "God-fearing" or "worshiping converts" who had been attracted to Judaism. At Iconium, as at Antioch, the Jews incited persecution; at Lystra success again till the Jews arrived from Antioch and Iconium and succeeded in having Paul stoned. But even so, the number of converts was so great that, after jaunting to Derbe, Paul and Barnabas, on returning to the cities visited, constituted presbyters and left well-organized communities (Acts 14:22).

Returning to Antioch, they related their success to the mother community. The joy this good news caused was soon chilled by the arrival of some members of the Judean church who, without authorization, came down to Antioch demanding that all, Jews and Gentiles alike, be circumcised and made to observe the Mosaic Law (Acts 15:1 ff.). This right-wing reaction coming from a Jerusalem party upset the community at Antioch. Paul and Barnabas then led a delegation to Jerusalem to discuss the question. In his account, Luke has apparently conflated two issues, the one of universal scope, the circumcision of the Gentiles, settled by Peter; the other about dietary laws, idol offerings and marriage within certain degrees of kinship, prescribed by James as articles of peace for Gentiles living in community with the Jews. Of the latter decree, Paul reveals no knowledge in his letters. There is no reference to it in 1 Cor 10, Rom 14 or Gal as something decided at the "Council." Acts 21:25 seems to indicate Paul first learned of the James decree when in Jerusalem at the end of his third journey. Likewise, though Luke's paraphrase in 15:22 makes it seem that Paul and Barnabas were the bearers of the letter, the *text* of the letter in 15:25 can be read to mean that Paul and Barnabas were among the addressees rather than the bearers. It would seem then that Paul had begun his second journey before this letter from James arrived and that the decisions Paul and Silas communicated to the churches on the second journey (Acts 16:4) were those authorized by Peter and not the letter of James.

Somewhere about this time, perhaps before Paul left on his second journey, Peter came to Antioch and in the spirit of his Jerusalem decision made nothing of eating with uncircumcised and hence Mosaically "unclean" men. But when another Judaizing group came from Jerusalem, Peter began to withdraw and eat separately with them, and soon the Jewish Christians, including Barnabas, were led "into the same dissimulation" (Gal 2:11–14). It was not a question of teaching but of example and practice, giving the impression that only Jewish Christians were real Christians. Paul sensed the danger and withstood Peter "to his face."

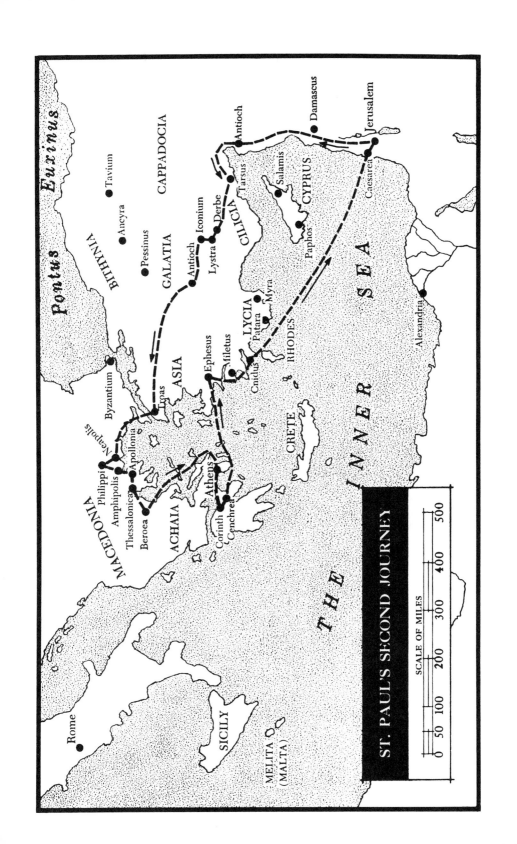

ST. PAUL'S SECOND JOURNEY

SCALE OF MILES

0 50 100 200 300 400 500

SECOND MISSIONARY JOURNEY

The Jerusalem decision and the dispute with Peter convinced Paul all the more that his mission was to the Gentiles. He prepared his second great missionary journey. Barnabas, however, separated from him over John Mark, whom Paul refused to take along because he had abandoned them in the midst of the first journey. While Barnabas and John Mark sailed to Cyprus, Paul set out overland, through Syria and the Cilician Gates to the churches he had founded in Asia Minor. Paul took with him Silas (or Silvanus), an eminent personage of the Church of Jerusalem, who was both Jew and Roman citizen, a Christian no doubt of the first hour. Silas had been chosen by the council of Jerusalem to return with Paul to Antioch and prove the fundamental accord of Paul's teaching with the mother Church. Paul's choice of Silas, whose orthodoxy and fidelity to the mother Church were above suspicion, shows his eagerness for unity in the Church, and for presenting a united front in the kerygma.

At Lystra Paul picked up Timothy, a young man, son of a pagan father and a Christian mother of Jewish origin, named Eunice. Marriages of Jews with Gentiles were tolerated in the Diaspora, but in a case like Timothy's, the child was supposed to follow the religion of the mother. Because Timothy was not circumcised, his presence with Paul would have presented an obstacle to the Jewish converts or prospective converts. Accordingly, Paul had Timothy circumcised before taking him along (Acts 16:1–3). The rest of the trip took the three through Cilicia, Phrygia, Galatia, to the borders of Mysia, and finally to Troas, where only a few miles of the Aegean Sea separated them from the continent of Europe. Luke joined them there. In a dream, Paul saw a mysterious Macedonian beckoning to him to cross the straits. Immediately the missionary party prepared for a Macedonian apostolate, setting sail from Troas and arriving, by way of the port Neapolis, at Philippi, principal city of the area. There was no synagogue there, but in spite of Paul's success in establishing a largely Gentile community (1 Th 2:2), the Jews stirred up a bitter opposition to him and had him and Silas imprisoned (Acts 16:19–34). The account of their release shows how Paul did not hesitate to use his Roman citizenship to make the local officials squirm (16:35–39).

Leaving the city by way of the *Via Egnatia*, the missionaries passed through Amphipolis and Apollonia and came to Thessalonica (Acts 17:1). This city, founded in 314 B.C. by Cassander, a general of Alexander the Great and named for his wife, Alexander's half-sister, had, at Paul's time, a colony of Jews large enough or wealthy enough to have a synagogue. Here, according to Luke, the Apostle preached on three successive Sabbaths, winning to the faith some of the Jews and a large number of proselytes and Gentiles and several notable women (Acts 17:1–5). Paul's first letter to the Thessalonians suggests that the community was chiefly a gentile one ("converted from the worship of idols," 1 Th 1:9). A difference of emphasis is probably due to the fact that Luke, following his typical style, had given an example of Paul's ministry to Gentiles in the Philippi section (Acts 16:11–40) and found it to his purpose to use Thessalonica as the stage for an example of his ministry to Jews and the consequent response. In Philippi, Paul's exorcising of a pagan prophetess in the name of Jesus provoked persecution by the anti-Semitic Romans (Acts 16:16–24). In Thessalonica, Paul's preaching of Jesus as Messiah occasioned Jewish accusations that Paul was proclaiming in Jesus Lord a rival to Caesar (Acts 17:1–9). Luke's programmatic intention in this whole section of Acts may also lead him to contract somewhat the time spent in Thessalonica, whereas the first letter to the Thessalonians suggests a longer apostolate there.

Opposition grew so hot in Thessalonica that Paul was sent away by night to Beroea, but he was soon trailed there by Jewish opponents, so that he had to be spirited away to Athens, leaving word for Silas and Timothy to join him as soon as possible. While awaiting there the arrival of his companions, Paul took up discussions not only in the synagogue but likewise in the marketplace, where he encountered the Epicurean and Stoic philosophers. Invited to address the Areopagus, a sort of "cultural council" of the city, Paul launched into a discourse which merits attentive reading (Acts 17:22–31), for the approach used to the Greeks differs radically from that used with the Jews (at Pisidian Antioch, Acts 13:16–41). Most striking, of course, is the absence of the long replay of sacred history. In its place Paul appeals to natural reason: God's creation and presence everywhere: "In him we live and move and have our being" (17:28). Behind Paul as he spoke loomed the Acropolis, at his feet temples and altars to every conceivable deity. The period of idolatry has been a period of ignorance in the human race; God has overlooked it, "but now he calls on all men everywhere to repent, inasmuch as he has fixed a day on which he will judge the world with justice by a man whom he has appointed, and whom he has guaranteed to all by raising him from the dead" (v. 31).

Note that the conclusion of Paul's sermon is the same as at Antioch to the Jews: the resurrection of Jesus, there seen as fulfillment of the Davidic messianic prophecies, here as a proof of the coming judgment.

To both Epicurean and Stoic this seemed utter nonsense. Though the mystery religions had given impetus to a belief in the immortality of the soul, the resurrection of the body was, in Greek thought, not only unheard of but not even conceived as desirable—at least to those who, to Plato's way of thinking, considered the aim of life to be the liberating of the soul from its mortal prison of flesh.

Paul's converts in Athens were few. He arrived in Corinth saddened and discouraged (1 Th 3:3 f.; 1 Cor 2:3), and resolved to abandon the "wisdom" approach and to preach the "folly" of the cross (1 Cor 2:2). At Corinth Paul lived with Aquila and Priscilla, who had come there from Rome, whence all Jews had been expelled by a decree of Claudius. Working with them at tentmaking, Paul first used the synagogue approach, and when this failed, he moved next door into the house of Titus Justus, a proselyte convert. Financial aid from the Philippians, brought by Silas and Timothy (2 Cor 11:9; Phil 4:16) enabled him to devote himself entirely to preaching. A more detailed picture of Corinth will be given later in the introduction to 1 Cor, where the information is more pertinent.

It was during his year-and-a-half sojourn in Corinth that Paul wrote 1 and 2 Thessalonians. The date generally agreed upon for the first letter is shortly after his arrival in Corinth, in early A.D. 51.

CHAPTER TWO

The Letters to the Thessalonians

1 THESSALONIANS

At Athens, before coming to Corinth, Paul made several attempts to return to Macedonia but was unable to do so (1 Th 2:18). So he sent Timothy back to Thessalonica "to strengthen you and encourage you in your faith" (1 Th 3:2), for Paul knew that the persecutions he had suffered there were no doubt now being directed toward the community (3:3–5). When Timothy returned from his mission, finding Paul in Corinth (Acts 18:5), the news he brought was encouraging indeed and compensated for the failure in Athens. The Christian community of

Thessalonica was, despite persecution, in a state of fervor (3:6). Nevertheless, Timothy's report may have included a letter to Paul with a number of questions, particularly concerning a point which may strike us as odd today: the order of events at the Parousia or Second Coming of Christ. The emphasis given the Second Coming in this letter is noteworthy, although we may be assured that Paul's attention to it is chiefly influenced by his readers' preoccupation about certain aspects of it.

OUTLINE

(The outline of each epistle is provided as a guide to the student's reading. The sections in boldface indicate those to be analyzed in detail in this text.)

THE ORDER OF THE PAROUSIA: 1 Th 4:13–18

[13]But we would not have you ignorant, brothers, concerning those who are asleep, lest you grieve as others do who have no hope. [14]For if we believe that Jesus died and rose again, so with him God will bring also those who have fallen asleep through Jesus. [15]We tell you this on the authority of the Lord: we who are alive, who survive until the coming of the Lord, shall not precede those who have fallen asleep. [16]For the Lord himself with cry of command, with voice of archangel and with trumpet of God, will descend from heaven, and the dead in Christ will rise first. [17]Then we who are alive, who survive, shall be caught up together with them in the clouds to meet the Lord in the air, and thus we shall ever be with the Lord. [18]Therefore comfort one another with these words.

With 4:13 Paul breaks into a new topic, the Second Coming of Christ, the Parousia. The plural *we* and the attention-arresting *brothers* mark the solemnity of the introduction. Paul's concern is not, however, with the Parousia in general, but rather with a hitherto unexplained point which is troubling the community: their fellow Christians who have died. If Christ, gloriously risen and reigning in heaven, returns to earth, will not the dead be at a disadvantage? How can they possibly share in his victory? At first sight, the difficulty of the Thessalonians seems to be their total ignorance of the Christian resurrection of the dead. At a time when it was not evident that Christ was not immediately returning, it would have been easy to jump to the conclusion that Christ was returning so soon that there was no need for resurrection, since all Christians would be living. The death of some of their members would raise the problem of how these would profit by Christ's glorious return, and, as a solution, Paul would have introduced them to the doctrine of the resurrection of the Christian dead.

Some exegetes have not hesitated to explain the Thessalonian problem in this way, as if Paul had preached the resurrection of Christ and his Second Coming, but not the resurrection of Christians. This, however, is highly unlikely, because Paul's kerygma (1:10) faithfully echoes that of Peter (Acts 3:19–20), who preaches Jesus as judge of the living *and the dead* (Acts 10:42). Moreover, it seems highly unlikely that the Thessalonians would have been ignorant of a hope which was already held by the synagogue. Paul himself will proclaim the resurrection of the just and the unjust before Felix (Acts 24:15), and will soon elaborate the reasons for the Christian resurrection in 1 Cor 15. The serenity and security with which Paul there argues from the resurrection of Christ to the resurrection of Christians on the principle of their solidarity with the risen Lord makes it much more likely that this was also part of his original message at Thessalonica, though not perhaps with the same clarity or emphasis.

Another solution offered is that the Thessalonians were expecting the Parousia to inaugurate a period of glorious reign on earth before the final resurrection, a joy of which the beloved dead would be deprived. But nothing in the text of Paul allows us to assume that; rather he presumes an immediate taking even of those living with the Lord (v. 17). The doctrine of a Christian millennium will not make its appearance until some fifty years after this letter.

It is best, then, to stay within the horizons suggested by the text. Some of the Thessalonian Christians had died. Emotions and grief similar to that of their former pagan days had gripped some of the community. There was occasion to recall the teaching of the resurrection of the just and to relate it to the coming of Christ, both truths which Paul had preached, without perhaps clarifying the intimate connection between the two. The fact of death does not put deceased Christians at a disadvantage, for they too will enjoy the triumphant Parousia by rising *first*.

The Christian dead are "those who are asleep." The image of sleep for death was a common one in antiquity and did not of itself connote immortality for the soul nor resurrection for the body. In pagan circles there was a hesitant belief in the former, strengthened and spread by the mystery religions; the latter, resurrection, was not even considered a possibility. For the Old Testament, "to sleep with one's fathers," originally meaning perhaps to be buried with one's family, came to be a cliché for death (cf. Gen 47:30). Those in this state were considered by the early prophetic apocalyptic literature to go to Sheol, a kind of shadowy dwelling place of the afterlife. In later Judaism, the belief in the resurrection of those *who have fallen asleep* was expressly affirmed: "Many of those who sleep in the dust of the earth shall awake; some shall live forever, others shall be an everlasting horror and disgrace. But the wise shall shine brightly like the splendor of the firmament, and those who lead the many to justice shall be like the stars forever" (Dan 12:2–3). A great grace is laid up for those "who have fallen asleep in godliness" (2 Mac 12:45). The way was thus laid for a new value to be given to the image "sleep" when used of death—and the value is underlined in Mt 9:24 and Jn 11:11—the daughter of Jairus and Lazarus are not dead but asleep, because they are to *rise*. From then on "to fall asleep" is a term for Christian death which looks to resurrection (Acts 7:60; 13:36; 1 Th 4:14; 5:10; 1 Cor 7:39; 11:30; 15:18, 20, 51). Thus in the third century burial ground came to be called a "sleeping quarters," *koimētērion,* whence the English "cemetery." At Thessalonica itself, an early Christian inscription reads "the sleeping-place (*koimētērion*) till the resurrection."

The figure of sleep, even in its Christian usage, tells us nothing in itself of the condition of the soul after death. Paul conceives the Christian mystery on this point always from the angle of its consummation. He does, however, state that for him, to die is to be with Christ, a lot he ardently desires (2 Cor 5:8; Phil 1:23).

The end or purpose of Paul's instruction is not to correct error but to comfort and console (v. 18). Paul may be contrasting Christian grief with pagan grief (so runs the interpretation of many of the Fathers of the Church), but more likely, he is not thinking of Christian grief at all, but rather of the hope which distinguishes Christians from pagans, whom he describes as "those who have no hope" (v. 14).

As a matter of fact, the pagan world confessed its hopelessness in the face of death. "When the dust has drained the blood of man, once he is slain, there is no return to life" (Aeschylus, *Eumenides*, 648). "Who prays to die is mad. Ill life overpasses glorious death" (Euripides, *Iphigeneia et Aulis*, 1252). "For us, when the short light has once set, remains to be slept the sleep of one unbroken night" (Catullus 5, 4). This thought dictated the frequent inscriptions: "Be consoled, no man is immortal," or "Sleep in peace, no man is immortal."

The shift in Christian inscriptions to "Live in God," "live in the Lord" "sleep in peace, in the Lord," was rooted in the new Christian faith of which our passage is a witness. *If we believe that Jesus died and rose . . .* (4:14) is a real condition, better rendered by *Since we believe. . . .* The object of this faith, that *Jesus died and rose again*, in modern terms would be stated, "rose from the dead." Paul's sequence is Semitic and the verb for "rose" is not the usual *egērgetai* he habitually uses elsewhere, but the unfamiliar *anestē*—indicating that Paul is reproducing an early Christian creed-formula, similar to the "suffered . . . died . . . was buried . . . rose again . . ." in our Apostles' Creed, except that it is limited to the two central acts: died and rose.

Now the death and resurrection of Jesus being absolutely certain, it is equally certain that with him God *will bring those also who have fallen asleep through Jesus* (4:14). This "through Jesus" is curiously unexpected and has given the exegetes occasion for discussion. Some take it as equivalent to "in Jesus," as Paul will speak of "the dead in Christ" in v. 16. But the more obvious reading is to take it just as Paul says it, the *through* expressing a causality, as in Acts 13:38, "*through* him the remission of sins." The only problem then is to explain how Jesus (note the name that recalls the historical, human personage in his suffering humanity) is the cause of the death of Christians. The author of life (Acts 3:15) is the cause not of death but of Christian death, which is a "falling asleep" in anticipation of the resurrection. Jesus' death has changed the meaning of death. Paul does not yet speak of a solidarity of Christians with Christ as Second Adam, nor of dying *with* Christ *or in* him—all points which he will develop later (1 Cor 15:20; Rom 6:4 ff.; Col 1:18).

What Paul now says, he says with the authority of the Lord—literally, "in the word of the Lord." The Gospels do not reveal any express equivalent of the apocalyptic description that follows; Paul must therefore be appealing to some unwritten statement of Jesus handed down in oral tradition (an *agraphon*), or to a private revelation made to him by Christ, or perhaps merely to an inspired commentary on the apocalyptic discourse of Jesus (Mk 13 and par.). At any rate, the certitude of it is as great as the facts of the death and resurrection of Jesus.

We who are alive, who survive until the coming of the Lord (4:15). This expression has been hotly debated among the exegetes. At first sight,

Paul seems to include himself among those who will be living at the Parousia, and thus it seems that he expected the great event to take place during his own lifetime. Many liberal exegetes conclude that Paul just made the mistake of foretelling an imminent return of Christ which really did not materialize (and the same exegetes say Jesus made a similar mistake concerning the end of the world). What is to be said of this? Aside from dogmatic considerations on the infallibility of Christ and the apostolic teaching, and the inerrancy of Scripture, there are other factors of a psychological and historical nature which this liberal interpretation overlooks or does not explain. Certainly Paul hoped for the quick return of Jesus, as did all the early Christians and particularly the Thessalonians (2 Th 2:1–3), for this meant reunion in him and victory for the Church (cf. Apoc 22:17–20). Paul, even on the eve of his death, defines the Christian as one who loves the coming of Christ (2 Tim 4:8). Did Paul in his enthusiasm pass from hope of an immediate return to an affirmation of it within his own lifetime? To do so he would have presumed knowledge which Jesus himself declared no man had, not even the Son (Mk 13:32; Mt 24:36). The contemporary Jewish apocalypses describe the coming of the kingdom as *near*, but they do not commit themselves to a mathematical calculation nor to absolutely definitive signs. Paul is using the same literary genre here. This in itself should make us hesitate to say he is affirming categorically that he himself will be among the living at the Parousia. The Protestant exegete Wohlenberg has observed that if "we the living" were taken in an extremely literal sense, it would lead to the conclusion that all Christians at the moment of Paul's writing would be living at the Parousia and that not one of them would die before, an affirmation which Paul would have considered absurd, since he knows of many Christians who have died—among them Stephen, who was stoned at Paul's feet (Acts 7:56–60).

Is this *we*, then, merely a rhetorical device by which Paul associates himself with those whose condition he is describing? This technique is well known to grammarians: the writer assumes the point of view of the person of whom he is speaking—much as a second-string halfback might ask, "What time are we going to play?", not knowing whether he personally will play or sit out the game on the bench. As a matter of fact, Paul does often use this technique—Gal 5:25–26; Rom 14:10; Eph 5:14—and, in this very letter to the Thessalonians, 5:5, 8, 9, and 10, where he says, "our Lord Jesus Christ, who died for us, in order that, whether we are awake or asleep (alive or dead), we may find life in union with him." Here the "we" is associated with both living and dead, it being uncertain in which state he and his readers will be at the Lord's coming.

Thus in 4:15, as St. John Chrysostom already remarked, "He does not say this 'we' of himself . . . but he speaks of the faithful."

In the Jewish apocalypses, it was commonly held that those living at the inbreaking of the kingdom—and they will be only a remnant of survivors—will indeed be blessed: "Blessed is the man who has patience and perseveres until the one thousand three hundred and thirty-five days" (Dan 12:12). "Know therefore that they who are left are more blessed than they who are dead" (4 Ezr 13:24). Paul uses similar terminology when he speaks of "we who are left," but his point is that there is no more advantage for the then living than for the dead, for the living *shall not precede those who have fallen asleep* (4:15).

In what follows Paul shows his dependence on Jewish and Christian apocalyptic and reflects the cosmology of the times. It would be wrong to imagine this scenario as a blow-by-blow description of the events; it is not always possible, in the apocalyptic genre, to distinguish figure and reality, and precisely how the future is to correspond to these images we cannot say. Paul's description is sober and retrained and goes swiftly to his point, which is that the resurrection of the dead is in the first scene of the drama, not in the finale.

The *Lord* here in v. 16 is expressly used as a name for Christ, for it means the divine royalty of the exalted Christ, particularly (in Th) as the coming judge of the world. The triplet, "with cry of command, with voice of archangel and trumpet of God" (4:16) may simply be three ways of saying the same thing—the solemn and cosmic announcement of the final moment, determined by God and executed by his creatures. Voice and trumpet are frequently found together in the apocalyptic genre: "I heard behind me a great voice, as of a trumpet" (Apoc 1:10). In the Old Testament, the trumpet seems to be a necessary accompaniment for great manifestations of God's majesty and power or the assembling of his people (Ex 19:13, 16, 19). The prophets use it as one of the sound effects of the "Day of the Lord" (Zeph 1:16; Jl 2:1, 15) or the inbreaking of the messianic victory (Zech 9:14) or the restoration of Israel (Is 27:13). We find it in the apocalyptic description of Mt 24:31, there called a "great" trumpet, and by Paul in 1 Cor 15:52, the "last trumpet."

Christ, in heaven since his ascension, descends, but he does not reach the earth. The faithful go to meet him. But before they do, the dead in Christ will rise first. In this instruction aimed at encouraging the Thessalonians, Paul does not speak of a resurrection of the infidels. Here the Christian deceased are not "those who sleep" but "the dead in Christ"—they died in union with him and even in death this union has never been severed. In Rom 8:11 Paul will give the profound basis of this union and its consequences: "If the Spirit of him who raised Jesus from the dead dwells in you, then he who raised Jesus from the dead will also bring to life your mortal bodies because of his Spirit who dwells in you."

And then all together, the living and the resurrected, will be taken on the clouds to meet the Lord in the air. The images again are those of the apocalyptic genre and the cosmology of the times. The clouds are not so much a necessary vehicle for flight as they are a vehicle for Paul's teaching on the assimilation of the faithful with Christ at the Parousia. As Christ comes on clouds (Mt 24:30; 26) or with clouds (Apoc 1:7), so Christians at that moment will have the same accoutrements as he. The cloud image has a theological content. The Greeks made it an attribute of divinity. The clouds serve as a chariot for the gods, and on a chariot of clouds Heracles was transported to heaven. In the Old Testament likewise the clouds are God's chariot (Is 19:1; Ps 104:3; Nm 10:36) but also his dwelling place or cloak (Ps 18:12; 2 Sam 22:12) or his footstool (Nah 1:3). The cloud was a symbol of God's presence over the meeting tent in the desert (Ex 40:34–38; Nm 14:10; 17:7) and of his guidance and protection of the Israelites in the desert (Ex 13:21 f.; 14:19). The cloud image was perhaps the closest the Hebrew mind came to the abstraction *divinity*. In theophany contexts, "cloud" is a label for the divinity, or at least the sign of its presence (cf. 2 Mac 2:8), and this is true in the New Testament as well as in the Old (the Transfiguration). In Dan 7:13, the "Son of Man" comes "on the clouds of heaven." The context tells us that the Son of Man is the victorious people of God in the final times; Jewish apocalyptic referred it to the Messiah, who according to 4 Ezra 13:1 ff., was to come on the clouds. At any rate, Hebrew thought did not clearly distinguish between the personal Messiah and the messianic kingdom, and Paul's imagery here stresses the final identity of the two in glory.

It is worth noting that the living and the resurrected do not await Christ's arrival on earth but go out to meet him. Some exegetes think that Paul is recalling the theophany of Ex 19:16–19, where, following the trumpet blast, "Moses led the people out of the camp to meet God, and they stationed themselves at the foot of the mountain. . . ." To go out to meet someone was a customary recognition of that person's dignity (Gen 14:17), and was the mark of honor extended in a special way to the king (2 Sam 19:16, 21). In the Hellenistic world which Paul certainly knew, part of the ceremonial at the *Parousia* or visitation of a city by the emperor or king was that of going out to meet him. The Jewish historian Josephus describes Titus' arrival at Antioch:

> The people of Antioch, on hearing that Titus was at hand, through joy could not bear to remain within their walls, but hastened to meet him and advanced to a distance of over thirty furlongs, not only men, but a crowd

of women and children also, streaming out of the city. And when they beheld him approaching, they lined the road on either side and greeted him with extended arms, and invoking all manner of blessings upon him returned in his train. . . .[1]

St. John Chrysostom uses the image of the imperial reception to explain the "going out to meet the Lord":

> When a city receives the emperor, the high dignitaries and those who are in his favor go out from the town to meet him, while the criminals are kept within the walls under guard, to await the emperor's sentence upon them. Likewise, when the Lord comes, those who are in his grace will go up to meet him in the air, while sinners and those whose consciences are darkened by many evil deeds, will remain on earth to await their judge.[2]

Canon Cerfaux follows a large number of the Fathers and moderns in extending the Hellenistic image to its subsequent details: After meeting Christ, the saints will come back with him to earth to judge the wicked. The day of Christ's return will also be a day of judgment (2 Th 1:7 f.; 2 Cor 5:10; 2 Tim 4:1), and the saints are to judge the world (1 Cor 6:2; Apoc 20:4). But this part of the program is not Paul's concern here. He says nothing about a return to earth but moves immediately to the goal: *and thus we shall ever be with the Lord* (4:17).

In thus describing the consummation of the Christian life, Paul reflects the constant doctrine of the early Church, drawn from the Master. The final reunion is described as a banquet (Lk 14:15; Mt 8:11), in which Jesus will feast with his disciples (Mt 26:29; Lk 22:30; Apoc 3:20) or as a kingdom in which they will reign with him (Mt 25:34; Apoc 5:10; 20:4–6). To the repentant thief Jesus promises, "Today you will be with me" (Lk 23:43; cf. Phil 1:23), and in John this union is described as "having part" with Jesus or simply being with him (Jn 14:3), which means *seeing his glory* (17:24). This latter relationship must have meant much to St. Paul, who had seen the glorious Christ on the Damascus road, and for whom Jesus is *Lord*, that is, enveloped in the glory of divinity.

That the just would possess glory in the kingdom was a commonplace in the apostolic kerygma (Mt 13:43; Apoc 22:5), and Paul's thought runs strongly in the same vein in the present epistle when he says that "God is calling you unto his kingdom and his glory" (1 Th 2:2). But we shall observe how in subsequent epistles Paul links the glory of Christians to its source, which is Christ (Phil 3:20 f.; Rom 8:17, 21), with whom Christians are already organically united (1 Cor), and that Christian life

---

[1] *Jewish Wars*, 7:100–103; tr. H. St. J. Thackeray (Loeb Classical Library, Harvard University Press).

[2] *P.G.*, 50, col. 450–451.

even now is a growth in glory (2 Cor 3:18). But for the moment Paul's thought is on the eschatological consummation, which he here describes simply as *being* with Christ or *living* with him (5:10), and this forever (4:17). Over, beyond and through the apocalyptic scenario, the essential of Paul's message is this: *and thus we shall ever be with the Lord* (4:17).

This is encouragement indeed, and encouragement to be shared. The closing v. 18 echoes the opening v. 13, and points to the fact that Paul's main purpose was not a discourse on a doctrinal topic, but a reassurance with the precision that the dead will share equally with the living in the joys of meeting Christ at his glorious return.[3]

THE MEANING OF THE PAROUSIA: 1 Th 5:1–11

¹But as to times and dates, brothers, you have no need that anything be written to you. ²For you yourselves know full well that the day of the Lord is to come like a thief in the night. ³At a moment when men are saying, "Peace and security," sudden destruction will fall upon them, like birth-pangs upon an expectant mother, and they will not escape.

⁴But you, brothers, are not in darkness, that the day should surprise you as would a thief. ⁵For you are all sons of the light and sons of the day. We are not of night nor of darkness. ⁶So then let us not sleep as do the rest, but let us be vigilant and alert. ⁷For sleepers sleep at night and drunkards are drunk at night. ⁸But let us, who are of the day, be alert and put on the breastplate of faith and charity, and for our helmet the hope of salvation. ⁹For God has not destined us unto wrath, but to gain salvation through our Lord Jesus Christ, ¹⁰who died for us in order that, whether we are awake or asleep, we should find life together with Him. ¹¹Therefore continue to encourage one another and build one another up, as you are doing.

With 5:1, Paul takes up another problem from the report of Timothy, one allied with the preceding but clearly marked as a separate question by the transitional expression, *But as to* . . . and the renewed address, *brothers.* The question voiced the preoccupation which goes back even to the time of Joel (400 B.C.) and is still with us today: *when* is the day of the Lord coming? The apocalyptic writings often took up the question, as for example Daniel's computation of the seventy weeks (Dan 9:20–27), but often the writer will confess his ignorance ("I know not what will happen to our enemies or when you will visit your works," Apoc Bar, 24:4; cf. 21:8) or simply ask the question, "how long?" (4 Ezr 6:59).

The disciples of Jesus were no less curious and asked, "When are these things (destruction of Jerusalem, end of the world) going to happen?"

---

[3]L. Cerfaux, *Christ in the Theology of St. Paul* (New York: Herder & Herder, 1959), 31–68.

(Mt 24:3; Lk 21:7). And even after the resurrection, "Lord, will you *at this time* restore the kingdom to Israel?" (Acts 1:6). The synoptic tradition is no less firm on the answer: "Of that day or hour, no one knows, neither the angels in heaven, nor the Son, but the Father only" (Mk 13:32; cf. Mt 24:36, 42), and, "It is not for you to know the times or dates which the Father has fixed by his own authority . . ." (Acts 1:7).

The expression "times and dates" is a biblical cliché expressing one thought through two words (technically, a *hendiadys*). The distinction between *chronos* (time in the sense of a sequence of events) and *kairos* (time in the sense of opportunity, suitable season, or date), both of which are used here, is not to be stressed; the "times and dates" referred to are the eschatological ones, soon to be described as the "day of the Lord." It is not necessary that Paul write them about this at any length, for what follows they know perfectly well. This whole instruction, like the preceding, is simply a recalling of previous teaching, with some supplementary touches.

The *day of the Lord* (5:2) is a Christian and Pauline use of the Hebrew *yom Yahweh*, the "Day of Yahweh," which appears in the prophetic literature as early as Amos (eight century B.C.), where it means the visitation of God's judgment on the nations, particularly on Israel, implying the vindication of God's rights accompanied by cosmic catastrophes. It is a day of punishment for sinners: "What will this day of the Lord mean for you? Darkness and not light! As if a man should flee from a lion, and a bear should meet him; or as if on entering his house he were to rest his hand against the wall, and a snake should bite him. Will not the day of the Lord be darkness and not light, gloom without any brightness?" (Am 5:18–20). Note that the image of light and darkness appears associated with the "day of the Lord" from the very beginning—and it is the darkness overtaking sinners that is first stressed, an aspect repeated by subsequent prophets (Zeph 1:15; Ezek 30:3; Jl 2:2). During the exile the expression "day of the Lord" came to mean the time when God would vindicate his own people against their oppressors and restore them (Jer 50:27; Ezek 30:3; cf. Jl 4). In Malachi the meaning is extended to that of the final judgment of the world, when the wicked will be punished and the good rewarded (Mal 3:19–24). A day of doom and darkness for the wicked, the "day of the Lord" will be a day of light for the just. "For you who fear my name, there will arise the sun of justice with its healing rays . . ." (Mal 3:20).

Paul keeps all of the Old Testament elements, transferring to the glorified Christ the title "Lord" in the "day of the Lord." The day of his appearance (1 Cor 1:8) as judge (2 Tim 4:8) will be a day of wrath (Rom 2:5, 16), of punishment for the wicked, but one of salvation, reward, and glorification for the saints (2 Th 1:10; 1 Cor 5:5; 2 Tim 4:8). Christian life is a preparation in love and holiness for that day (Phil 1:10). In Thessalonians Paul concentrates first on its suddenness and its unexpectedness (which, we should be careful to observe, is not the same thing as its imminence). Joel had described it as the pouncing of a lion (Jl 3:16); Jesus, using a popular Old Testament figure of the thief (Jer 49:9; Ob 5; Jl 2:9) who comes at an hour unexpected, had counseled watchfulness (Mt 24:43 = Lk 12:39). From this it was but a step to add *in the night* (5:2), a further touch of incertitude (as in Mt 15:6). The point of the image is obviously not that Christ's coming is a theft but that it is so sudden that the time cannot be foretold, no more than one can foretell when a thief will attempt robbery.

When men [*they*] *are saying* (v. 3). The impersonal "they" in the literal translation refers doubtless to unbelievers, in contrast to "you, brothers" in v. 4. True to the apocalyptic and prophetic genre, and echoing the cry of the false prophets of peace (Jer 6:14; Ezek 13:10, 16), Paul describes the period as one of great complacency—adding *security* to the simple "peace" of Jeremiah and Ezekiel, to underline the pejorative meaning of peace here, corresponding to the attitude skewered in Lk 12:19. In this Paul is simply summarizing the synoptic descriptions in Mt 24:37–39 and Lk 17:27–30. In the midst of the feverish activity of making merry and making a living, comes *destruction*. The fate of destruction which befalls the wicked is contrasted with *salvation* for the elect in v. 9, and confirms that the latter is thought of here as something yet to come.

The "pangs of childbirth" was a constant image of the Old Testament prophets, particularly to stress the sudden inbreaking of suffering or catastrophe (Is 13:8; Jer 6:24; 13:21; Ps 48:7), and here again Paul reflects the genre and the links his thought has with the apocalyptic discourses of Jesus (Mt 24:8; Mk 13:8). St. Thomas sums up the traits of this visitation described by Paul as: *sudden, deadly, afflictive, inevitable.* "From the wrath of God now one may flee to his mercy, but then the time will not be one of mercy, but of justice."

Whereas infidels are in the darkness, and consequently subject to surprise, Christians are not. Darkness is a biblical figure for death—it is the lot of the stillborn (Job 3:16; Ps 6:3–6; 58:9) or the dead in the nether world (Job 10:22), whose light has gone out (Job 18:5 f.; Prov 13:9; Sir 22:9), who do not "see the light" (Ps 49:20; Job 33:30). "Darkness" also symbolizes great adversity or disaster (Job 30:26; Ps 23:4; Is 8:22; Jer 23:12; Lam 3:2) or simply evil (Is 5:20). The suggestion here is that darkness has its moral sense of infidelity to God, and really therefore the darkness is a blindness within, like that visited on those unfaithful to Yahweh, who grope about even at midday (Dt 28:29).

The "day" that surprises those in this kind of darkness is not the natural dawn that follows night, but the "day of the Lord" that bursts suddenly on the unprepared. It is for these that, according to the prophets, the day of the Lord brings darkness rather than light (Am 8:9; Jer 4:23; Jl 2:1–2; 3:4; 4:14 f.; Is 24:4 f.; 34:4).

Christians, however, are by their very being made for light and day. In contrast to darkness, the biblical figure of light stands for life (Job 38:15), or for divine favor (Job 22:28; 29:3), so that to pray God for light is to pray for better times (Ps 4:7). It stands especially for God's salvation (Ps 27:1), portrayed as a deliverance of the prisoner from the dungeon to the light of day (Is 42:16; 49:9), or the raising of the defeated to victory. "Though I have fallen, I will arise; though I sit in darkness, the Lord is my light. . . . He will bring me forth to the light" (Mic 7:8 f.). The eschatological city of the redeemed is quite naturally therefore portrayed as a city of light that is perpetual (Is 60:19 f.) and sevenfold in its intensity (Is 30:26). The messianic city will know one continuous day (Zech 14:7; cf. Enoch 58:6; 92:4 f.).

When Paul tells his readers that they are all sons of the light, sons of the day, he means that they already share in this eschatological salvation. Reinforcing the statement with, *We are not of night nor of darkness* (5:5), Paul makes it clear that the difference between the Christian and the pagan is not one of degree but one of being. Although he does not use the term "sons of darkness" (the now famous antithesis with the "sons of light" in the Dead Sea Scrolls), the contrast and the incompatibility are just as absolute. The difference between being a Christian and not is a difference between day and night (2 Cor 6:14).

The attitude toward the Parousia is one of the points of difference. The Christian is already part of that new world to be made at the "day of the Lord." Unlike the pagan, he welcomes the Parousia as something for which he was made, much as a fish seeks water or a trapped miner air and light. The Hebraism "son of" often means "destined for" (2 Sam 12:5; Jn 17:12) or "specially characterized by" (Mk 3:17; Lk 10:6) or "belonging to" (Mt 8:12). "As of light is made the day, so of faith in Christ is made the day, i.e., the beauty of good works" (St. Thomas).

Why should Christians be alert? Lest they be surprised, "caught" by Christ's sudden return? No. We might have expected that, for the synoptic tradition does stress the unexpectedness of the return as a motive for "watching." For Paul, however, we must watch not because we know not the day nor the hour (Mt 25:13) but because *"we are of the day,"* because we *are sons of the light and sons of the day* (5:5). That is, the Parousia corresponds to what we are essentially as Christians; for us it is not an ambush but a consummation. Made for the day and eagerly awaiting it, let us show it by living as befits the daylight hours—by staying awake and working.

Sleeping and drunkenness are characteristic of the night and symbolize the stupor of those unaware of the coming judgment. The Christian's attitude is one of being constantly "on his toes," alert, possessing all his faculties, and capable of meaningful action at all times. Today we might say less figuratively, "Let us live in the state of grace and work at our salvation," with the coming of Christ on the horizon of our thoughts.

The image of being on full-time alert evokes military preparedness, and for this Paul uses the description of the armor of his day—the breastplate, which symbolizes faith and charity, and the helmet, which is the hope of salvation. The figures are manifestly borrowed from Is 59:17, where the Lord, the redeemer of Zion, is said to have "put on justice as his breastplate, salvation as a helmet on his head." It is worth noting that Paul substitutes "faith and charity" for justice. The technical term Paul will develop in Galatians and Romans ("justice") does not even appear in 1 or 2 Thessalonians, but Christian life is considered to consist essentially in faith and charity, which are themselves impelled by hope, the three summarizing the essential equipment of the soldier of Christ. Note that hope here appears in the final position (unlike our better-known order of "faith, hope, and charity" of 1 Cor 13:13). This order is characteristic of our letter (1 Th 1:13) because Paul's point of view is not the relative importance of these virtues in themselves, but rather their role in the motivation of the Christian community. Faith and charity look to the person of Christ in himself and in one's neighbor, hope to the consummation of the final day (see Col 1:5). The salvation that is hoped for is manifestly eschatological, and stands in contrast to the coming wrath of God (v. 9), which the Christian is to escape through Christ (1:10; 2:16). The term "salvation" will recur often in the Pauline epistles. For the time being, it suffices to remember that here it refers not to the present but to the future.

The reason for living in constant alert is paradoxical: because God has not destined us for his wrath but to attain salvation. A moralizing preacher might more easily have said we must act because salvation is up to us. Instead, he says it is up to God, who has already determined to save us. However, instead of engendering the complacency based on a mere emotional conviction that "I'm saved," Paul considers the destiny as one demanding constant diligence, the best of one's efforts. The image is not one of partnership but of total subordination (though free and active) of man's action to God's.

The salvation which is to become the property, the "domain" of the faithful, is attained *through our Lord Jesus Christ* (5:9), the title "Lord" here indicating that Christ effects our salvation not merely through the once-done action of his death but likewise through his resurrection and his present glorified humanity, in virtue of which he is "Lord." The resurrection of Christ is, therefore, as much as his death, a cause of our salvation.

The past act to which the future salvation is linked is the death of Christ, which was *for us*. Paul's constant doctrine is that Christ's death was a death *for us* (Rom 5:6–8; 14:15; 2 Cor 5:15) or for our sins (1 Cor 15:3). Later he will describe it especially as a *giving* or *handing over* of himself for the sake of the faithful (Gal 1:3; 2:20; Rom 8:32). This is the only time in 1 and 2 Thessalonians that Paul speaks of the death of Christ, and the formula he uses reflects the tradition of the "Servant of Yahweh" which he received from the earliest Palestinian communities— that Jesus fulfilled the role of the innocent and suffering "Servant" who according to Is 53:5–6, "was pierced for our offenses, crushed for our sins; upon him was the chastisement that makes us whole, by his stripes we were healed . . . the Lord laid on him the guilt of us all." Paul does not pause here to develop the theology of Christ's death as he will do later in Galatians and Romans. In referring to this basic truth in which his readers had been instructed, Paul stresses that the end or purpose of Christ's death was that we might *find life together with him*—that is, share in the risen life he now leads. It is in this, ultimately, that the salvation of which Paul has spoken, consists. *That . . . we should find life* is probably what the exegetes call an ingressive or inchoative aorist, the meaning being "that we may begin to live the new life with him"—that is, whether we are awake (= living, 4:17) or asleep (= dead, 4:16) when the Lord returns, we may join him in his risen life—as Paul will elaborate later in 1 Cor 15:1–11. As pointed out above, Paul here associates himself equally with those living or dead at the Parousia—and thus nullifies any attempt to prove he taught that the Parousia would arrive before his death.

Paul here considers Jesus essentially as the *living* one, the one risen from death, with whom all Christians are called to live. The future glorious life of Christians is inconceivable apart from Christ. The antithesis death-life appears for the first time, but in quite elementary form.

The aim of Paul's instruction is to strengthen and to build up the community, or rather, to give the community additional matter to communicate this "consolation" and "edification." The verb *parakalein*, from which "paraclete" comes, means to comfort and console, but not in the modern sense of extending sympathy in the face of the inevitable, but rather in the sense of "encouraging" and "strengthening." Note that it is based on a truth of faith which the members of the community are to share and more deeply penetrate. Like "encouraging," "building up" is likewise an important function of each member of the community and will be discussed at length later in our study. Note here that it does not mean "edification" in the modern sense of giving an exteriorly good example of pious conduct, but is connected with a deepening of the faith. Paul's counsel ends with a compliment, "as indeed you are doing."

2 THESSALONIANS

1. Authenticity

There is no doubt as to the canonical authenticity of 2 Th, which the Church has always accepted as belonging to the inspired corpus of the New Testament. But the Pauline authenticity of this letter in the course of the last two centuries has been either questioned or denied.[4] F. C. Baur, founder of the Tübingen school of exegesis, already in the mid-nineteenth century denied the authenticity of both epistles to the Thessalonians. Exegetes today recognize that Baur's arguments were too much influenced by his limited conception of St. Paul. (According to Baur, Paul had no other interest than establishing a Hellenized church and fighting any Judaizing elements.) Those who contest the authenticity of 1 Th today are rare. Nevertheless, Baur has maintained his influence as to 2 Th principally through the work of W. Wrede, who in 1903 took up the question of the second letter. The letter is, he said, a careful construction by some other author between the years A.D. 70–110. His work was an imitation, with expressions borrowed from the first letter to give his work an air of authenticity. However, the arguments against the Pauline origin of this letter are not at all compelling: (1) Granted that the view of the end-time in 2 Th provides for signs preceding the end whereas in 1 Th the end comes suddenly, both these concepts are found side by side in the Jewish apocalyptic literature of the time; (2) The great similarity of style between the two letters is best understood not as a literary forgery but as what might normally be expected of a writer addressing the same audience about the same matters within a short period of time and drawing much of his teaching and vocabulary from traditional Jewish sources. The alleged parallels are not in the same sequence and cover only about one-third of 2 Th. Finally, early tradition favors the authenticity of 2 Th, for it is alluded to by Polycarp and Justin, and by the *Didache*—all of the second century. The Muratorian fragment (an early "canonical" draft) likewise knows the epistle.

---

[4]On the general question of the authenticity of the Pauline letters, see B. Ahern, "Who Wrote the Pauline Epistles?" *TBT* 12 (April 1964), 754–760.

2. Occasion and Purpose

Paul's first letter answered the question concerning the role and order of the deceased at the time of the Parousia, urging his readers not to be troubled about the time or date of the event, but to live in readiness, as belonging already to the day. Some within the community had concluded that the day had already arrived—and had apparently appealed to a letter or sermon of Paul's as substantiating this teaching. From this theoretical error they had drawn a practical conclusion: to stop work. Thus a false interpretation of the Parousia and the abuse of idleness brought a second letter from Paul not long after the first, and hence in the summer or fall of 51.

OUTLINE

THE PAROUSIA, ITS SIGNS, ITS DELAY, ITS ELEMENTS, ITS MEANING FOR THE FAITHFUL: 2 Th 2:1–17

[1]*We beseech you, brothers, concerning the parousia of our Lord Jesus Christ, and our assembling unto him,* [2]*that you be not hastily shaken from your right mind, nor be terrified, whether by spirit, or by utterance, or by letter purporting to come from us, to the effect that the day of the Lord is already here.* [3]*Let no one deceive you in any way. For [that day will not come] unless the apostasy comes first, and the man of iniquity is revealed, the son of destruction,* [4]*who opposes and exalts himself above everything that is called God or is an object of worship, so that he takes his seat in the temple of God, proclaiming himself to be God.* [5]*Do you not remember that when I was still with you, I used to tell you these things?*

[6]*And now you know by experience the Enchanter who is to be unmasked in his proper time.* [7]*For the mystery of iniquity is already set to work. Only the Enchanter appears active now, until he is ousted.* [8]*Then the wicked one will be revealed, whom the Lord Jesus will slay with the breath of his mouth and will destroy with the epiphany of his coming.*

⁹The coming of the man of iniquity is according to the working of Satan, with every kind of power, signs and deceptive wonders, ¹⁰and every seduction to wickedness for those who are perishing for not having accepted the love of the truth that they might be saved. ¹¹Yes, that is why God sends them a misleading influence so that they believe falsehood, ¹²so that all may be justly condemned who have not put their faith in the truth but have taken their delight in wickedness.

¹³But we are bound to give thanks to God always for you, brothers beloved of the Lord, because God has chosen you from the beginning for salvation through sanctification by the Spirit and belief in the truth. ¹⁴To this he called you by means of our gospel, to possess the glory of our Lord Jesus Christ. ¹⁵So then, brothers, stand firm and cling to the traditions you have learned from us, whether by word of mouth or by letter. ¹⁶And may our Lord Jesus Christ and God our Father, who gratuitously loved us and gave us everlasting encouragement and good hope, ¹⁷himself encourage and strengthen your hearts in every good work and word.

This section of the epistle is a celebrated one, and many of its elements have given rise to the most divergent opinions. Before examining it in detail, it is important to recall: (1) that Paul is here contemplating the final times. He ardently desires that the "day of the Lord" come soon, but he knows too that the apostolic tradition confessed a total ignorance as to the date. From our twentieth-century perspective, we would expect Paul to allow for a long interim, but his ignorance of the length of the interim is total. His concern here is not the date of the Parousia but the whole eschatological process in which his readers are already involved. (2) The literary genre here is apocalyptic, and as such it belongs to a conventional type which has its own laws: highly imaginative and dramatic, abounding with symbol and metaphor, it stresses the progressive separation of the grey of the present world into the black and white of consummate evil pitted against good, a cosmic struggle led by God against the wicked angels. As Old Testament apocalyptic grew out of Holy War imagery projected to the final times with the occasional help of Persian imagery, so Paul's apocalyptic is an implementation and adaptation of Old Testament apocalyptic to the basic tenets of the Christian faith.[5] Faithful to the genre, Paul displays his thought in a highly generalizing dramatization. This section complements the two previous ones of 1 Th.

We beseech you, brothers is a conventional transitional phrase from thanksgiving (1:3–10) and prayer (1:11–12) to instruction. What follows is the topic to be discussed. It is solemnly introduced by using all Paul's

---

[5]For examples of Jewish apocalyptic texts very similar to 2 Th 3:3–4, see 2 Baruch 83:4–9; 1 Henoch 91:3–10.

customary titles for Christ, *our Lord Jesus Christ*, and by underlining the social and collective character of the meeting with him. The Jews certainly thought of the future salvation as a collective thing, an "ingathering" of whatever fragments of the people might be dispersed: Read 2 Mac 2:4–8, and notice how the time of God's final saving act is described as the moment when God will "gather together the assembly of his people" (v. 7, with *episynagogē*, the same word Paul uses here). In the apocalyptic genre, Is 27:13 reads, "On that day, a great trumpet shall blow, and the lost in the land of Assyria and the outcasts in the land of Egypt shall come and worship the Lord on the holy mountain in Jerusalem." To pray for God's salvation is to ask him to "gather all the tribes of Jacob" (Sir 36:10). It was this that constituted the increasing hope expressed in 2 Mac 2:18: "For we have hope in God that he will soon have mercy on us and will gather us from everywhere under heaven into his holy place." The ingathering would naturally be the characteristic work of the Messiah (Ps 17:28, 50). The failure of this messianic invitation underlies Jesus' lament over Jerusalem, "How often would I have gathered your children together, as a hen gathers her young under her wings, but you would not!" (Mt 23:37; Lk 13:34). The invitation rejected, Jesus will achieve the same end more universally through his sacrificial death, which will be not for the people only but "to gather together the sons of God scattered abroad" (Jn 11:52). The Parousia will be the rallying call, when the angels, at the sound of the trumpet, will gather the elect from the four corners of the globe (Mt 24:31; Mk 13:27).

Thus Paul returns here to the thought of 1 Th 4:15. There the image was that of a processional meeting (*apantasis*) of the Lord, after the Greek custom at a visitation of king or emperor. Here it is the Hebrew eschatological ingathering represented by *episynagogē*. The noun appears elsewhere only in Heb 10:25, where it refers to the assembly of the Christian community for worship. Those who "forsake our assembly" do not realize that the day of the Lord is drawing near. The assembly for Christian worship is a preparation for the eschatological assembly at the Lord's Parousia.

The object of Paul's entreaty is that they be not easily shaken—the verb evokes the tossing of waves in a heavy sea (Lk 21:25), or the shaking of a reed in the wind (Mt 11:7), both favorite images of psychological or doctrinal instability (Mt 11:7; Lk 7:24; cf. Eph 4:14) or fear (Ps 9:27; 10:6; 30:7). In Pauline psychology the mind (*nous*), used here in 2:2, is the faculty which renders the spirit (*pneuma*) intelligible, and Paul has little respect for a man's "spirituality" when the *nous* is absent. Paul's 21 uses of *nous* against three in all the rest of the New Testament (Lk 24:45; Apoc 13:18; 17:9) indicates the high store he places on the intellectual dimension of the Christian life. The bizarre and the erratic have no place in the mature Christian, for his "good sense," his "judgment," anchor of mental stability, is not removed but rather perfected by the Spirit (Rom 12:2; Eph 4:23). The addition of *nor be terrified* (2:2) echoes the word of Jesus in his own apocalyptic discourse (Mk 13:7 = Mt 24:6). Paul, like Jesus, wishes to put his readers on guard against a frantic agitation concerning the last things.

It is less easy to determine precisely what the sources of this worry are: *whether by spirit, or by utterance, or by letter purporting to come from us* (2:2). What is the meaning of the phrase "purporting to come from us," literally "as by us"? And does it refer to the letter only, or to the utterance also, or possibly the spirit as well, hence to all three?

The trouble in the community seems to have been caused by an erroneous appeal to Paul's authority. It is easy to see how a letter might be attributed to Paul, for this would be the best way to secure apostolic authority for new doctrines. Paul expresses a fear of false letters in 3:17. But one might wonder why, if there were a real letter circulating falsely, he would have not more explicitly and roundly condemned it. Hence some exegetes think Paul is simply trying to correct a misinterpretation of his first letter to the Thessalonians. But if this were so, then the misinterpretation was due to a gross misreading, for nothing in 1 Th indicates Paul thought the day of the Lord was "already here." A too literal understanding of "we are of the day" (1 Th 5:8) could have been understood in this sense, but only if one ignored the express statement of 5:1.

"Spirit" used in contrast to "utterance" may mean oracular utterance (*pneuma*) in contrast to intelligible speech or teaching (*logos*). Both could be abused contrary to the apostolic tradition. We know from 1 Th 5:19–21 that the Spirit was active in the community and that prophecy abounded. At the same time Paul counseled them to "test all things"— no doubt to check the revelations of the Spirit against the rule of faith and the apostolic tradition. Hence a "prophet" may be meant here, one perhaps who linked his message with that of Paul.

But perhaps the triad is simply meant to be a rhetorical way of saying, "whatever be the source or manner of its coming." The theological sense is nowise changed in any case. The verb *enestēken* (2:2) does not mean that the day of the Lord "is imminent" but that it "is here"—or at least that it "is just at hand." Paul is interpreting the agitators' doctrine from the consequences some have already drawn from it: they have quit work, a thing imaginable only when the day of the Lord itself "is here" (3:6–15).

But such is not the case. For there are two signs which must precede that day. The first is the *apostasy* (2:3). The word is used by profane authors for a political defection, as Plutarch speaks of "an apostasy from Nero," or Josephus of an "apostasy from the Romans." But in the Bible it becomes a technical term for religious defection (Jos 22:22; Jer 2:19; the verb "to apostatize," Jos 22:18–19; Dan 9:9; Jer 3:14; Is 30:1). It means a rebellion against God or against the covenant (1 Mac 1:15) or against the worship of the fathers (1 Mac 2:19). It is virtually equivalent to "serving strange gods" (Dt 7:4; cf. 32:15), and is used in the New Testament for infidelity, a "turning away from the living God" (Heb 3:12; cf. Acts 5:37; 15:38; 19:9). Characteristic of the reign of the Seleucid Antiochus Epiphanes (1 Mac 2:15), the "apostasy" came to be a constant element in descriptions of the final times (Jubilees 23:14 ff.; 4 Ezr 5:1 ff.) It reappears in 1 Tim 4:1, where Paul says that a departure from the faith will take place "in the final times." There is again no indication as to when this will take place, except that Paul affirms that it is not taking place at the time of his writing.

The *man of* iniquity (2:3), called simply "the wicked one" in v. 8, is literally, "he who is without, or against, law." "Iniquities" in the plural means simply "sins." In the singular it expresses the essence of rebellion against God, and is paralleled in 2 Cor 6:14 with unbelievers, darkness, Belial, idols. "Man of iniquity" is one whose nature it is to be in open rebellion against God. The epithet "son of destruction" does not mean that he is the source of destruction to others, but rather that, expressing the totality of evil, he will be the first to experience God's vengeance. "Son of" here has the same sense as "son of death" in the Old Testament (1 Sam 20:31; 2 Sam 12:5; 1 Kg 2:26), that is, deserving of death and destined to it. Here the vengeance is not death but the total loss which is opposed to life (Mt 7:13) and to glory (Rom 9:22).

He who opposes (2:4) is a biblical term for enemy (Ex 23:22; 2 Sam 8:10; 1 Kg 11:14; Is 41:11), and specifically for Satan, "the Adversary" (Zech 3:1; 1 Tim 5:14). Although the title Satan does not appear in our text until v. 9, it is possible that Satan is meant. At least the "adversary" is his instrument. He will, in any case, be an incarnation of pride, like the kings mocked by the prophets for having aspired to raise their thrones over the stars of heaven to be like the Most High (Is 14:13 f.) or for saying, "I am a god" (Ezek 28:2, 6, 9).

The description of the adversary's blasphemous self-exaltation is manifestly borrowed from Daniel's description (11:37 f.) of the Seleucid king Antiochus Epiphanes (175–164 B.C.), who profaned the temple, destroyed the holy books, forbade circumcision, pillaged the temple treasure, and set up in the temple an image of Baal Shamem (the Olympian Zeus), referred to in the Bible as "the abomination of desolation." Of him Daniel says, "The king shall do as he pleases (act according to his own will), he shall exalt himself and make himself greater than every god and he shall utter blasphemies against the God of gods" (11:36–37). In the apocalyptic literature for which Daniel stood as a kind of model, the images used of Epiphanes' reign became types for the outbreak of evil and godlessness in the final times. The synoptic apocalypses use the same imagery (Mk 13:4; Mt 24:15).

The adversary will carry his impiety to the extent of taking his seat in the temple of God itself, proclaiming he is God. Opinions differ as to what is meant by the temple. Some, following the early opinion of Irenaeus, hold it to be the temple of Jerusalem. As a matter of fact, the Jewish temple still existed at the time Paul wrote, and in the Danielic tradition which our passage reflects, the temple profaned is that of Jerusalem. Others, following Chrysostom and Jerome, see the temple as signifying the Church. This interpretation has the difficulty of explaining how in this case the Church could even be called the "temple of God," for if the Antichrist is at its head, it is no longer the Church of God at all. A third group holds that Paul is speaking figuratively, meaning that the Antichrist will try to usurp the rights of God. The last interpretation seems the soundest. The genre of this whole passage, we should never forget, is apocalyptic, and Paul is borrowing images and expressions from elsewhere. "Temple" here no doubt means that of Jerusalem, but only as a vehicle to express the adversary's blasphemous action of claiming for himself the worship due God.

Is this "man of iniquity" an individual person or a collectivity? Or both? And is he something presently at work or only something future? All are questions to which only the rest of the passage can give a clue.

Paul gives no apodosis after the condition begun in v. 3. If the translator supplies one (e.g., "that day will not come"), he must be careful not to make it the primary point of Paul's teaching here, since Paul himself omits it and focuses not on the future but on the present danger of deception. We think it better to leave the text as Paul wrote it—as if he were reciting his previous teaching from memory, then suddenly interrupts the recitation to say, "Don't you remember my telling you these things?" Paul thus concludes with a gentle rebuke indicating that his previous teaching was clear enough on the coming of the Lord, the suddenness of it, the signs preceding. The explanation just given is not, therefore, hastily made up to answer the question of the moment, but belongs to the original teaching of the Apostle.

Verse 6 is a celebrated dilemma for the exegete. Literally it says, "And now you know the *katechon*, that he may be revealed at his proper time." Taking the word to mean "restrainer" or "preventer," many interpreters have understood it as a benevolent power presently holding back the full unleashing of the powers of evil. Thus Tertullian took it to be the Roman Empire, which at the time of Paul's writing was not openly hostile to the new religion. Others have linked this restrainer to Jewish legends concerning a good angel. Still others see in it a good force like the two witnesses of Rev 11:3–12: the beast of the abyss unleashes his power only after the witnesses, symbol of the gospel preaching, have been done away with. Following the N. T. indications elsewhere that the end will not come until the gospel has been preached universally (Acts 1:3; Mark 13:10; Mt 24:14), these authorities would identify this beneficent restraining force as the gospel.

But C. H. Giblin (*The Threat to Faith: An Exegetical and Theological Re-examination of 2 Thessalonians 2*, Rome, 1967), following L. Sirard, has shown that the meaning "to restrain" is not found in any of the 16 other N. T. texts where the verb occurs and that the philological evidence from the papyri and the O. T. as well favors the meaning "to grasp," "to seize," and in this case would mean "he who exercises control" (Giblin, 180), or a power "grasping for control" (ibid., 230). Giblin translates, "seizing power" or "seizer," while noting that in the case of the Thessalonians they have certainly not fallen (to any great extent at least) under this malevolent power. But there has been a manifestation of that power, and the use of the Greek word *katechon* is perhaps deliberate because of the similarities this verb would evoke with the ecstatic seizures associated with the cult of Dionysus which was widespread at Thessalonica (Giblin 202 f., 235 f., 239, 241a). "You know" would then refer to experiential knowledge of some manifestation of that psuedo-prophetic mania in the community, perhaps the same alluded to in v. 2 above (Giblin, 224). Inasmuch as the attempt to seize control is of the demonic and pseudo-prophetic order, the transferred meaning, "Enchanter," seems justified.

This interpretation receives support from what immediately follows: "For the mystery of iniquity is already at work. . . ." That is, the Thessalonians have had occasion to verify it in the activity of the "Enchanter," which can stand for any threat to the faith but chiefly for that threat which is such a mixture of truth and falsehood, of light and darkness, that the faithful become easily confused and seduced. When the *katechon* is ousted, that is, when the community has been freed from all ambiguous and seductive influence, then the man of iniquity, the

Antichrist, will be revealed for what he is. Since the ousting of the *katechon* coincides with the revelation of the man of iniquity, it would seem that the *katechon* exercises his seductiveness precisely because it is not yet perfectly clear to many of the faithful that he is the instrument of Satan, as will become clear with the "man of iniquity." If this interpretation is correct, then the *katechon* is a very rich image indeed and it corresponds to Christian experience of every age. For what leads most men astray is not consummate evil but the evil that seems to be a fantastic good. In synoptic terms, it is the wolf that comes in sheep's clothing, the false prophet, whose falsity is not immediately obvious.

Beginning to describe the Parousia of the wicked one (v. 8), Paul interjects the counter description of the Parousia of the Lord Jesus, in a couplet of rhythmic parallels, the first of which echoes Is 11:4: "He shall strike the ruthless with the rod of his mouth, and with the breath of his lips he shall slay the wicked." To this Paul adds, in the second line: *and will destroy with the epiphany of his coming.* Both express the same reality—the ease with which the Lord will accomplish his victory—as one might extinguish a taper. It suffices for the Lord to appear, and the enemy is vanquished. The word translated sometimes "brightness" or "manifestation" or "appearance" is *epiphaneia*, epiphany. We have kept epiphany in the translation because it is a technical term. To the Jewish reader it would evoke the majestic manifestations of God in the Old Testament (2 Sam 7:23; Ezr 5:1; Am 5:22; 2 Mac 2:9; 5:8, 51; 15:27), and to the Hellenistic reader the visitation of the king or emperor, whose *Parousia* was considered an *epiphany* of the divinity.

Returning in v. 9 to the Antichrist, Paul describes his appearance with traits characteristic of the apocalypses of the synoptics, with special emphasis on the element of falsehood and seduction. His great power will be in dragging along others in his wake. In v. 10, *and every seduction to wickedness for those who are perishing*, the use of *adikia* for "wickedness" is instructive. Literally meaning "injustice," it has practically the same value as *anomia* (iniquity) in vv. 3 and 7, and is constantly used to describe the state of things in the final times. The work of the Messiah will be to abolish injustice (Enoch 91:8; Ps Sol 17:24–27). It is opposed not only to justice (Rom 6:13) but also to truth (1 Cor 13:6, as it is here). Akin to ungodliness (Rom 1:18), it is a power which one obeys, as one may also obey the truth (Rom 6:13).

The signs and wonders may present a temptation for the just, but they lead to destruction those *who are perishing* (2:10). The use of the middle voice stresses their own responsibility for their destiny—"who are ruining themselves"—and the present tense indicates that the final judgment is something for which one's present attitude is the determining factor.

Being in this state is the self-inflicted punishment for not accepting the *love of the truth* (2:10). "Truth" here does not have the restricted meaning of "the conformity of the mind to reality" but the biblical meaning which is a religious one. The truth is not only something which one knows (1 Tim 2:4) but something which one does (Is 26:10; Jn 3:21). It is a way of life. The members of the community of Qumran are gathered "to practice the truth" (1 QS 1:5; 8:2), to have their knowledge purified by the truth (1 QS 1:12, 16); they form the community or house of the truth (1 QS 2:26). For Paul, truth stands for the content of the gospel, his preaching (2 Cor 4:2; 13:8), which is the "message of truth" (2 Cor 6:7; Col 1:5; Eph 1:3), so that to obey the gospel (Rom 10:16) and to obey the truth (Gal 5:7) are equivalents. Thus to become a Christian is "to come to a knowledge of the truth" (1 Tim 2:4; 2 Tim 3:7). This knowledge comports a penetration of its intellectual content, certainly, but beyond that it is knowledge of a person ("the truth is in Jesus," Eph 4:21), involving a total commitment (Rom 2:8).

That is why the truth is not only something to be known but also something to be loved. The love which responds to the truth must be of the same order—divine—and hence is possible only by God's gift. Before the assent to faith, God offers man a prior grace, love for the truth, which disposes and connaturalizes him to it and prompts him to identify it when he hears it. But like any gift, this love must be accepted. The decision is crucial for man's destiny. Acceptance places him on the path to salvation. Refusal brings the withdrawal of the subsequent grace—a withdrawal which Paul describes in Old Testament terms as God's sending them an "influence of error" (*a misleading influence*, 2:11) by which they give their faith to falsehood. Hebrew thought did not distinguish between God's causative and permissive will, nor did the language lend itself to such refinements. Though this is certainly a punishment, it results from a man's lucid refusal of God's gift, for which he bears the total responsibility. The final result is a judgment, or rather a condemnation visited upon all who have not made the act of faith in the truth. The aorist tense refers to the act of refusing to believe.

Instead, they have chosen to make wickedness their delight. Again the aorist tense more exactly rendered "*took* their delight" refers to the act of lucid and deliberate choice, and the verb used indicates that the choice was not one of weakness but of total commitment, a kind of relishing. By contrast, the suggestion is that he who believes makes the truth his delight—which is exactly what Paul will say in 1 Cor 13:6— love does not rejoice over wickedness but rejoices with the truth. Hence the real bifurcation—the real crisis, judgment—is made by man's response to the initial gift of love. The same thought is expressed by Jn 3:19–21: "Now this is the judgment: The light has come into the world, yet men have loved the darkness rather than the light, for their works were evil. For everyone who does evil hates the light, and does not come to the light, that his deeds may not be exposed. But he who does the truth comes to the light that his deeds may be manifest, for they have been performed in God." These texts go a long way toward showing, on the one hand, the gravity of refusing the gift of God, and, on the other, how baptism of desire can exist even in one who has not yet heard the gospel.

From this severe judgment of conscious infidels, Paul now turns to a thanksgiving for his readers, whose lot he contrasts with that just described. His "brothers" are first of all "beloved of the Lord," Christ being meant here as the Father was meant in 1 Th 1:4. The divine love always being an efficacious and manifest love, it has shown itself in the choice God has made of Christians. However deep the mystery may be, it does not help to say that those who assent to the gospel make themselves thereby "beloved of God" as if God had nothing to do with it. Pushed to a deeper level, the Christian is defined here not as one who loves God (although this sense is found in Rom 8:29) but as one whom God has loved and as a result chosen. Man's choice of God is God's choice of him; realized in time, its source is ultimately in the act of God *from the beginning* (2:13). (Some texts read "as firstfruits" instead of "from the beginning.") Personal love always involves a "singling out"—a truth of which the Old Testament Jews were strongly convinced and proud, as witness Dt 26:18, a close parallel to our text: "And the Lord has chosen you today to be a people for his own possession." As in marriage, love ends in choice and perpetual commitment, so the divine love has resulted in a covenant or alliance expressing choice and commitment. Theologically there is great significance in the fact that Christ's love for the faithful has become manifest in the Father's singling them out for salvation. Father and Son are united in one act of love and choice.

The salvation to which they are called is the final consummation corresponding to the first act. It is prepared for now by means of *sanctification by the Spirit and belief in the truth* (2:13). The present Christian life is a process of sanctification—that is, of progressive separation from the impure and profane and a strengthening of one's state of consecration or belonging to God. It is authored by the Holy Spirit, whose presence is both challenge and agent of the Christian's growth in holiness (1 Th 4:3–9; Rom 15:16; 1 Cor 3:16–17).

Sanctification is thus primarily the work of God, but it is not an automatic thing. It supposes faith in the Christian—not merely the once-made act of faith but the abiding and energetic virtue of faith by which man accepts the truth and lives by it. Here, then, is a formula which indicates that salvation is attained through the inseparable synergism of God's action and man's cooperation—the Holy Spirit's work of sanctification and man's docility to that work through his submission to the Christian truth.

To this—namely to the sanctification of the Spirit and the faith in the truth as the intermediate phase to salvation and glory—God has called the faithful. "Vocation" according to Saint Paul refers primarily to the call God gives every Christian (1 Th 5:24), so that "the called" is a synonym for Christians (Rom 1:6; 8:28; 1 Cor 1:24). It is a call to God's eschatological kingdom and glory (1 Th 2:12) but intermediately to a life of sanctification (4:7; 5:23–24) and faith (here).

The instrument of God's calling is the gospel, and its ultimate end is to place the Christian in possession of the glory of our Lord Jesus Christ. Christ possesses the divine glory as Lord (Phil 2:9–11; Mt 25:31) and communicates it at his coming (Tit 2:13; 2 Tim 2:10). Into this glory the Christian is called to enter (Lk 24:26; 2 Th 1:10). The possession of glory is the positive side of *salvation*, a concept with which it is frequently linked as here (v. 13; cf. 1 Th 5:9; 2 Tim 1:10).

From this doctrine, expressed in the form of thanksgiving, Paul draws a practical conclusion. Since the truth, communicated through the gospel, is that which leads to salvation and glory, it is important to *stand firm and cling to the traditions you have learned from us* (2:15). The word *stand* is a favorite of Paul's (1 Th 3:8; Phil 1:27; 4:1; 1 Cor 16:13; Gal 5:1; Rom 14:4) and is always used as meaning "hold firm," "hold your ground," or "persevere." Here it is explained as meaning fidelity to the "traditions" received. Paul, so often accused of being an innovator, was a "man of tradition." The gospel itself he received and handed on; it is a sacred tradition (1 Cor 15:3–11; Gal 1:11–12; Col 2:6–8), but it bears with it certain Christian ways and practices which are the common standard of life in the Christian communities. Having the force of law, these are "traditions" (1 Cor 11:2; 2 Th 3:6). Here (2 Th 2:15) the distinction between the two senses of "tradition" is not clearly defined, since Paul wants them to cling to the whole of his message "handed down" to them. Note that for Saint Paul tradition may be written or oral. It is something prior to its forms. It is not "what is not written." On the other hand, as St. John Chrysostom comments, "It is clear that not everything has been transmitted to us in writing; there are many things that have come down to us without being written, and these are also worthy of faith. That is why we hold tradition worthy of faith. It is tradition—look no further" *P.G.* 62:488).

This Pauline text stresses the priority of the apostolic tradition to Scripture. In ecumenical theological discussions this is generally admitted as common ground. The problem is how the apostolic tradition can be known. Is our only tool today Scripture? But Scripture demands interpretation. Who authentically interprets Scripture? Is Scripture to be isolated from the life of the Church by exegetes who then become the ultimate interpreters of Scripture's meaning for the Church, or is there something in the self-consciousness of the Church, called "tradition," which, along with Scripture and inseparable from it, guarantees the permanence of the apostolic tradition, yet in such a way as to transcend the limits of mere exegesis? Saint Thomas already perceived the significance of this problem in his concise commentary on our present Pauline text: "From this it is evident that many unwritten things in the Church were taught by the Apostles *and therefore to be preserved.*" *Et Ideo servanda*—which could also mean "observed"—the point being that if Paul could command the early Christians to observe (i.e., practice, cling to) things he has taught them orally, the obligation of observing these things, if they concerned the universal Church, could conceivably devolve on succeeding generations. But in this case, how could the succeeding generations know that oral apostolic tradition, if they could never get beyond the material limits of the Apostle's written word as determined by mere exegetical science?[6]

If perseverance in the apostolic tradition is their responsibility, it is also a grace, and Paul now turns to a prayer for it. He addresses both the Father and the Son, here placing the Son first (unlike 1 Th 3:11–13). Oddly, however, the pronoun *himself*, which is meant to stand for both persons, and the verbs predicating their action, are all in the singular! Paul could not more strikingly have suggested the intimate

---

[6]This is one of today's most central ecumenical questions. Protestantism has come to a greater understanding of the importance and necessity of tradition in the interpretation of Scripture (cf. the statement on "Tradition and Traditions" issued by the Faith and Order Conference at Montreal in 1963); on the other hand, the teaching of Vatican II on Divine Revelation has, in contrast to the rigid "two-source" theory of earlier manuals, stressed the basic unity and harmony of these two modes of transmission. For a typical statement of the problem from the ecumenical standpoint, see *Scripture and Ecumenism*, ed. L. J. Swidler, a seminar of Catholic, Protestant, and Jewish scholars (Duquesne University Press, 1965).

union of Father and Son in the bestowal of grace. The divine principle of the Christian's strength is thus not the Father alone, nor the Son alone, but both of them working together.

The divine action requested is prepared for by a confident recalling of the love both Jesus and the Father have shown the Thessalonians in the past. The Greek participles *loved* and *gave* (2:16) are in the aorist tense. As such they do not exclude a continuation into the present, but they do mark a past act, a previous proof of love. Since it is a question of the common love of the Father and Jesus, the "loved" and "gave" must refer to the sending of Christ and his passion, which are both a historical event and a mystery of salvation, but above all—the point stressed here—a tangible manifestation, a proof of the divine love. God's love: "God proves his love for us in this, that while we were yet sinners Christ died for us" (Rom 5:8). Christ's love: "I live by faith in the Son of God, who loved me and gave himself up for me" (Gal 2:20; cf. Eph 5:2). The two loves are really one: "the love of God which is in Christ Jesus" (Rom 8:39). Christians are equivalently "the beloved of God" (2 Th 1:4) and "the beloved of the Lord" (2 Th 2:13).

Now the strength Paul asks comes precisely from this mystery of God's love for Christians: "In all these things (tribulation, distress, persecution, hunger, nakedness, danger, the sword) we triumph *because of him who loved us*" (Rom 8:37). God's love for him, and his consciousness of it, makes the Christian omnipotent.

There is more, however, than just consciousness of that love. To evoke God's love is to evoke the idea of gift or efficacious aid, for God's love is always an active, dynamic love (Gal 2:20; Eph 5:2; Apoc 1:5). This explains why Paul should join the thought of God's love with a prayer for his readers' progress. For if God's love is realized by faith, it is attained properly by hope which leans on the manifestations of that love given in the past and guaranteed for the future. Some commentators find in the closely knit construction of love-gift, a reference to the initial gift of the Spirit (1 Th 4:8; Gal 4:6; Rom 5:5), whose lasting effect is indicated by "eternal consolation." Thus from the love of the Father and the Son would come the gift of the Spirit.

At any rate, the Father and the Son have given an everlasting *encouragement*, the courageous confidence, inspired by the Spirit, that nothing, whether persecutions (1:4; 1 Th 3:3) or disquieting utterances concerning the time of the Parousia (2:2 f.) can prevent the Thessalonians from sharing the future glory of Christ. This divine encouragement is likewise "consolation" or "comfort," for the two ideas are hardly separable in the Greek *paraklēsis*.

Along with it, the divine persons have given *good hope*, that is, hope that is guaranteed realization precisely because it flows from the Holy

Spirit given (Rom 5:5) and leans on the magnificent testimony of God's goodness already shown Christians on Calvary: "He who has not spared even his own Son but has delivered him for all of us, how can he fail to grant us all other blessings with him?" (Rom 8:32). St. Thomas comments laconically, "Good hope, that is, the infallibility of the eternal goods."

We cannot escape taking a deeper look at the notion of consolation, given so much importance here by Paul as part of the divine action furthering Christian growth.

In classical antiquity, to console or comfort those in need was considered a social duty. One of the functions that made the philosopher and the poet an important cog in society was his ability and duty to console. Needless to say, both philosopher and poet received payment for their works of consolation in the same way that hired mourners did. The names of Plutarch, Seneca, and Cicero are only a sampling of the many writers who undertook to compose something "On Consolation." Often the author's main attempt was to console himself. Advice was given on how to assuage one's sorrow: read a work of consolation, busy yourself with study, tell your sorrow to another, accomplish your duties, think that you or the lost one have lived purely and justly, sing, marry again. Suicide itself was not excluded; the sword and the hemlock are no mere literary creations.

Antiquity ultimately had no answer to the riddle of life, and death itself was an unresolved mystery. The disciples of Epicurus who considered death an absolute end, a return to nothingness, used this motive to console by urging one another to make the most of life: think of every day as your last, and then every hour will seem a gift (Horace, *Ep.* I, 4, 12–14). In the face of death, the ancients in general sought consolation in the thought that all men must die. Carved into many an ancient tombstone are the words: "Be consoled—no man is immortal!" Plato had indeed offered the thought of the immortality of the soul as a consolation at death, and the mystery religions lent it their support. Death was presented as a liberation from the body, the transient bodily life on this earth at its best being merely the condition for the soul's entering happiness in the next life. However, often that belief is stated with tongue in cheek, for it is accompanied with the conditions, "if it is true," or "perhaps" or "if the departed one is now a partaker in some life more divine" (Plutarch). As the German exegete Gustav Staehlin has said, "Surely for the best of them the thought of eternal life was scarcely more than a comforting metaphysical hypothesis." And that hypothesis was powerless to lift the great shroud of despair and pessimism from the ancient world. The saying of Theogenes was often repeated: "It is best for mortals never to be born, and for those already born to die as soon as possible."

What role does the divinity play in the consolation writings? The evils and boons of life are looked upon as measured out by the gods, and thus it is some consolation to accept their decrees (such was Achilles' consolation from Priam in the *Iliad*). Especially do the gods determine the moment of death (Seneca), and it is considered a divine favor if a man dies in the fullness of his age (Xenophon). There is one instance (in Julian) in which it is stated that when a favorite of the gods dies, the god will not abandon him who lived under the divine protection. But beyond this instance, hardly once is a divinity considered a consoler, for *there was no divinity in antiquity whose role it was to console.*

To this concept the Old Testament presents a striking contrast. Man's sorrows indeed may be deep-felt, at times so great as to make man reject any comforting (Ps 77:3). But comforting there is, and if it may come from man (Job 21:2; Jer 16:7), genuine comforting comes from God alone (Is 57:18). In contrast to the divine consolation, all other is empty. God turns sorrow into perfect consolation, whether this be for the individual (Ps 23:4; 71:21; 86:17; 94:19 and esp. 119) or for the people (Is 54:11 ff.; 51:19 ff.). The role of God as consoler underlies his self-revelation as shepherd of his people (Is 40:11) or as mother. "As a mother comforts her son, so will I comfort you" (Is 66:13). If it is by his deeds that God consoles his people, it is likewise by his efficacious word (Ps 119; 2 Mac 16:9) or through Wisdom (Wis 8:9) or through the prophets (Is 40 ff.; Jer 30 ff.). But particularly it will be through his *Servant* that God will bring comfort to all who mourn (Is 61:2). The notion of consolation in the Old Testament, then, in the last analysis, is bound up with God's future salvation (Is 40:1 f.).

And this is the sense we first meet in the New Testament, where to look for the Messiah is to "await the consolation of Israel" (Lk 2:25). Those who mourn now are in the new dispensation already blessed, for they are certain of comforting (Mt 5:4). This comforting will be consummated in the eternal reign with God in the new Jerusalem (Apoc 21:3–5); that is why the consolation God has already given Christians is *eternal* and is so intimately linked with *good hope* (our passage). "What is this consolation?" asks Chrysostom. "The hope of things to come" (*P.G.* 62:488).

To ask God to comfort the Thessalonians' hearts is therefore to ask him to increase their conviction and their hope; for the consolation God gives engenders hope (Rom 15:4). And if Paul begs this of God before he begs for strength, it is because the divine consolation alone can make man unshakable and fearless (Is 51:12; Sir 30:23). Now this is precisely what the Thessalonians need, and Chrysostom has seen it well:

> As long as one is not a victim of unnerving agitations, one can put up with whatever happens with great patience. But if the soul is troubled, no longer can one expect of it good and generous actions. As paralysis disables the action of the hands, so does trouble seize the soul that lacks faith and does not hold to the hope of a future good (*P.G.* 82:489).

For Christians to grow firm and fixed in every good work, they need the divine comfort, which is not ao sentimental sedative but a courageous confidence inspired by a conviction of the reality of the good things God has promised and the certainty of attaining them. It is an interior comforting and strengthening which does not necessarily remove one's sufferings nor reduce their poignancy, but nevertheless brings joy in the midst of them because they are endured in union with Christ: "For as the sufferings of Christ abound in us, so also through Christ does our comfort abound" (2 Cor 1:5).

This is, of course, a development which grew deeper as Paul lived through the apostolic experiences of his life. In the light of his later development, to pray Christ to comfort Christians is to pray him to increase the conviction of their union with him, that they may be heartened in the knowledge that not only did Christ suffer before them, but that he likewise assumes their sufferings and communicates to them the power of his sufferings, so that it is one mystery of redemptive suffering, one Christ who suffers (Col 1:24). It is therefore a favor not only to believe in Christ but also to suffer for him (Phil 1:29).

Not only was this source and motive of consolation the antipode of pagan antiquity's noblest efforts at consolation, but the idea of suffering with the Messiah was unheard of in Judaism.

The divine consolation is no palliative. It results in a more vigorous and dynamic Christian life—the strengthening in *every good work and word* (2:17).

CHAPTER THREE

The Letter to the Philippians

Assigned Reading: Acts 18:12–19:40

PAUL CONTINUES HIS MINISTRY:
THE THIRD JOURNEY—MINISTRY AT EPHESUS

It was during Paul's stay at Corinth that Gallio came into office, in the spring of 51; the Jews at this time made a concerted effort to win a condemnation from the proconsul but were dismissed when Gallio discovered it was a religious issue among the Jews. After some time, Paul took Priscilla and Aquila with him to Ephesus, where after a brief discussion in the synagogue, he sailed to Caesarea and journeyed from

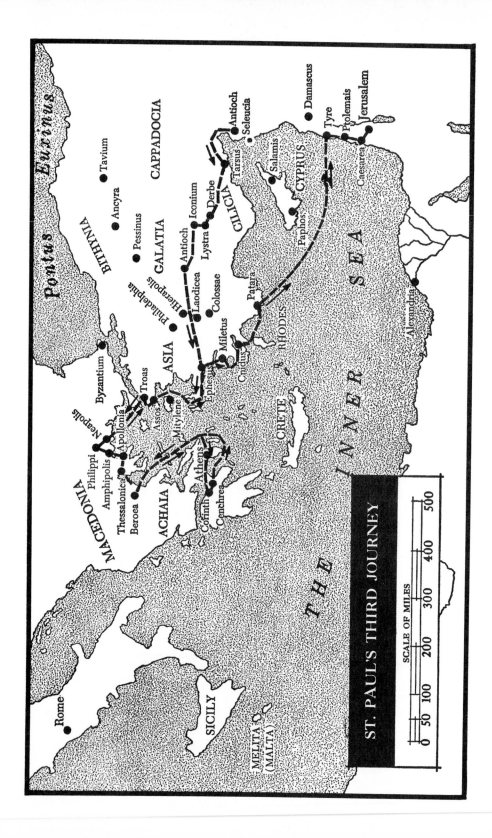

ST. PAUL'S THIRD JOURNEY

SCALE OF MILES

0 50 100 200 300 400 500

there to Jerusalem "to pay his respects to the church" and then returned to Antioch.

The third great missionary journey Paul undertook in the year 53, again from Antioch. This journey, like the second, was overland. He passed through the Galatian country and Phrygia, strengthening the communities he had founded (Acts 18:23). He came then to Ephesus and there began a ministry that was to last for almost three years (Acts 19:1, 8, 10; 20:31). Before Paul's arrival, however, a brilliant convert from Alexandria named Apollos, "an eloquent man and mighty in the Scriptures" (Acts 18:24), had come to Ephesus and begun to preach the way of the Lord in the synagogue. It was clear to Paul's intimate associates, Aquila and Priscilla, however, that Apollos' instruction in the faith had been quite rudimentary, so they took him home and completed his instruction. Then the Christian community sent him with high recommendation to Corinth, where he was of great service by his eloquence and knowledge of Scripture. This incident is of importance for understanding Paul's first letter to the Corinthians, in which Apollos figures.

After three months' efforts to convince the synagogue Jews, Paul withdrew his disciples and turned chiefly to the Gentiles, occupying the school of one Tyrannus, probably a Greek teacher of rhetoric. It was here that the power of the name of Jesus appeared in exorcisms, to such an extent that many magicians were converted and burned their magical books publicly. Luke also gives a graphic account of the riot in the theater, excited by Demetrius the silversmith who saw in the new religion preached by Paul the death of his market for images of Artemis, the fertility goddess whose gigantic shrine sprawled over an area roughly corresponding to that of an American football stadium, with one hundred twenty-seven columns sixty feet high, thirty-six of them sculptured.

Paul's three years in Ephesus were perhaps the most successful of his entire career. Demetrius could exclaim that because of Paul's efforts the new religion had spread "almost over the whole province of Asia" (Acts 19:26). Paul would write from Ephesus that here "a door has been opened to me, great and evident" (1 Cor 16:9); through his efforts and those of his companions, Timothy, Erastus, Gaius, Aristarchus, and Epaphras (Acts 19:22, 29; Col 1:7), Christian communities were founded in Colossae, Laodicea, Hierapolis (Col 1:7; 2:1; 4:12 f.), Troas (2 Cor 2:12; Acts 20:5–12) and most probably the other Christian communities in Asia referred to in Apoc 1:11: Smyrna, Pergamum, Thyatira, Sardis, and Philadelphia.

But the success was not without its counterpart of danger and persecution (Acts 20:19; 21:27). Although it is not clear whether the "combat with wild beasts" (1 Cor 15:32) is to be taken literally or as a figure for his struggles with ferocious men, Paul was at one point "crushed beyond measure—beyond our strength, so that we were weary even of life" (2 Cor 1:8) and in serious danger of death (2 Cor 1:9 f.; 11:23, 26). The Acts are silent about these latter distresses, but their silence should not be a considered proof that Paul was never imprisoned in Ephesus, if there are other reasons pointing to such an incarceration. One of Paul's letters certainly written in prison is that to the Philippians. Many authorities in the past have held that Phil, like Col and Eph, was written during Paul's imprisonment in Rome. But in recent years more and more exegetes are accepting the reasons favoring the composition of this letter during an imprisonment of Paul during his three-year stay in Ephesus.

The reasons for preferring the Ephesian origin to the Roman are many. Chief among them is the fact that this origin fits the chronology of Acts and Corinthians perfectly. The numerous comings and goings which the letter supposes between the Philippians and the prisoner would demand an extremely long time if he were in Rome, whereas they could easily be made in the seven-day journey that separated Philippi from Ephesus. The fact that the Philippians and Paul assume (4:10) that they had no occasion to help him since his first visit would be hard to explain if Paul were in Rome, for by that time he had visited them twice on his third missionary journey, whereas at the Ephesus date he had not returned even once. Finally, the references to the Pretorian Guard (1:13) and the house of Caesar (4:22), which had led many commentators to choose the Roman origin of the letter, are now known to fit equally well the situation in Ephesus, where there was a detachment of the Pretorian Guard, and where there was also a group of slaves and freedmen of the emperor who belonged to the "house of Caesar."

The letter to the Philippians was written from Ephesus, then, very close to 1 Cor, probably before it.

THE LETTER: OCCASION AND PURPOSE

We have already discussed Paul's first missionary visit to Philippi, the principal Macedonian city which he evangelized on his second missionary journey (Acts 16:11–40). The details of the account in Acts tell us of an exorcism Paul worked there and of his brief imprisonment, but not a great deal about the community established there. Paul's letters, however, give us to understand that the community in Philippi was a fervent and stable one. Certainly it was one that showed great devotion to Paul, for although quite poor (2 Cor 8:2), the Philippians sent him aid at Thessalonica (Phil 4:16) and again at Corinth (2 Cor 11:9). It was the Philippians who first responded generously to Paul's collection for the poor in Jerusalem (2 Cor 8:2; Phil 4:15). The fact that Paul himself accepted their gifts to him attests to the exceptional confidence he had in them, for it was his practice not to depend financially on his communities, lest his motives be suspected.

Now, hearing of Paul's imprisonment, the Philippians have responded once again with financial aid, sending it through Epaphroditus, no doubt one of the leaders in their community (Phil 4:18). This manifestation of their great concern for Paul prompts him to open his heart in a letter which breathes the affection he has for them. Epaphroditus had fallen ill after his arrival, and the Philippians had sent word inquiring about him. By this time, however, their envoy had recovered. Paul sent him back to Philippi with this letter.

There is no dogmatic issue at stake in this letter, no attack of an adversary to answer, no interior trouble to reassure, no abuse to correct. The letter is the most personal of Paul's, and for this reason the most interesting, for its shows the thoughts which are dominating his meditation at this point in his ministry, when he has no polemic to carry on.

If the authenticity of this letter of Paul's is not generally contested today, the same cannot be said for its integrity. By the integrity of an epistle is meant the question as to whether all its parts are a single writing or whether it is a fusion of different letters written at different times with different aims. In our present letter there are certain abrupt changes of thought (for example 2:19; 3:2; 4:2, 10), which might suggest that Phil represents scraps of correspondence sewn together. One proposed reconstruction would see three different components: (1) 4:10–23, a note sent immediately after the arrival of Epaphroditus; (2) 1:1–2:18; 3:1–4:1; 4:8–9, a letter of a more doctrinal nature telling the Philippians of Paul's condition and urging them to stand firm in the faith; (3) 2:19–30; 4:2–7, a note entrusted to Timothy and Epaphroditus.

Such divisions are interesting and would explain how part of Phil may have come from a Roman captivity, whereas another part may have come from the Ephesian captivity, but it is a risky thing to apply twentieth-century scissors to a first-century document merely on the basis of internal criticism. The abrupt change of topics can just as readily be explained by the absence of polemic over a contested point and the unrelated nature of various topics Paul wished to cover in this letter—a common occurrence in personal correspondence.

Of particular interest is the appearance in the opening lines of the letter of the terms *Bishops (episkopoi)* and *deacons (diakonoi)*. This is the first mention in the epistles of official titles of the hierarchy. Paul had spoken in 1 Th 5:12 of those established in authority over the community. The more common name *presbyters* was used for those established, usually in collegial fashion, over the community, to exercise a limited authority under close supervision by the apostles. The *presbyters* were called *episkopoi* or "overseers" in relation to their function of ruling the Church (Acts 20:17, 28), which involved presiding at the assemblies, at the Eucharist, preaching, instructing catechumens, and administering church property. The *episkopos* or overseer is the Christian equivalent of an office already known at Qumran as the *Mabbeqer*.[1] The term *episkopos* at this time is thus simply a synonym for presbyter, stressing the function (overseeing) where *presbyter* (elder) stresses the dignity of the office. Both therefore correspond rather closely to today's parish clergy. The apostles did commit plenary apostolic authority to trusted fellow workers (1 Tim 3:1–15; Tit 1:5), and these are no doubt the forerunners of the *episkopoi* of a later time, who appear in the letters of Ignatius of Antioch (A.D. +107) as the equivalent of our modern "bishops."

Deacons assisted the *episkopoi* in fulfilling certain important functions in the community, whether temporal (as in Acts 6:1 ff.) or spiritual, as in preaching the gospel, teaching and baptizing converts (Acts 6:8– 8:40). Their qualifications are given in 1 Tim 3:8–13.

The message from the Philippians probably came from the "bishops" and deacons, whom Paul names in the address of the reply.

OUTLINE

---

[1]Cf. R. E. Brown, *New Testament Essays* (Milwaukee: Bruce, 1965), "The Qumran Scrolls and the Johannine Literature."

KENOSIS, THE CHRISTIAN FORMULA FOR GREATNESS: Phil 2:1–11

[1]*If then there is any encouragement in Christ, if there is any solace from charity, if there is any fellowship from the Spirit, if there are any feelings of compassion,* [2]*make my joy perfect by thinking alike, having the same charity, with one soul and one mind.* [3]*Let there be no spirit of contention or vain-glory among you, but rather let each one in humility regard the others as his superiors,* [4]*not seeking his own interests, but those of others.* [5]*Have this attitude which was also in Christ Jesus,*

[6]*Who, though he was in the form of God from the start,*
Did not consider equality with God
A thing to be clung to
[7]*But emptied himself,*
Taking the form of a slave,
Made in the likeness of men.
[8]*And looking outwardly like any other man,*
   He humbled himself,
Becoming obedient unto death,
Even to the death of the cross.
[9]*Therefore also God has exalted him*
And bestowed on him
The Name above all names,
[10]*So that in Jesus' name*
Every knee should bend
Of those in heaven, on earth and below,
[11]*And every tongue acclaim*
That Jesus Christ is Lord
Thus glorifying God the Father.

After encouraging his readers to firmness, Paul launches into an exhortation to fraternal union and charity, basing his appeal first upon the Philippians' own cherished values (1–4) and then upon the example of Christ (5–11). The appeal of the four introductory "if" clauses, as St. John Chrysostom already interpreted them, is apparently meant to lead up to the point Paul wants to make about the unity of sentiments. Some authors think that the four elements refer to the community's affection for Paul ("If you have any comfort for *me*," etc.), but there is no reason for limiting them to this, particularly since Paul has found their charity already active (1:9) and wishes precisely that the community achieve unity not with him but with one another. The "ifs" would rather express real conditions in the Philippian community, "If there is any encouragement in Christ among you (as I know there is). . . ."

Encouragement (paraklēsis) is a technical New Testament word and a favorite of Paul's. It is sometimes translated *consolation* or *comfort*, but even in this case it always bears the notion of an interior, spiritual strengthening in the faith (2 Th 2:17; Rom 1:11). It is a gift of God (2 Th 2:17) but is ordinarily channeled through instruments, either Scripture (Rom 15:4) or a stirring speaker (Rom 12:8) or one's fellow members of the community (Rom 1:11; 1 Th 4:18). In any case, it is found in the Christian's union with Christ.

The *solace* (2:1) that comes from charity is closely allied to the "encouragement" in Christ but expresses the nuance of alleviation of sorrow. *Fellowship (koinōnia)* is another technical New Testament word, used in Acts 2:42 to describe the intimate union of the first Christian community as it came regularly together and "broke bread." In the Pauline literature, it is used to described the many-faceted *union* effected by the new life in Christ: union with Christ (1 Cor 1:9), with the Holy Spirit (2 Cor 13:13), with the body and blood of Christ (1 Cor 10:16), with the sufferings of Christ (Phil 3:10), and of Christians with one another or with the apostles (Phil 1:5; 2:1). Here it means the fraternal union which is the gift of the Holy Spirit. With the first three appeals, we have a discreet allusion to the Holy Trinity, love being the characteristic gift of the Father (cf. 2 Cor 13:13; Rom 5:5). To this Paul now adds a motive more human: *any feelings of compassion*, perhaps here especially for Paul in his imprisonment.

Make my joy perfect by thinking alike. . . . We may sense here that some elements of division have arisen in the community—not a matter of false teaching but more probably the problem of compatibility of temperaments and views inevitable in a growing community. Echoes of this problem occur elsewhere in Phil (1:27; 2:14; 4:2; and Paul's stress on appealing to them all together: 1:1, 4, 7, 8, 25; 2:17, 26; 4:21). If there is any obstacle to reconciling these differences and forgetting them in Christ, it can only result from a spirit of contention and vainglory. For charity to flourish, these two attitudes must be replaced by the humility which prefers to consider others as one's superiors and the seeking of others' interests instead of one's own.

For that is precisely the example Christ has left us. The imitation of Christ goes to the very assimilation of his interior attitudes, his way of thinking. "Take the attitude which was that of Christ Jesus. . . ."

With v. 6, Paul slips into a new section which, although skillfully woven with the preceding, is different in literary form and new in the theological depths to which it leads the motivation for Christian unity and humility.

The first thing that comes to light on careful examination of vv. 6–11 is that here is neither rambling prose nor staccato of elliptical phrases such as Paul is at times capable of, but rather a veritable hymn, carefully structured into strophes, with balanced phrases, parallelisms, antitheses, assonances—all of which betray a careful and artistic composition. The vocabulary is unusual; many of the expressions are non-Pauline, several are even exceptional in common Greek usage. The theme developed here suggests Is 52–53, where we find the title *servant* (or *slave*) given to an individual whose voluntary humiliation is rewarded by his exaltation by God. V.11 in our present text is an explicit reference to Is 45:23. "Every knee shall bend . . . and every tongue shall swear (confess). . . ." Now Paul himself does not elsewhere use the Servant-of-Yahweh theme of Christ; the theme was nevertheless a central one of the self-revelation of Jesus according to the kerygma and the theology of the primitive Jerusalem community. All these considerations argue strongly for the original composition of this hymn in a Palestinian community or in some community strongly stamped by the Jerusalem conception of Christ as the Servant of Yahweh.[2]

The one concerning whom this entire hymn is predicated is Christ Jesus of v. 5. This is neither *merely* the historical Christ nor *merely* the transcendent Christ. Paul never isolates these two aspects of the same person, and there is no logic to the argument advanced by some that the transcendent Christ could not be proposed as a model, for in the

---

[2]D. M. Stanley, "The Theme of the Servant of Yahweh in Primitive Christian Soteriology, and its Transposition by St. Paul," *CBQ* 16 (1954), 420–425; "*Carmenque Christo quasi Deo dicere* . . ." *CBQ* 20 (1958), 180–182; "The Divinity of Christ in Hymns of the New Testament," in *Proceedings: Fourth Annual Meeting of the Society of Catholic College Teachers of Sacred Doctrine* (Notre Dame, Indiana, 1958), 12–29; *Christ's Resurrection in Pauline Soteriology*, 94–102.

New Testament even the Father is presented as a model to imitate (Mt 5:48; Eph 5:1).

Christ was from the start in the form of God. The verb used here (*hyparchōn*) is not the mere verb "to be" given in some translations but another verb meaning "to begin," or, in the intransitive, "to be already in existence." In Paul's usage of the verb elsewhere it has this same meaning—"Man is the image and glory of God *hyparchōn*," i.e., he is this by nature from the beginning, from his creation (1 Cor 11:7); or in Gal 2:14 Paul tells Peter, "If you *being* a Jew *from birth* live like a gentile . . ." (cf. also Acts 16:20, 37; 17:24). And thus it refers to an existent state of Christ rather than to any historical or singular manifestation of his glory such as would be his miracles or the Transfiguration. The present participle indicates a state which endures throughout the actions which follow.

Paul does not say that Christ was in the *nature* of God, but the word *form* (*morphē*) which he uses is closely allied to the idea of nature. It is not easy to determine how much Paul's conception of *form* reflects the Greek philosophical notion, but it is a fact that in Paul's usage *morphē* stands in stark contrast with *schēma*, which means what is only exterior, unstable, and transitory. Thus the "fashion of this world" which "passes away" is *schēma* (1 Cor 7:31), whereas the inner life, the achieving of genuine likeness with Christ, is described by a verb formed from *morphē*—"Be transformed by the renewal of your mind" (Rom 12:2; cf. 1 Pet 1:14). Even in profane Greek, the word *schēma* refers to something exterior—the costume, manner of acting, often with the pejorative sense of being ostentatious or false. *Morphē*, in Paul's usage, stands for something much more akin to the inner nature of the being. "Like the Latin 'forma' and the German 'Gestalt,' it signifies the form as it is the utterance of the inner life, not 'being' but 'mode of being' or better, 'mode of existence.' "[3] We can conclude that this first verse is telling us that the person of Christ was preexisting in a state or condition which was divine, a condition which he possessed in virtue of his very being.

St. Thomas, in commenting on this passage, asks why Paul uses the word *form* instead of *nature*. Form, he says, "befits those special names given to the Son in three ways. For he is called Son and Word and Image. The Son is one who is begotten, and the end of begetting is the form. And therefore, that he might be shown the perfect Son of God, Paul says *in the form*, as having the perfect form of the Father. Likewise a word is not perfect unless it leads to a knowledge of the nature of the thing it represents; and thus the Word of God is said to be in the form

---

[3] R. Trench, *Synonyms of the New Testament*, 65.

of God, because he has the complete form of the Father. Likewise neither is the image said to be perfect, unless it have the form of one whose image it is." This is a theological inference, of course, but it does not do violence to Paul's thought.

The interpretation of the next line depends on the translation of *harpagmon*, which admits of various meanings, for each of which some authority can be cited. The sense of "robbery," exegetes today generally agree, is to be discarded. The two meanings most probable are "a precious thing to be seized" or "a precious thing to be retained." If the first, then the equality with God was something Christ did not desire to acquire. But this would have no sense if, as the previous line indicates, he already somehow possessed the divine character.[4] Hence, the better interpretation is that of the earliest patristic citation we have (second century, *P.G.* 20:433B), that Christ, who possessed the immeasurable good of being equal with God, nevertheless refused to exploit it. This fits best with the parenetic character of the passage, too, in which Christ is held up as a model of disinterestedness and unselfishness.

Equality with God (2:6) is one of the strongest expressions of the New Testament. The only other passage that comes near to it is the later Jn 5:18, where the Jews accuse Jesus of making himself *equal* to God. In the latter passage the adjective *equal* in the Greek is in the masculine singular, as would be expected. But here in Phil 2:6, it is in the neuter plural—thus suggesting the divine attributes rather than divine personality. Since these things that belong to him in his divine state permit their being laid aside, they must be the attributes inasmuch as manifested visibly, the *brilliance* of the divine, the divine privileges. Just as "form of God" described Christ's inner divine character which never changes, this "equal to God" describes the external, divine brilliance which he has but does not cling to, for it can be renounced.

He emptied himself (2:7) not of the form of God which he possesses in a permanent way, but of this equality of privilege with God. The verb *empty* in Greek has the same root as "vainglory" in v. 3 and suggests by contrast that whereas that vice is a seeking of a glory that is vain, Christ deprived himself of a glory that was his due. St. Thomas sees in Paul's choice of the verb "emptying" a beautiful expression of the Incarnation:

> What is empty is opposed to what is full. Now the divine nature is full enough, for in it is all the perfection of goodness. . . . But human nature, and the human soul, is not full but rather in potency to fullness, because from its inception it is like a *tabula rasa*. Human nature is therefore empty, and thus he says "emptied" because he assumed human nature.

---

[4]But see P. Schoonenberg, *"He Emptied Himself" Philippians 2:7* in *Concilium* II, 47–66.

For the preexistent Christ, therefore, theIncarnation was no "addition" but rather a "subtraction," not indeed of his divine nature, but of the divine glory. From the verb *ekenōsen* the technical word *kenōsis* has been formed to signify the process of *emptying* with which this hymn deals.

Equivalent to the act of emptying, therefore, is that of taking the form of a slave. The word *slave* does not imply that Christ belonged to the social class of slaves among men. It refers rather to the condition of his humanity in contrast to his condition of Lordship coming up in v. 11. Above all, it has the religious sense in which Paul uses it of himself as one totally consecrated to God's service (Rom 1:1), but particularly with the note of humiliation and suffering which Second Isaiah had prophesied of the Servant of Yahweh, with whom Jesus had explicitly identified himself (Mk 8:31; 9:31; 10:32–34, 45). To adequately appreciate the Isaian background the student should at this point reread the Fourth Servant Song in Is 52–53. The contrast of Lord-Servant is strong in both the synoptic and the Johannine traditions (cf. Mk. 10:43–45; Jn 13:14–16; Gal 4:1).

Saying that Christ took the *form* of a slave does not imply that it was mere appearance, for as Theodoret already remarked, the same term *form* was used in v. 6 for God himself, who certainly has no visible or tangible appearance, and "thus the form of a slave does not designate merely what is seen but human nature as a whole" (*P.G.* 82:572D–573A). St. Thomas' theological insight on this phrase is again instructive:

> Why is it more fitting for the author to say 'the form' of a slave rather than 'a slave'? Because the term *slave* designates the hypostasis or supposit [the person], which was not assumed, but rather the nature. Now what is assumed is distinct from the one assuming. The Son of God, therefore, did not assume a man, for that would imply that the man was other [in person] than the Son of God, whereas it was the very Son of God who became man. He therefore took the nature in his own person, that the Son of God and the Son of man might be the same person.

The term *assume*, used by later theology for the action of the Incarnation, is simply an outgrowth of the word Paul uses here, *taking*.

Christ took a nature like ours in everything "except sin" (1 Cor 5:21). The word *likeness* in Paul stresses more the formal identity, at times visible, of the beings compared, rather than their distinction (cf. Rom 1:23; 5:14; 6:5; 8:3). We have already discussed the difference between form (*morphē*) as being interior and profound and figure (*schēma*) as being more exterior and superficial. *Likeness* (*homoiōma*, 2:7) is between the two. "Whereas *form* indicates something absolute, *likeness* refers to a relation to others of the same condition, *figure* to looks and appearance" (Bengel). It is this real solidarity with men which the epistle to the Hebrews extolls: "It was right that he should in all things be made *like* his brethren . . ." (2:17).

The beginning of v. 8 is literally "and in appearance found as a man. . . ." The thought of Christ's solidarity is here pursued in its external manifestations—dress, learning, gestures, eating, speech, actions. Everything that men could see and hear and touch in Christ proclaimed that he was one of them, "lost in the crowd," as it were. If there was already an *emptying* in the taking on of a human nature (v. 7), there was a true humiliation in taking one subject to pain, suffering, and death. There is a progression here which echoes the Song of the Servant: "There was in him no stately bearing to make us look at him, nor appearance that would attract us to him. He was spurned and avoided by men, a man of suffering, accustomed to infirmity . . . yet it was our infirmities that he bore, our sufferings that he endured . . ." (Is 52:2–4).

Thus Paul is speaking here not only of the preexistent Christ nor of the Incarnation in an ontological sense; he is now speaking also of the historical Christ and of his Incarnation as a phenomenological event, perceptible in all its pathos to men. Even in his humanity he does not appear as Lord but as servant.

The most characteristic virtue of a servant is obedience. Christ was born under obedience to the Law (Gal 4:4); he obeyed men (Lk 2:51), delivering himself freely even to his unjust judge (1 Pet 2:23), but here it is his obedience to God which is extolled. Christ's passion and death was essentially an act of obedience, repairing for the race what was lost through the disobedience of the first man (Rom 5:19). There is no mention of the redemptive value of his death here as there is in Rom 5:19 and Heb 5:8 f., because Paul is concentrating on Christ's personal abasement and reward. Now of all deaths, that of the cross was·the most shameful, both in Hebrew thought (Dt 21:23 = Gal 3:13; Heb 12:2) and in Roman (Cicero, *Verr.* 5:64), because it was the type of capital punishment meted out, precisely, to slaves.

Suddenly there is a reversal of action and of agent. Whereas Christ has been the subject of all the preceding deeds of emptying and humiliation, now he becomes the object of God's action upon him: exaltation and bestowal of the name Lord. The emphasis falling on the initial *therefore* (2:9) relates the divine exaltation directly to the self-humiliation of Christ—the kind of divine seesaw which comes repeatedly in the New Testament: to be exalted by God one must first plunge to the depths of annihilation of self (Lk 14:11; 18:14; 1:52; Prov 3:34). The exaltation consists, of course, in Christ's resurrection (constantly referred to the Father as its cause), and his enthronement as Lord. The use of the intensive form *hyperypsōsen* may indicate that Christ now has *more* than what he started with in the form of God, in the sense that he now has a glorified humanity; it may also be intended to convey the very Pauline idea that God's reward always surpasses in glory what man has endured in suffering (Rom 5:15, 20; 8:18).[5]

The bestowal of a name means much more in Semitic and early Christian thought than in modern naming or christening. In the context of the divine plan it refers to the manifestation of God's glory, power, or presence in his saving deeds, by which he "makes himself a name" (Is 63:12; Jer 32:20). Here, of course, it is a name that is *bestowed*, that is, given as a reward. The name above all names is not that of Jesus, or Christ, or God, but, as v. 11 indicates, the name *Lord*, *kyrios* in the Greek, *Yahweh* in the Hebrew, the name used constantly in the Old Testament for the God of Israel. Here it is the superiority of this name above all others that is stressed, as in Eph 1:21 and Heb 1:4. Christ then enters into divine honors, not as though he *became* God through his resurrection, but now in his humanity that obeyed and suffered, he is constituted in that glory which was his *right* in virtue of his preexistence, and is now his *reward* in virtue of his sacrifice.

The greatest proof of Paul's faith and proclamation of the divinity of Christ lies in v. 10—"that at the name of Jesus every knee should bend. . . ." Paul is consciously applying an Old Testament text used of the adoration given to God alone and applying it to Jesus (Is 45:23: "to me every knee shall bend and every tongue shall swear . . ."). A similar transfer of the divine names to Christ is made in Rom 14:11. We do not yet have the technical term *"consubstantial* with the Father," which will come out of the Arian controversy, but to a Jew of Paul's time, using the divine name as he does could only mean an affirmation of the divinity of Christ in the fullest sense of the term.

The being *in heaven, on earth, and below* (2:10) refer to the angels, good and bad (Col 1:16–20; 2:15), to men and the forces at work on the earth, and to the souls of the deceased—the "sheol." The triple enumeration is a rhetorical device to express the universality of Christ's Lordship, and the meaning of the distinct spheres of influence need not be pressed.

The acclamation "Jesus is Lord" was a summary of the earliest Christian creed (1 Cor 12:3; Rom 10:9). *Lord* here stands in sharp contrast to *slave*, and in Pauline theology it means the state of glory Christ now enjoys as a result of being raised from the dead and exalted to the right hand of God, making him Son of God *in power* (Rom 1:4);

---

[5] F. Martin, "And Therefore God Raised Him on High" (Phil 2:9), *TBT* 11 (March 1964), 694–700.

that is, the instating of the integral Christ, now with his human nature, in that glory which was his by right through preexistence but now in his nature or form as servant has been won through obedience, suffering, and death. By the very fact, this exaltation makes him Lord of the universe and demands that every creature acclaim him as such. It is the Father who has exalted and glorified the Son, but he has done so in order that all creatures in their turn so acclaim him—this very movement of adoration of the Son having as its fruit the glorification of God the Father. In Jn 17:1–5 the Father glorifies the Son in order that the Son glorify the Father. For John, this takes place already during the earthly life of Jesus. This corresponds to the general Johannine manner of conceiving the earthly life of Christ as a manifestation of God's glory in the flesh (1:14; 2:11; 12:23–24, 28; 18:6). For Saint Paul the earthly life of Jesus was a hiding, or really a sacrificing of that divine glory that was his by right and a fulfillment of the role of the Suffering Servant in its most humiliating aspects. The outbreak of the divine glory appeared only at the resurrection, itself a promise of the Parousia, when all creation will be compelled to confess that Jesus Christ is Lord.[6]

* * *

This text is a dense theology of the Incarnation. Without ceasing to have the character of God, the Son foregoes that external glory which is his by right, in order to assume the nature of the Servant, becoming like men in all things, one among many. He went farther still, submitting to humiliation and becoming obedient even to death and to the supreme ignominy of death on a cross. The Father has rewarded this abasement by raising Christ from the dead, thus constituting him now in his humanity in the glory that is properly divine, declaring him worthy and deserving of the worship given to God alone.

In all this Christ is given to Christians as an example that the way to glory is not through glory but through the emptying of self even of legitimate satisfaction in order to serve.

THE KNOWLEDGE AND POSSESSION OF CHRIST: Phil 3:7–16

[7]*But the things that were an advantage to me, these for the sake of Christ I have counted loss.* [8]*More than that, I count everything loss in comparison with the supreme advantage of knowing Christ Jesus, my Lord. For his sake I have suffered the loss of all things, and I count them refuse, that I may gain Christ* [9]*and be found in him, not with a*

---

[6]M. Trinitas, "Jesus is Lord," *TBT* 11 (March 1964), 701–708.

justice of my own derived from the law, but with the justice that comes from faith in Christ—the justice that God gives on the basis of faith.
[10]*And this in order that I might learn to know him, and what a power his resurrection is, and what it is to share his sufferings. Growing conformed with his death,* [11]*I hope that I may somehow attain to the resurrection from the dead.* [12]*Not that I have already attained or have already become perfect. No—I press on, hoping to overtake and seize, for I myself was overtaken and seized by Christ Jesus.* [13]*Brothers, I do not pretend that I have already laid hold. But one thing I do: forgetting what lies behind and straining toward what lies before,* [14]*I press on toward the goal, to the prize of God's heavenward calling in Christ Jesus.* [15]*Let us, then, as many as are spiritually mature, be of this mind. If you see it another way, God will clarify the difficulty for you.* [16]*It is important that we continue on our course, no matter what stage we have reached.*

V. 6 ended on the note of justice, that state of blamelessness which the Pharisees, and Paul before his conversion, thought came uniquely from a meticulous observance of the Law and all the legal traditions with which it had been embroidered. In this Paul was an irreproachable model. He had considered this an immense good, a gain for him, until he met Christ on the Damascus road. Now all those things are for him loss—and all else, i.e., all human values apart from Christ become subtractions, a waste of time and energy, not because of any intrinsic evil in themselves, but because they cannot compare with the surpassing *knowledge of Christ Jesus my Lord* (3:7). It is Paul's own experience of Christ that he is here appealing to (*knowledge* here has the fundamentally Semitic sense of personal union), but always with the idea of holding this up as an example of what every Christian's life should be (v. 17). For the sake of Christ, that is, with the purpose of attaining him perfectly, Paul has willingly suffered the loss of all things; he considers them *skybalon*—literally meaning "what is thrown to the dogs," by usage meaning the scraps left over from eating, offscouring of pots, garbage, or even dung.

That I may be found in him . . . (3:9). It is not easy to say whether Paul is thinking of what he has already gained in Christ by comparison with what he has rejected, or whether he is looking still to the more perfect possession of Christ and by Christ at the Parousia. The two senses are not necessarily exclusive and, in the sequence, Paul has in mind both the future (the goal, the prize) and the present (faith, sharing Christ's sufferings). "In Him" expresses the essence of the Christian life, which the sequence now describes in terms of "justice." This theme will be developed at length in Gal and Rom, where it reveals the tones of polemic. Here we have a first sketch, and a precious one, and we shall at this time only underline the traits it bears here: (1) *It is not a self-produced justice,* "mine" in the sense of a salary paid for work. (2) Nor does it come from the Law—theme to be developed in Gal 3:21 f.; Rom 3:21 f.; 10:3, where the attempt to attain justice through the Law alone is caricatured precisely as attempting to establish one's *own* justice. (3) It comes through *faith* in Christ. Man's response of faith is here presented as the instrument or vehicle (the preposition *dia*) of justice. (4) It is a justice *from* God, hence not a reward or a salary but a gift. "Justice" here, then, does not mean an attribute of God (although this thought of the "justice of God," to be developed in Romans, may be here in germ) but the justice that comes from God and is given to man. Here it is an attribute of man which changes him from a sinner to a friend of God, but even so it remains a gift. And thus man, even transformed, has nothing wherein to glory, except in the goodness of God to him. (5) It *rests upon faith.* The preposition *epi* represents an advance over *dia.* It suggests that this gift of justice is an abiding reality, and that just as faith was the door by which God's justice entered man's being in the first place, so faith is also the foundation on which the life of justice rests. (6) It makes possible three great goods: (*a*) The knowledge of Christ. This is not the initial knowledge which comes upon conversion but a deepening of it to which Paul aspires (as in Eph 3:19)—as indicated by the ingressive aorist purpose infinitive, which R. Knox translates, "Him I would learn to know. . . ." There is then a growth in the knowledge of Christ which is rooted in faith. It is a personal knowledge, the verb *ginōskein* expressing here as it does elsewhere a personal relation between the knower and the known (1 Cor 2:8; Jn 2:24, 25; 1 Jn 4:8). (*b*) An experience of the power of Christ's resurrection. *His resurrection* (3:10) is best interpreted appositively, as the power which is resurrection is—not merely showing Christ to be divine (2:10 f.; Rom 1:4), manifesting the glory of the Father (2:11; Rom 6:4) and guaranteeing the future glorious bodily transformation of Christians (Phil 3:21), but—and this is the meaning here—acting as a vital force in Paul's daily life. This thought of the present power of Christ's resurrection is an advance over the theology of Thessalonians, where the resurrection is viewed as an eschatological event; the "immanent" transforming power of Christ's resurrection will be developed in 2 Cor 3:18 where Paul states that to be united with Christ is to be under the constant influence of his glorified humanity. (*c*) A communion with Christ's sufferings. Paul's ministry and his present imprisonment have taught him this in a very real and experiential way. His conversion on the Damascus road involved first seeing the risen Christ (Acts 9:4 ff.) and then learning how much he must suffer for him (v. 16). Now Paul has come to see the full meaning of that experience; he knows that conformity with Christ means an identification with Christ in suffering, and this is something to be desired. Paul will say in 1 Cor 15:31 that he "dies daily." Here the present participle *symmorphizomenos*, "becoming conformed," is a word of Paul's coining; it is found nowhere else in Greek. It stresses his eagerness to *grow* in conformity with the suffering Christ.[7]

Whereas in Col 1:24 Paul will find the great motive for these sufferings in the good they bring to the Church, here it is his own personal goal that inspires him. Indirectly, of course, he is using his own example as an argument *a fortiori* to show what his readers' attitude should be.

It is above all his realization that he is "not yet there" (v. 12) that fires his desire for progressive assimilation or "embodiment" of the mystery of Christ's death. This growth is the only path that gives him any hope of attaining the glorious resurrection. And lest any of his readers think that by seeing Christ on the Damascus road or by his subsequent career he has "arrived," Paul wishes expressly to correct this impression: "Not that I have already attained." It may well be that Paul, having disposed of the Judaizers in vv. 2–11, now turns to Christian enthusiasts of the other extreme who think that they have already attained the resurrection. At any rate, the aorist indicates he is referring to the moment of his conversion: that was only the beginning; it was not the immediate reaching of the goal.

Not once does Paul tell us the object of his pursuit or of his seizing, and there is no sense trying to supply one in the translation. He evidently wishes to underscore not the term but the fundamental attitude which should characterize progress to it. We would say today: "I don't mean to say I have arrived," to stress not where we have arrived but the satisfaction we do not yet have of getting where we were going.

It is this satisfaction that Paul rejects. The fact of his conversion gives him no right to it. And his attitude toward what has happened since then is expressed by the following, "nor have I now become perfect." Since in v. 14 he considers himself among the perfect, the perfection which he denies himself here must be the absolute perfection of final reunion with Christ. It is possible that some might judge that Paul's identification with Christ unto chains has now made him "perfect"? The thought would later be denounced by Ignatius of Antioch in

---

[7]The chapters entitled "The Power of His Resurrection" and "The Fellowship of His Sufferings" in B. M. Ahern, *New Horizons* (Notre Dame: Fides, 1963); also *CBQ* 22 (1960), 1–32; P. Hinnebusch, "Christian Fellowship in the Epistle to the Philippians," *TBT* 12 (April 1964), 793–798.

similar circumstances: "Even though I am in chains for the sake of the Name, I am not yet perfected in Jesus Christ" (*Ephesians* 3, *P.G.* 5:645–648). And "Being in chains for his sake I am all the more apprehensive, since I am not yet perfected" (*Philadelphians* 5). At any rate, the prisoner does not hesitate to say that even in chains he continues in hot pursuit. For Paul the spiritual life is not merely a walking (Gal 5:16; Col 2:6; Phil 3:17; Eph 4:1) nor merely a running (Rom 9:16; 1 Cor 9:24, 26; Phil 2:16; Gal 5:7) but a pursuit. When Paul thinks of acquiring virtues, he thinks of *pursuing* them: the good (1 Th 5:15), justice (Rom 9:30 f.), hospitality (12:13), charity (1 Cor 14:1), the things of peace (Rom 14:19). The image both stresses the goal and suggests its elusiveness. Not only the desire of the goal but the anxiety caused by its absence spurs the Apostle's efforts. The expression "that I may somehow attain" is not so much an expression of uncertainty about attaining the goal (cf. 2:16) as a diffidence in the worth of his acquired gain to bring him to it.

The verbs "pursue" and "lay hold of" are paired in military contexts to express pursuit of fugitives with the determination to capture them, and in the figurative sense for the pursuit of an ideal unto perfect attainment (Rom 9:30 f.; Sir 11:10). The verb *katalabō* represents an advance over the previous verbs. It means to "overtake and seize," to "make one's own." This advance parallels perfectly what Paul teaches in 1 Cor 13:12: "Now my knowledge is incomplete, but then I shall have complete knowledge," the contrasting expressions themselves paralleling the contrast between vague, mirror-type sight and vision face to face. These parallels, and the lingering force of "to know him" (v. 10) justify interpreting this "seizure" which marks the final triumph as the knowledge of perfect vision.

What follows may be taken as the object of seizing: *Hoping to overtake and seize that for which I myself was overtaken and seized.* . . . In this sense, the Apostle's ambition would be to reach the ideal contemplated and fixed by Christ when he converted Saul on the Damascus road. Or the verb "seize" may be taken absolutely and the sequence as meaning "*because* I was seized by Christ." The latter interpretation enjoys the support of the majority of commentators, ancient and modern. Paul would then consider his striving as the paying of a sacred debt, as Chrysostom already observed. In the same tradition, Theophylact glosses: "When I was counted among the perishing and condemned, Christ pursued me as I fled from him and captured me and converted me to himself. I must, in turn, follow him hereafter so as to seize him." As a matter of fact, the verb *diōkein* can mean either "pursue" or "persecute." Paul may be playing on the double meaning of the word: "At conversion Christ said: 'I am Jesus whom you are *persecuting*' (pursuing to destroy, *diōkeis*, Acts 9:5). His seizure of me was a conversion, but not the end of pursuit—rather, only its beginning. For it fired me more than ever to *pursue him* (*diōkō*), not to put him in chains but to possess him in consummate union." We cannot overestimate Paul's conviction of his being conquered and captured by Christ. If he has become an Apostle with the mission of preaching the gospel, it has been by force (1 Cor 9:16). If he is now a soldier of Christ, doing his work and borne in his victory parade (2 Cor 2:14 f.), it is because he was first conquered and captured by the divine Warrior on the Damascus road.

Whatever be the translation of this segment, the basic idea is that to the action of Christ's seizing of Paul must correspond Paul's seizing of Christ—but not as a mere analogy, for Paul's grasping is made possible by Christ's and is founded therein. It seems that this is simply a variation of Paul's favorite theme that the aim of the Christian life is to know Christ (or God) as perfectly as one has been known by him (1 Cor 13:12; cf. Gal 4:9 and Jn 10:14; 2 Tim 2:19). Paul's strenuous efforts have their source and term not in a Stoic ideal of self-mastery, but in Christ.

What Paul has said in v. 12—disavowal of satisfaction with his attainment and declaration of his strenuous pursuit of the ideal—he substantially repeats in vv. 13–14, but more vigorously. *Brothers*, he begins, with an evident view to arresting attention. *I do not pretend that I have already laid hold (of it).* The Greek construction underlines Paul's emphasis on himself, less perhaps to contrast his lowly opinion of himself with others' high opinion of him than to contrast his opinion of himself with others' opinions of themselves. Paul fears an excessive self-estimation or self-satisfaction on the part of his readers and in the gentlest way warns them by appealing to his own example: "I myself . . . what about you?" Chrysostom comments:

> Most certainly he who thinks himself perfect, he who thinks he lacks nothing for possessing perfect virtue, will cease running, as if he had already made the goal. But he who considers himself still far from the finish-line, will not slacken his drive (*P.G.* 62:271).

Paul fixes his efforts on one single aim. Forgetting what lies behind, he strives for what lies ahead. The "landmarks already passed" does not refer to his life under the Law, for this interpretation would go against the whole context of vv. 12–14, and although he *forgets* the ground covered, he does not say it is loss, as he does of his pursuits before the race started (vv. 7–9). It rather refers to the portion of his *Christian* course already traversed. This he forgets. It is not that he is ashamed of the progress he has made thus far, for it manifests the grace of God and stimulates greater strivings (1 Cor 4:11–16; 9:19–27; 15:10; 2 Cor 11:23–12:6). The attitude he skewers is the lingering on the past which leads to a slackening of efforts through discouragement, or, more to the point here, through self-sufficiency. "We have our full ardor," comments Chrysostom, "only when we throw the whole striving of our soul toward the remainder of the struggle and cast the past into oblivion" (ibid.). Paul's whole striving is for what lies before him. He is "straining every nerve and muscle" for the higher attainments of the Christian life. The participle "straining toward" is clearly lifted from the imagery of the arena, and particularly of the footrace, as is shown in Lucian's description of the runner:

> The sort of thing which occurs in the athletic contest takes place in a foot-race. Here too the good runner, as soon as the first barrier is dropped, strives only for what lies ahead. He has his mind set on the goal alone. He trusts in his own feet to bring him victory, and he is all fair play to the contestant next to him; what the other runners are doing is no concern of his (*Calumn.* 12).

From this image, English usage has coined the expression "the home stretch."

I press on toward the goal (3:12). *Skopos* as the word for goal appears only here in the whole New Testament. It is that on which one fixes the eye. Used in classical Greek and in the Septuagint for a mark to be shot at, it took on also the metaphorical sense of end, aim, object. Paul's image is clear:

> For the runner in the arena to look back is not only useless but dangerous. He must keep his eye fixed constantly before him to keep from swerving from the straight line and likewise to foresee the unexpected— accidents or obstacles that would slow his pace or cause his fall. The desire to win gives him wings, and he strives for the goal with every nerve and thought, knowing well that a moment's slack could lose the victory. The classic images evoke those agile racers, feet skimming the ground, head and chest straining forward, arm stretched toward the goal their eye devours.[8]

The accumulation of objectless verbs bears, like the runner, on the long-awaited *prize*, whose modifying "of the upward calling" lights up the spiritual meaning of the metaphor. The prize is the "crown of righteousness" as in 1 Cor 9:24–27 and 2 Tim 4:8 (cf. Apoc 2:10), the share in the glory of the exalted Christ (Rom 8:17 and 2 Tim 2:10 f.), the eternal life with which one already comes to grips in the struggle (1

---

[8]F. Prat, "Un aspect de l'Ascèse dans S. Paul," *Revue d'Ascétique et Mystique* (January 1921), 14.

Tim 6:12). This prize is attached to the act by which God calls, is offered in it, contained in it. The call is literally *upward*, hence not heavenly but *heavenward* (as in Jn 11:41; Heb 12:15), stressing the goal of a movement. Chrysostom explains the image:

> Christ has willed that the theater of the struggle be here below; and there above, the crowning. . . . Even in our cities, when the champion athlete or horseman goes to receive the prize, he does not remain below in the arena. He goes up, called by the emperor, who from his elevated throne crowns him (*P.G.* 62:272).

The total significance of the metaphor will now come to light if we compare the "prize of the calling" with its parallel "hope of the calling" in Eph 1:18 and 4:4. The calling, involving as it does the prize, engenders hope, which here is the vigorous energy firing the "do-better-yet" of the race. Impelled by the prize, the Christian deploys every faculty and every ounce of energy to cover the remaining stretch. Courage, strength, perseverance, generosity, wholeheartedness, endurance are all evoked by the image; but the point highlighted here is that, just as the passion to win rules out any reliance on the stretch traversed—and even any thought of it—so too the Christian will not linger upon past gains or present virtues; the hunger for perfect union with Christ, which marked his conversion, will only grow more acute as the race advances. One single intention obliterates every other consideration: consummate possession of Christ.

Paul's example has been an implicit sermon for his readers. Lest they miss the point, he now invites them to join him in the same pursuit. He even presumes that many of them are far advanced, like himself, on the road: "Let us then, as many as are spiritually mature (*teleioi*) be of this mind." The word *teleioi* cannot mean "the perfect" in the sense of "consummated in perfection," as it does in 1 Cor 13:10 ff., for Paul has just denied this in verse 12. Nor does the term reveal an influence of the mystery religions so as to be rendered "initiated." When it does not mean those consummately perfect, it means one who is spiritually an adult. Its counterpart is "infant" (*nēpios*, Eph 4:13 f.; cf. 1 Cor 14:20), which is applied to those Christians making their first faltering steps in their new life, capable of assimilating only the milk of elementary doctrine, not the solid food of which the "spiritual men" (*pneumatikoi*) are capable (3:1). These have not merely received the Spirit but likewise live according to the Spirit (Gàl 5:25); they are moved by the Spirit (Rom 8:14) and show their adulthood by standing firm against the changing winds and waves of false doctrines (Eph 4:14) and—our present text makes it clear—by striving for constant progress. The *teleioi* here, then, are those who progress—those whom later spirituality would call "proficients." It is a title which challenges one to attain perfection and to act in accord with his call thereto—"You are perfect, think of doing perfect things," writes Ignatius to the Smyrnians (11:3). It imposes the conviction that one is far from perfection; as if Paul said, "Let us then, as many as are perfect, realize we are not perfect." The ancient commentators were impressed by this paradox: To the remark of Chrysostom, "the mark of perfection is not to believe oneself perfect," Theophylact adds, "This is perfection, not to lean upon it." And St. Thomas: "The more perfect one is, the more imperfect he knows himself to be."[9]

But at the same time this realization conveys a confidence in one's virility to attain the desired end. The word *teleios* seems made to describe athletes capable of magnanimous efforts: "Bear the infirmities of all like a master athlete (*teleios athlētēs*). The greater the toil, the greater the reward" (Ignatius to *Polycarp*, 1:3). And that on which all are to agree is the ideal of continual progress just depicted by Paul. "If then we are spiritually mature," Paul would say, "let us show it by making ever greater progress."

If you see it another way, God will clarify the difficulty for you (3:15). It is not that Paul would countenance disagreement with his teaching on the uselessness of circumcision or the moral demands of the gospel; but he has just held up an ideal of progress so lofty—*continual* progress—that his slower-paced followers may not think it possible—or this sublime ideal may have opened up new avenues as yet beyond their grasp. Hence God himself will take care of clarifying Paul's teaching and bringing it to profit (cf. 2 Tim 2:7). Such is the interpretation of Chrysostom, who goes on to remark that the use of the verb *reveal* shows that their inadequacy would be merely a matter of ignorance:

> These words do not concern the teaching of doctrine but the *perfection* of morals. They prescribe that no one regard himself perfect; for, as soon as one thinks himself in full possession of virtue, one has absolutely nothing (*P.G.* 62:272).

With v. 16 Paul concludes the discussion. Literally, the text reads: "Still, whatever we have attained, let us hold to the same." The same *what*? The commentators try to supply a complement here; but much is merely conjecture. The best explanation seems to be that Paul, having held up the ideal of continual progress and having realized that the sublimity of the ideal may leave some aspects not yet understood, now

---

[9] J. T. Forestell, "Christian Perfection and Gnosis in Phil 3:7–16," *CBQ* 15 (1953), 163–207.

says that *in any case* they should hold on to the progress they have made and moreover hold to the direction, the line which has led them where they are, finding therein the principle of new progress. Or, to exploit the lingering figure of the footrace, progress does not mean getting out of line or thinking that the running is better in another's path. Rather, in order to progress, they must hold to the same line and directions which have led them where they are. The Greek infinitive used for the imperative and its final position give the character of an exclamation and stress the urgency of the command. "You are in the clear. All you need is full speed ahead. Whatever you do, don't change your tactics!"

No other text of St. Paul presents so vividly and vigorously the progressive nature of the Christian life.

COLONISTS AND VICTORY: Phil 3:20–21

[20]Our commonwealth, however, exists in heaven. It is from there that we expect as Savior the Lord Jesus Christ, [21]who will transform our lowly body, conforming it to his glorious body, in keeping with that power enabling him to subject the universe to himself.

Against the way of acting described in v. 19, which manifests that its authors have made their home the things of this earth, stands the Christian attitude flowing from a consciousness of its origin in a different commonwealth.[10] The *our* is emphatic—but as for *us*. *Politeuma* does not mean citizenship but commonwealth; it is often used for a colony of foreigners. The city of Philippi consisted mainly of Italian colonists and hence was essentially a Latin city, with its administration modeled on that of Rome. The Philippians could easily therefore understand Paul's figure of a homeland elsewhere. "Our home is in heaven," comments M. Dibelius, "and here on earth we are a colony of heavenly citizens." With this line Paul has set the cornerstone of the Christian's view of the world, on which Augustine will raise the first Christian "theology of history" in *The City of God*. Paul does not condemn real human values (as is shown a few lines later—4:8–9), and he himself gives the example not only of being debtor to Greek and foreigner, to learned and unlearned (Rom 1:14) but of incarnating himself and the gospel into the world about him with its preoccupations, making himself all things to all men (1 Cor 9:22). But at the same time, when the Christian works in this world he does not lose himself in it, but with a continual restlessness for the better city of heaven, he alone can keep the world from losing itself, for not looking beyond its own horizons. Here,

---

[10]N. Flanagan, "A Note on Philippians 3:20–21," *CBQ* 18 (1956), 8–9.

however, heaven is not some place to go, but the place whence Christ will come, his "capital" as it were. Christian life transcends the earthly because Christ, its source and inspiration, is in heaven and will return. This latter portion of the verse mirrors perfectly the eschatology of the early Jerusalem community, as revealed in the preaching of Peter in Acts 3:20–21:

> "in order that so the times of refreshment may come from the presence of the Lord, and that he may send him who has been destined beforehand for you as the Christ, Jesus. Heaven must receive him until the time of the restoration of all things. . . ."

In v. 21, Paul describes the resurrection with a vocabulary that echoes the kenotic hymn of 2:6–11. There Christ: (1) in the *form* of God takes the *form* of a slave, (2) in outward *appearance* (*schēma*) found as a man, (3) he lowered himself. Here the process is reversed, Christ: (1) taking Christians' *lowly* body and (2) changing its appearance (*metaschēma*) (3) makes it have the same *form* as his glorious body.

The final phrase casts the whole process into a cosmic reference. The power Christ exerts in raising Christians is the same power by which he is capable of subjecting the universe to himself and actually does so (cf. 1 Cor 15:27; Heb 2:6–8). We may wonder why Paul makes so much of the victory of Christ over all things, even giving it the emphatic position in this sentence, when the most important, the essential victory is surely that of the resurrection. Our modern manner of regarding the world, even as Christians, is unfortunately so easily reconciled to partial victory that we have a psychological difficulty understanding the basic restlessness of the Jewish and early Christian soul with the world around it. For the early Christians, heirs to the Old Testament conviction that all creation is made for the spirit, the neo-Platonic victory by escape from the world was incomprehensible. Resurrection that would not also entail a remaking of the universe would be only a half-victory. If there is to be resurrection, this is only the initial conquest, the fall of the citadel of Satan, and the first step toward repossession of all of creation which sin has wrenched from God.

In our present verse, the moment of this total victory is the Parousia, something yet to come. We shall see later how the interiorization of this view also affects the Christian's present attitude toward the world.

CHAPTER FOUR

The Letters to the Corinthians

CORINTH—THE CITY AND ITS EVANGELIZATION

In classical times, Corinth had enjoyed an international prestige—it was a center of pottery and bronze work, an enterprising seaport city that established colonies as far west as Syracuse. But in 146 B.C. the Roman consul Mummius, wishing to favor the Italian merchants of the more recently established rival port of Delos, razed the port of Corinth. On its ruins a century later (44 B.C.) Julius Caesar founded the Roman colony called *Laus Julia Corinthus,* comprising chiefly the veterans of the army defeated at Pharsalus, soon to be joined by an influx of immigrants from neighboring states. The new city thrived, situated as it was on the isthmus, with its port of Cenchrea looking to the East and Lechaeum to the West. So heavy grew the shipping traffic that a stone-paved road called the Diolkos was built joining the two ports and boats were "ferried" on rollers or sleds from one port to the other. Nero began the construction of a canal, completed only at the end of the nineteenth century under French and Greek direction.

No little boost to the city's renown came in 27 B.C. when, as a result of the division of provinces between Augustus and the Senate, Achaia fell to the latter and Corinth was made its capital and seat of the proconsul. By the time of Saint Paul, the population of "greater Corinth" had grown to such an extent that according to one estimate, surely exaggerated, the number of inhabitants was 600,000. Around the nucleus of Latin residents was an agglomerate of Greeks and Near-Easterners of every provenance, including a considerable number of Jews, attracted by the commercial advantages of the city. Economically, the city was composed of a small number of wealthy merchants, a large number of poor workmen, and the rest—a good two-thirds of the population— slaves (cf. 1 Cor 1:26–31). In addition to the Jewish synagogue, there were temples to Apollo, Asclepius, Athene, Zeus, Cybele, Isis, Serapis, Melkart, Aphrodite. The cult of Jupiter Capitolinus and of Artemis of Ephesus, the Great Mother, flourished, as did most probably certain "mysteries," those of Isis surely, and probably those of Bacchus. Of all these most prominence was claimed by the cult of Aphrodite (Roman Venus), whose sanctuary dominated the city from the Acrocorinth (the high acropolis of the city), where in classical times, according to Strabo, some one thousand female hierodules practiced sacred prostitution. In the excavations of the theater, a stone seat was discovered bearing the inscription "of the girls," indicating these hierodules had their reserved seats there.

The effect of the cult of Aphrodite on the morality of the city was obvious. The term "Corinthian girl" came to mean "prostitute" and *korinthiazesthai*, "to Corinthianize, live like a Corinthian," came to signify living a dissolute life. If Aelius Aristides' remark is true, "No other city has fascinations more powerful to draw men of every race—it is the city of Aphrodite," still it was an expensive venture to go there as a playboy, as was reflected by the proverb, "Not every man has the means to go to Corinth."

The isthmic games flourished at Corinth (cf. 1 Cor 9:26 f.); but of all the Greek cities, Corinth was virtually alone in its enthusiastic adoption of the homicidal games of the Roman amphitheater.

This was the city in which Paul arrived from Athens, discouraged at his failure to win the Areopagite Greeks through the approach of natural theology. In this port city now, after employing his usual method of preaching first to the Jews, Paul turned to the Gentiles. In spite of initial success, Paul's depression must have lasted some time, until the reassuring vision in which Christ told him, "Do not fear, but speak and do not keep silence; because I am with you, for I have many people in this city" (Acts 18:10 f.). As a matter of fact, Paul's ministry of nearly two years must have been an extremely fruitful one, fanning out to other areas, for 2 Cor speaks of the "churches" of Achaia.

To these people, of generally poor culture (1 Cor 1:26), many of whom had led depraved lives (1 Cor 6:11), Paul, abandoning the "wisdom" approach he had attempted in Athens, preached the folly of the cross (1 Cor 1:17). The spirit of this religion was so different, the reversal of values so cataclysmic, that it won great numbers and fired the enthusiasm of the new community. On the Hellenistic soil of Corinth was proved once more what had happened in Palestine, that sinners and harlots would precede many others into the kingdom of God.

The community forged by the gospel of Paul differed not only in moral background but in race and social position as well: Jews, Greeks, Orientals, immigrants from everywhere found themselves suddenly brothers in Christ. Slaves, too, found themselves alongside the nobility of the day. Among the latter was Crispius, the former president of the synagogue, and Erastus, the city treasurer (Rom 16:23; Acts 19:22), who seem to have been quite wealthy. Women, too, formed an important part in the community, taking an active part in its life—to an extent that would call for some regulation later (1 Cor 11).

During Paul's stay there, things apparently went well, but it is obvious how easily such a community might be upset by factions, by moral backsliders, or by a spirit of rivalry. It is precisely these difficulties that appear after Paul's departure and explain much of the subject matter of our 1 and 2 Corinthians.

THE WRITING OF 1 CORINTHIANS

First Corinthians was certainly written from Ephesus during Paul's ministry there, before the riot of the silversmiths which forced him to leave the city (Acts 20:1). When Paul arrived in Ephesus, the brilliant Alexandrian convert Apollos, instructed and no doubt baptized by Aquila and Priscilla, had already been sent to Corinth, where he was of great service to the church (Acts 19:27–28), watering where Paul had planted (1 Cor 3:6).

Apollos' rhetorical brilliance had no doubt won over certain elements in Corinth which Paul had not been able to reach. Yet for all that Apollos on his return to Ephesus must have reported that not all was perfect in the Corinthian community. It was perhaps on this occasion that Paul wrote a letter to which he refers in 1 Cor 5:9, where he gives us this much of a clue to its contents—that it warned them vigorously against "fornicators," that is, baptized Christians who were falling back into pagan practices. This letter has not come down to us, but it is the first of at least four letters we know Paul wrote to the Corinthians. For our purposes, we shall call it Letter A. It must have been effective, but it raised many questions as to Paul's exact meaning. The church also no doubt wished to speed the return of Paul and Apollos. It thus wrote a letter expressing these sentiments and sent it most probably by a delegation of three of the leaders of the community, Stephanas, Fortunatus, and Achaicus (1 Cor 16:15 ff.). The missive was mainly a list of questions requesting clarification of the Apostle's first letter and listing a series of "cases of conscience" which the complexion of the community and their daily association with pagans inevitably raised.

Behind these questions and in the light of other reports received, Paul sensed the gravity of the situation in Corinth: a ferment of moral indifferentism was attempting to justify pagan moral standards in the Christian camp by appealing to the new *gnosis* and liberty of the gospel; an incestuous man was welcomed publicly in the community. Above all, the community was torn by factions: a group of ascetics in reaction to the libertines; public litigations of Christians before pagan courts of law; but especially a division and rivalry over the different leaders to whom the Corinthians claimed allegiance. The spirit of division even entered the common worship, so that the Lord's supper became a scene of various groups eating apart. Meantime, the use of the charisms (tongues, interpretation, prophecy), which the charismatic has the power of controlling (1 Cor 14:32), had become so disorderly that the Christian assembly was becoming a source of scandal to pagan visitors.

The letter, the second of Paul, letter B, our canonical "First Corinthians," aimed at putting order into this enthusiastic chaos and was obviously pastoral in nature. But no other letter of Paul is so rich in the variety of doctrinal points it introduces: Eucharist, Baptism, resurrection, the nature of the Church as the body of Christ, eschatology, charity and its relation to Christian wisdom and knowledge, tradition, the role of the Holy Spirit, charisms, Christian liberty, marriage, virginity. Little wonder that selections from this letter should appear so frequently in our liturgy.

OUTLINE

THE UNITY OF THE CHURCH: 1 COR 1–3

1. Introduction: 1 Cor 1:1–9

    ¹Paul, called to be an apostle of Christ Jesus by the will of God, and Sosthenes the brother, ²to the church of God which is in Corinth, to the sanctified in Christ Jesus, called to be saints, with all those who everywhere call on the name of our Lord Jesus Christ—their Lord and ours. ³Grace be yours and peace from God our Father and the Lord Jesus Christ.

⁴I give thanks to my God continually for you—for the grace given you in Christ Jesus. ⁵For in him you have been made rich in everything—in every kind of (gift of) speech and every kind of knowledge, ⁶in the same degree in which the testimony of Jesus Christ has been confirmed among you, ⁷so that you are not lacking in any gift while you await the manifestation of our Lord Jesus Christ. ⁸He will also continue to strengthen you unto the end, blameless on the day of our Lord Jesus Christ. ⁹Faithful is the God by whom you have been called into fellowship with his son, Jesus Christ our Lord.

This is the first introductory salutation we have examined. The letters of antiquity normally bore an external address, which, like our envelope addresses today, remained visible after the letter was sealed. It was customary within to begin with an address often more formal, and a greeting, often quite stereotyped. Paul uses both of these with a sovereign liberty, which regularly sets the tone for the whole epistle.

If our chronology of the epistles is correct, this is the first time we encounter the title *apostle* used in the address. In 1 and 2 Th he uses no title at all, in Phil he is "servant." The use of *apostle* here is an affirmation of the authority with which he writes and a discrete lesson to those in the community who were claiming other authorities in opposition to Paul. An *apostle* is one *sent from*, an ambassador, in this case of Christ, who gave a select number of his disciples this name (Lk 6:13). The synoptics insist on the solemn and deliberate choice Jesus made of the twelve (Mk 3:13). If Paul is an apostle, it is only in virtue of a similar call, that which he received on the Damascus road, showing God's deliberate determination.

We have no way of knowing whether the Sosthenes mentioned in the introduction is the same as the head of the synagogue in Corinth whom the Jews beat in front of Gallio's tribunal (Acts 18:17). All we know for certain is that he was well known to the community of Corinth (the Greek article before *brother* indicates this). Perhaps he acted as Paul's secretary.

The designation *church* for the community is the Greek *ekklēsia*, literally, "convocation," the word used in profane Greek for the assembly of citizens called together by a herald to deliberate public affairs (cf. Acts 19:39); it is the usual Septuagint rendering of the Hebrew *qahal*, designating either "assembly" (Dt 9:10; 18:16) or as *qahal Yahweh* Israel itself, the people of God (Dt 23:4; 1 Chr 28:8; Mic 2:5; cf. Neh 13:1). It applies in the latter sense even when the people are not all assembled in the same place. It was the term *ekklēsia* rather than *synagōgē* that the primitive Christian community took over from the Old Testament, because the latter term was already used by the Greek-speaking Jews for their synagogue meetings. The addition "of God" manifests Paul's desire to identify the Christian community as the "assembly of Yahweh." In the light of Paul's rich theology of "calling," there can be little doubt that he thinks of the community as called together by God.[1]

The term *church* was first assumed by the early Jerusalem community, and as other communities were formed in other towns of Palestine, they too called themselves "churches"—Paul calls them "the churches of God in Judea" (1 Th 2:14)—but at the same time the singular noun *church* was applied to all of them together: "the Church throughout all Judea and Galilee and Samaria was at peace" (Acts 9:31). So likewise the term "church of God," in the singular can refer to the local assembly (as it does in 1 Cor 10:32; 11:22) or it may refer to the universal Church (Phil 3:6; 1 Cor 15:9).[2]

Does Paul's expression here, then, mean, "the local church of Corinth" (Cerfaux) or "the one Church of God, such as it exists in Corinth" (K. L. Schmidt)? Certainly, the individual community itself has all the pre-requisites to be called the "Church of God," and yet it is so because everything that constitutes the new People of God is found there, as the universal is found in the particular. And Paul never considers the individual church an autonomous reality—the apostolic authority and the traditions of the universal Church are binding upon the individual church—as the Corinthians will have to learn in this very letter (1 Cor 4:17; 7:17; 11:16; 14:34).

A second designation for the faithful is "the sanctified." Really this term means "consecrated," set apart from profane existence and belonging to God as his chosen property. It was a common designation, especially in the later Jewish literature, for God's people (Dt 33:3; 4 Mac 17:19) and was transferred to the community of Christian believers (Acts 20:32; 26:18; Heb 10:14), who by their act of faith have entered into union with Christ, thus sharing in his own consecration to God. To this state corresponds the profession of sanctity to which God has called

---

[1] J. Guillet, "From Synagogue to Early Christian Assembly," in *Mission and Witness,* ed. P. J. Burns (Westminster: Newman, 1964), 3–24; D. M. Stanley, "Kingdom to Church," ibid., 25–60; and L. Cerfaux. *The Church in the Theology of St. Paul* (New York: Herder and Herder, 1958), 95–117. But cf. James Barr, *The Semantics of Biblical Language* (Oxford: Oxford University Press, 1961), 119–129.

[2] On this last point, we do not think Canon Cerfaux's arguments are adequate to impair the interpretation of these texts of the universal Church. When Paul says he persecuted the Church of God, it was not only in Jerusalem but wherever he could find Christians, even if he had to go to Damascus!

them: "having as your vocation to be saints." Paul does not hesitate to call these Corinthians saints, knowing full well that abuses abound in the community. For sanctity, in the genuine biblical sense, means first of all an objective consecration, by which all the members of God's people are set apart from the world to belong to God—and only then implying the *noblesse oblige* of an ethical holiness.

Finally, Christians are *those who call on the name of our Lord Jesus Christ*. To call upon the divine name is a frequent Old Testament expression for adoring God (Ps 99:6; Jl 3:5); used here for Christ, it means divine honor is given him. As the invoking of the name of Yahweh made the unity of the people in the Old Testament, so does the name of Christ make the unity of Christians wherever they are.

Instead of the common Greek greeting *chairete, rejoice*, Paul adroitly substitutes the similar sounding *charis, grace*. The meaning of the latter term is the divine benevolence (as we might say, "God love you!") or the effective gifts by which this benevolence is manifested. *Peace* is the Jewish greeting signifying prosperity, but Paul means it no longer in a material sense but in the sense of the interior gift that flows from the indwelling Spirit and from charity (Gal 5:22), the spirit of harmony and well-being in the soul reconciled with the Father in the Son, whose joint gift is both grace and peace.

The common epistolary practice of an introductory thanksgiving Paul likewise transforms by a Christian perspective—here to thank God for the *grace* already bestowed on the Corinthians. Vv. 5 to 7 spell out what Paul means by *grace* here. It is not primarily the grace of personal sanctification that he has in mind but rather the spectacular profusion of charisms which accompanied their conversion and which continues to operate in the community—especially the gifts of tongues and of knowledge, that is, those of an oratorical and intellectual nature, which, like the Spirit falling upon the household of Cornelius (Acts 10:44–47), confirmed the divine origin of the message they heard and the genuineness of their faith. In the light of the whole epistle, there is an almost imperceptible irony in this *captatio benevolentiae*, for Paul does not praise their moral gifts, nor their charity, as he did these qualities of the Thessalonians and the Philippians, but only mentions those gifts on which the community itself is setting highest store (cf. 8:1–13; 14:6–40). He then proceeds to say that Christ will pursue his work *unto the end* (1:8), that is, unto perfection, so that they may be blameless on the day when Christ comes as judge. Paul thus gently introduces the theme of moral perfection, which the rest of the letter will show glaringly absent, in order to suggest that they are not yet at the goal of their new life but have still a long way to go, particularly in the area of that ethical holiness without which they cannot be ready for their returning Lord.

But Paul is confident that this work will move ahead (cf. Phil 1:6), not because of their fidelity but because of God's. No attribute of God is more extolled in the Old Testament that his fidelity (Dt 7:9; Is 49:7), based on his own sworn word (Dt 7:8). It plays an important role in the theological thought of Saint Paul (1 Cor 10:13; 2 Cor 1:18; 1 Th 5:24; 2 Th 3:3; Heb 10:23), for the object of God's call is now more than a call from Egypt to a promised land; God has called them to a *fellowship* with his own Son (1:9). This *koinōnia* which expresses a common life of Christians with the Son, and of Christians with one another, is the basic principle to which Paul reduces all his considerations in this letter. Whether expressed in terms of fellowship or in the concept of the body of Christ, or in the prepositions *in* and *with* Christ, this union and solidarity is the keystone of Paul's entire theology. It is particularly important here as Paul prepares his readers for some down-to-earth applications of the principle of fellowship to life in the Corinthian community. In the first ten verses of this letter the name of Christ appears ten times. The name is the basic rallying sign for a divided church. "See how he always fastens them as with nails to the Name of Christ. It is not any man nor teacher but continually the Desired One himself whom he remembers" (Chrysostom, *P.G.* 61:19).

2. The Factions in Corinth: 1 Cor 1:10–17

> [10]*I appeal to you, brothers, by the name of our Lord Jesus Christ, to be united in the way you talk, and not to have divisions among you, but to be restored to the same attitude and the same spirit.* [11]*For it has come to my attention, through those of Chloe's household, that there are quarrels among you.* [12]*What I mean is that one of you says, 'I am of Paul,' another 'I am of Apollos,' another 'I am of Cephas,' another 'I am of Christ.'* [13]*Is Christ divided up? Was Paul crucified for you? Or were you baptized in the name of Paul?* [14]*I thank God that I baptized none of you except Crispus and Gaius;* [15]*lest anyone should say that you were baptized in my name.* [16]*I did baptize the household of Stephanas also. Beyond that I am not aware of having baptized anyone else.* [17]*For Christ did not send me to baptize, but to preach the Gospel—but not with the wisdom of eloquence, lest the cross of Christ be robbed of its force.*

The theological value of Paul's treatise on Christian wisdom (1:18–3:4) can be appreciated only by careful study of the circumstances which provoked it. Paul will have many abuses to correct in this letter, but chief among them is that of the party spirit. He plunges into his subject with a cry of urgency. The verb *parakaleō* here means more than encouraging or exhorting, but not quite "command." It is almost an adjuration, as the mention of the *Name* suggests, yet tempered with affection and directness, by the term *brothers*, which Paul often uses when he has something painful to relate (1:26; 3:1; 7:29; 10:1; 14:1). The most obvious symptom of the party spirit is their open and verbal wrangling. "To speak the same thing" (a literal translation which we have rendered *to be united in the way you talk*, 1:10), was a classical expression for peace, or for settling a dispute (Aristotle, 3 *Polit.*, 3:3). The spirit of concord should be visible and audible in a community bearing the name of Christ. The divisions are not heresies but simply factions or cliques which militate against charity; they could in the long run precipitate defections in graver matters. The word we have translated *restored* (1:10) is used of nets that after use must be cleaned, repaired, and folded together (Mt 4:21; Mk 1:19), or of parts of a whole that are harmoniously organized and work smoothly together. Applied to persons, it has the notion of being reconciled and readied for a common task. Here, it is the interior sentiments and points of view that must be in agreement.

Paul's concern is based on a recent report from *those of Chloe's household* (1:11). We know nothing of Chloe otherwise, but these informants, whom Paul delicately avoids naming, lest personalities become involved, belonged to the household either as members of the family or as slaves, or, according to one suggestion, as agents of a commercial house, whose duties brought them frequently to Ephesus.

The nature of the quarrels now becomes apparent in the way Paul dramatizes them: it is a division not over doctrine but over personalities. Paul reproves first of all those who claim him as their hero in opposition to the others—diplomatically challenging first those who should be most willing to give him ear. Paul's title to prestige in the Corinthian community lay of course in his title as founder and in his labors of nearly two years there. The Roman element of the community may have especially rallied to Paul's side after the riot of the Jews, the favorable decision of Gallio, and Paul's choice of the house of Titus Justus as headquarters for his preaching (Acts 18:7 f.). When, after Paul's departure, Apollos arrived and began to preach, he must have presented a considerable contrast with his predecessor, especially by his Alexandrine erudition and the brilliance of his oratory. He was a man made to appeal to the Greek passion for the beautiful and the mystic. The converted Jews and neophytes would be more inclined to claim Peter (Cephas) as their symbol, for he not only had the prestige of head of the twelve but also represented the Palestinian roots of the early Church. If, as Dennis of Corinth attests (around A.D. 170, *P.G.* 20:209), Peter came to Corinth, it was certainly after the foundation of the community (3:6, 10; 4:15). That the community knew him would explain the frequent references to Peter in this epistle (3:3–8, 21–23; 4:14–16; 9:4–6; 15:5).

The meaning of the party *of Christ* (1:12) has divided the exegetes. Some see in it Jews of Palestinian origin who had known Jesus "in the flesh" and who now are appealing to their "primitivism" as justification for their party and perhaps for Judaizing practices they wish to promote. Others see in it the expression a group of well-intentioned Christians reacting fittingly to the party spirit of their confreres— though this is unlikely in view of their own condemnation along with the others. Finally, other exegetes find in these a group of laxists disavowing dependence on any authority and cloaking their position with a name "above" that of any human intermediary.

This party spirit involves an absurdity, and Paul uses the ironic question typical of the diatribe to underscore it: Is Christ cut into pieces, so that each of the four persons would have a part, or, better, that Christ be divided against himself? The absurdity implied is that there would be more than one Savior. "Is the passion of Paul the cause of our salvation, so that through him Baptism has its power to save? . . . No, he says, for it is proper to Christ to have wrought our salvation through his passion and death" (St. Thomas). Baptism ascribes one *unto* the name, in the same sense in which contemporary commercial papyri declare purchased goods to have passed "to the name"—i.e., to the account—of their new owner. The one baptized becomes the possession of the One whose name he bears and stands under his effective power. In the Old Testament, the invoking of the divine name upon the people is simply another way of saying that God has consecrated them by making them his own (Dt 28:9 f.; Is 63:19; Jer 7:10; 14:9), a guarantee of the divine protection (Jer 14:9; 2 Mac 8:15). Baptism "unto the Name" of Christ (cf. Acts 2:38; 8:16; 10:48; 19:5) means therefore that the Christian now belongs to a new Lord. Baptism indeed has given Christians new life; but it is not the minister who counts but he into whose name one has been baptized (Chrysostom). The efficacy of Baptism does not depend on the minister.

The ministry of Baptism Paul left to others—it was a fatiguing work, and Paul, whose health was never robust, was probably already over-worked with his other duties. But his motive lies basically in the commission of Christ to the Apostles: "He constituted the twelve . . . that he might send them forth to preach" (Mk 3:14). Paul, having seen the risen Christ, and having been commissioned by him, is an apostle of equal rank with the twelve (1 Cor 1:1; 9:1); if he baptizes it is only incidentally, as it were, to his apostolic mission, which is to excite men to that faith which can come only through hearing, and hearing only through preaching (Rom 10:17). This is no depreciation of Baptism, which is the sacrament of faith (Mt 28:19), but others can easily perform this rite, whereas there is a uniqueness about the Apostle which makes him a founder or an architect of communities (3:10) inasmuch as, endowed with divine authority, he presents to men the call of God and thus forms the *ekklēsia*, the assembly of God.

The second half of v. 17 serves as a transition to Paul's message on wisdom. Whereas the Corinthians, particularly the party of Apollos, were basing their partisanship on the eloquence of the speaker, as if the preachers were to be judged like the rhetoricians of the day whose only wisdom was that of words, Paul insists that the message he brings derives its power from its content, which is the cross. Not the wisdom of discourse but the discourse of (true) wisdom (1 Cor 12:8) will later merit his praise, and in what follows Paul, no slouch at rhetoric himself, gives a beautiful example. But to reduce Christianity to a philosophy, even under pretext of winning adherents, would be to ask the hearer to attach himself to ideas, whereas the basic challenge of the kerygma is a fact and a person. The language in which this fact is presented must be adapted to its object, stripped therefore of anything that would smack of eloquence for the sake of eloquence.

3. The Gospel: Divine Paradox: 1 Cor 1:18–25

[18]*For the message of the cross is foolishness to those who are perishing, but to those being saved, to us, it is the power of God.* [19]*For it is written, 'I will destroy the wisdom of the wise, and the cleverness of the clever I will thwart.'* [20]*Where is the wise man? Where is the scribe? Where is the disputant of this world? Has not God made foolish the wisdom of the world?* [21]*For since in the wisdom God offered, the world did not through wisdom come to know God, it pleased God through the absurdity we preach to save those who believe.* [22]*The Jews demand signs and the Greeks look for wisdom,* [23]*but we proclaim a Christ that is crucified, to the Jews a stumbling-block and to the Gentiles an absurdity,* [24]*but to those who are called, to the Jews and the Greeks alike, Christ, the power of God and the wisdom of God.* [25]*For the foolishness of God is wiser than men and the weakness of God is stronger than men.*

The snobbish rivalries of the Corinthians derive from a misunderstanding of the nature of Christianity and of the kerygma which drew them from the anonymity of pagan individualism into the unity of the people of God. The object of that message is essentially the cross—namely, the proclamation of a divine deed which topples humanly constructed values by transcending them. The cross would seem the instrument least calculated to win adherents, for in the ancient world it evoked not merely pain but especially shame and derision. Yet it is the essence of the new message preached—and it divides men.

It is to some a stupidity. The Greek word here (*mōria*) suggests something that is flat, dull, insipid—what is foolish not in the sense of being publicly dangerous but rather publicly despised, ignored because it is ridiculous. However, those who have judged it so are in reality perishing—the present participle here meaning that by this judgment they have put themselves on the road that is leading them to perdition. Those, on the contrary, in the process of being saved, take quite a different view of the message of the cross. It is the power of God. Unlike the noisy rhetoricians, it has an inherent dynamism. It is action and deed. This cryptic description prepares for Rom 1:16, where the gospel is defined as "the power of God unto salvation to everyone who believes." The word of God already in the Old Testament was conceived as deed as well as idea, and as having an inherent efficacy. But here it is the specific content of the cross which possesses this dynamism—and it was precisely this that makes the message so paradoxical and so difficult for the mind to grasp. Chrysostom, who knew well the Greek mind, saw this, and gave the answer, perfectly in line with Paul's theology as developed elsewhere:

> Now observe: when I say, "He was crucified," the Greek says, "And how can this be reasonable? He did not help himself when undergoing crucifixion and sore trial at the moment of the cross: how then after these things did he rise again and help others? For if he had been able, before death was the proper time. . . . But he who did not help himself, how did he help others? There is no reason in it," he says. True, O man, for indeed it is above reason; and the power of the cross is beyond words. For it was by actually being in the midst of horrors that he showed himself above all horrors; and by being in the enemy's grasp that he triumphed—and this comes from infinite power. For, just as in the case of the three young men, their entering the furnace would not have been so astonishing, as the fact that having entered it they tramped upon the fire. . . . So also with regard to Christ. His not dying would not have been so inconceivable as is the fact that having died he should loosen the bonds of death. Do not ask, then, "Why did he not help himself on the cross?", for he was hastening on to come to grips with death itself. He did not descend from the cross—not because he could not, but because he would not. For how could the nails of the cross hold back him whom the tyranny of death itself did not restrain? (*P.G.* 61:31).

The principle of the dynamism of the cross is simply the consummate application of God's tactics already illustrated in the Old Testament, as witness the citation of Is 29:14, which refers to God's will to save Jerusalem from the Assyrians without political intrigues and alliances. In the foolishness of the gospel, remarks Chrysostom, God destroyed the wisdom of the wise: "He cast out Plato, for example, not by means of another philosopher of more skill, but by an unlearned fisherman. For thus the defeat became greater, and the victory more splendid" (P.G. 61:33). "The Greeks feel not so much shame when they are defeated by means of the 'wise,' but are then ashamed, when they see the artisan and the sort of person one meets in the market more of a philosopher than themselves" (P.G. 61:40).

The *wise man* (1:20) typifies the Greek, the *scribe* the Jew, and both are summed up in the *disputant* of this world. The Greek word means "debater," here certainly in the pejorative sense of one constantly discussing and disputing more for the art than for the matter, and one whose view in any case is limited to the horizons *of this world. World* or *age (aiōn)* here too has the pejorative sense of a purely natural erudition, a purely human way of looking at things, myopic by comparison with God's view and opposed to the intrusion of the divine—what Paul elsewhere calls the "wisdom of the flesh" (2 Cor 1:12). This type of wisdom God has *made foolish* (1:20), either "addled" or *shown* to be foolish, by his own intervention, "like the needle of a compass maddened by the approach of a magnetic force too great" (C. Spicq).

Up to this point the "wisdom of the world" has been presented in such unfavorable light that one would think it totally depraved. Yet in this pre-Incarnation state of man there was a wisdom offered by God (when translated "wisdom of God," "God" indicates the source rather than the possessor of this wisdom), and it was not totally at odds with human wisdom, for the created universe itself spoke to men something of the nature of God—enough to make man's incomprehension of it a sin as well as a mistake (Rom 1:20 ff.). But this way failed. Saint Thomas' masterful commentary on this passage leaves nothing to be added:

> Divine wisdom in making the world inscribed its judgments in the things of the world, as is said in Sir 1:10: "He has poured her forth upon all his works"; so that creatures themselves, made by the wisdom of God, are related to the wisdom of God in the same way that a man's words are related to his wisdom which they signify. And as a student comes to know the wisdom of his teacher through the words he hears from him, so man could come to know the wisdom of God by studying the things made by him—as Romans 1:20 says, "His invisible attributes are clearly seen . . . being understood through the things that are made."

> But because of the vanity of man's heart, man went astray from the right path of knowing God. Whence John says (1:10): "He was in the world, and the world was made by him, and the world knew him not." And therefore God led the faithful to a saving knowledge of himself through certain other things that are not found in the patterns of creation—and for this reason they are thought stupid by worldly men who consider only the patterns of human things. These other things are the facts of faith. God's manner of acting therefore is like that of a teacher who, realizing that his meaning is not being grasped by his hearers, strives to use other words to explain what he has in his heart.

This new way was not that of order and harmony, so extolled in the wisdom literature and valued by the Greek mind:

> Here, not content with merely showing himself, he wishes to unite himself with his creature, the Infinite with the finite—there is no more proportion or measure to keep; he comes forward now only by foolish steps; he jumps mountains and hills, from heaven he bounds to the crib, from the crib to the cross, from the cross to the tomb and the depths of hell, from there to the highest heaven. All is without order, without measure. If the finite is to rise to the Infinite, it can only be by the same steps the Infinite took to join itself to the finite. It must free itself and escape the rules of prudence, which imprison it within itself, and lose itself in the Infinite; because it rises beyond all rules, it has the appearance of going astray (Bossuet, *Oeuvres oratoires,* ed. Lebarq. 6, 2).

It is for this reason that it takes faith to perceive the wisdom of God's new way of dealing, the way of salvation which is the way of paradox. By natural temperament (v. 21) the Jews demand signs—miracles, spectacular deeds of power (as the Gospels bear witness, Mt 12:38 ff.; Lk 11:29 ff.) and the Greeks wisdom—that is, a religion which will captivate but not disturb the cultured mind. Paul here shows that perfect grasp of the psychology of the Hebrew and the Greek which made him the apt instrument to bridge the gap between the two. He does so by proclaiming something that goes counter, because going beyond, the natural tastes of each—Christ crucified. The Jews indeed looked for a Messiah, but the fact that Jesus perished on the cross proved to them that he was not the glorious liberator they desired.[3] The cross was thus for them a stumbling block, an obstacle to faith.

---

[3]Trypho the Jew, in his later discussions with Justin, argues precisely this point: "Our entire race awaits the Christ, and all the Scripture texts which you have quoted we too recognize as having been said about him. . . . But, as to the question of knowing whether the Christ should be dishonored unto crucifixion, we doubt; for in the Law it is said of the crucified that he is accursed (cf. Dt 21:23), and, for the present I would not easily believe it. The Scriptures foretell a suffering Christ, evidently; but that this should involve a suffering cursed in the Law, we should like to know whether you can demonstrate it" (Justin, *Dialog,* 89, 1, 2).

The Greek idea of religion was not eschatological at all. A religious founder should therefore be one who more than any other would lead man to contemplate the order and harmony of the universe and make meaningful the cycle of time and lead man to a more harmonious subjection to its inevitability. In short, he should be a philosopher. A founder who would disturb this comfortable, cultured settling-in-the-world by reversing its values and going to death on a cross, fate of the irrational dregs of humanity, would indeed have no chance of winning the Greek.

That is why it takes a special grace, a divine call, to read in the cross more than stupidity and weakness. The surprising thing is that the message of the cross *did* win adherents, and in great numbers:

> When therefore those who seek signs and wisdom not only do not receive the things they seek, but even hear the contrary to what they desire, and then by means of these contraries are persuaded—does this not show the unspeakable power of him who is preached? As if to someone tempest-tossed and longing for a haven, you were indeed to show not a haven but another wilder portion of the sea, and yet he would follow you with gratitude. Or as if a physician could attract to himself the man that was wounded and in need of medicine, by promising to cure him not with drugs, but with burning him again! This is the result of great power indeed. So also the Apostles won the day, not simply without a sign, but even by a thing which seemed contrary to all the known signs (Chrysostom, *P.G.* 61:33).

Surely here Paul has in mind not only the cross but the resurrection which showed it to be the power of God and the wisdom of God. Implicit in this emphatic repetition here (v. 24) is that God has put more power into the cross and its message than he has put in the material universe. And if the universe can tell us something of God ("the wisdom of God," v. 21), the cross-resurrection tells us infinitely more—and saves us besides.

This is precisely the thought Paul develops in his powerful conclusion (v. 25). The foolishness of God is wiser than men—that is, having the appearance of folly, it is really the supreme wisdom, just as having the appearance of weakness, it is the supreme strength. In short, here is affirmed the "wholly other" nature of this wisdom and power (what today we call "the supernatural"), and at the same time the analogous kinship it retains with man's desire for wisdom and power. Lilly thus translates, "Why, there is more wisdom in the 'absurdity' of God than in all the 'wisdom' of men and more might in the 'weakness' of God than in all the might of men."

The real folly, then, is not in God's instrument, the cross and its message, but in the myopia that cannot perceive the superior wisdom of the paradox. Chrysostom, writing from the vantage point of the fourth century, when the power of the cross had proven its efficacy by rendering the Empire Christian, could say:

> How greatly did Plato labor, endeavoring to show that the soul is immortal! Yet even as he came he went away, having spoken nothing with certainty, nor convinced any hearer. But the cross achieved persuasion by means of unlearned men. Yes, it convinced the whole world—and not about common things but it wrought its conviction discoursing about God and the godliness which is according to truth, and the gospel way of life, and the judgment of the things to come. And of all men it made philosophers: the very rustics, the utterly unlearned. Behold how "the foolishness of God is wiser than men," and "the weakness stronger?" How stronger? Because it overran the whole world, and took all by force, and while men were endeavoring by tens of thousands to extinguish the name of the Crucified, the contrary came to pass: the name of the Crucified flourished and increased more and more; while the persecutors perished and wasted away. The living at war with the dead were powerless (*P.G.* 61:34).

*   *   *

Chief among the truths affirmed in this passage are: (1) The ability to know God through natural reason; (2) the historical insufficiency of this knowledge; (3) the "wholly other" and infinitely superior revelation of God through the scandal of a crucified Savior, bringing an infinitely superior wisdom and power to save.

4. Their Own Case as an Example: 1 Cor 1:26–31

> *26Just consider, brothers, your own call; not many of you were wise according to the flesh, not many influential, not many of the upper class. 27But what the world holds foolish God chose to put to shame the wise, and what the world holds weak God chose to put to shame the strong, 28and what the world holds ignoble and despicable God chose—the things that are not—to paralyze the things that are, 29so that no flesh may glory in God's sight. 30But from him you now exist in Christ Jesus, who has become for us the wisdom from God, and justice and sanctification and redemption as well—31so that, just as it is written, "Let him that takes pride, take pride in the Lord."*

This section is an argument *ad hominem* to reinforce what Paul has established in the preceding section. Having shown that humility is demanded by the object of the kerygma, the cross, he now shows that it is demanded by the very complexion of the Corinthian community itself. If God has shown a lack of "wisdom" in determining to save the world by the cross, he has shown the same folly in the type of persons he has chosen to receive the gift. The *call* which Paul asks them to consider picks up the "called" theme already introduced in v. 24, and refers it to the concrete circumstances of their introduction to the faith. There are few among them who *according to the flesh* (1:26), that is, according to human standards, were wise or influential or "noble"— that is, belonging to the urban bourgeoisie, the dominant upper class, with its accompanying prestige. The handful of notables, among whom we know of Erastus, the city treasurer (Rom 16:23), and Crispus, president of the synagogue (Acts 18:8; 1 Cor 1:14), were surely the exception in the mass of the faithful at Corinth. Here more than anywhere else perhaps was manifested God's choice of the poor and the little (Lk 1:52; 10:21). The threefold *"God chose"* (1:27) stresses the divine initiative in bypassing the world's wise and powerful, in order to select "vessels of clay" in which God's wisdom and power might be manifest. *The things that are not* (1:28), a technical philosophical term witnessed by Philo and the payri, climactically summarizes the Corinthian status—those considered to be nothing because of their insignificance. These God chose to *paralyze* those who are—that is, to nullify or make ineffective, powerless, in the sense of not granting them contact with the power and the wisdom of the gospel. God's purpose in so doing was to show that all is due to his gift and that mere men (flesh) has, before God, nothing with which to barter or beg. One of the divine credentials of the gospel is its effectiveness despite human support.

From him (1:30), that is, from God's gift alone, comes the state in which Christians now find themselves. The verb *este* here can be taken as merely copulative—"you are"—but the contrast Paul is making with "the things that exist not" in v. 28 makes it more probable that he is pressing the word for its meaning "to exist." Union with Christ, elsewhere described as a new creation (2 Cor 5:17), fills the void of nonexistence which summarized their previous state, confers on them that existence which they had not, and in so doing gives them entry into a new kind of wisdom, the "wisdom from God," without which man can gain no real esteem (Wis 9:6). This transcendent wisdom is not merely a speculative thing—for two reasons: (1) In apposition to it are: *justice, sanctification and redemption. Justice* as a term for the new state of righteousness of man before God will be developed at length in Galatians and Romans. *Sanctification* is here the process (*hagiasmos*) and not just the state, by which a man's belonging to God and consequent purification of the profane are deepened. *Redemption* in Rom 3:21 means the eschatological consummation, but here it has already taken place in the past (*he has become for us*) and hence is somehow already possessed. (2) Above all, the reason this wisdom is not merely speculative and that all these other themes converge with it is that their meeting point is not a mere body of truths (a "philosophy") but a person. In Christ are found all the treasures of wisdom (Col 2:3); and what Jeremiah said of the God of the Old Testament, "Yahweh is our justice" (Jer 23:6), Paul transfers to Christ. In 2 Cor 5:21, Paul will say that in Christ "we have become the justice of God," but here Christ is our justice, just as he is our wisdom, sanctification, and redemption. The reason for Paul's choice of this manner of expression is given by Chrysostom:

> But why did he not say, "He has made us wise," but rather "was made for us wisdom"? To show the copiousness of the gift—as if he had said, "He gave to us his very self" (P.G. 61:42).

The Corinthians can legitimately be proud of their union with Christ, and we can be sure that in citing Jer 9:22 f., Paul understands by *Lord* the risen and glorious Christ in whom the Corinthians have not merely become "wise" but possess an everlasting source of an ever-growing wisdom, as also of justice and sanctification, the process which in Christ will lead to the consummation of the redemption.

5. The Foundation of Faith: 1 Cor 2:1–5

> ¹*And when I came to you, brothers, it was not with pretentious speech or wisdom that I announced to you the testimony of God. ²For I decided not to know anything among you but Jesus Christ and him crucified. ³It was rather in weakness and fear and much trepidation that I presented myself to you. ⁴And my speech and my preaching did not consist in the persuasive words of wisdom but in a convincing display of the Spirit's power—⁵that your faith might rest not on the wisdom of men but on the power of God.*

The same divine paradox, shown in the content of the preaching (1:18–25) and in the social position of the hearers (1:26–31), applies equally well to the preacher from whom they first heard the good news. This good news did not demand, but rather forbade pretentious speech and this-worldly wisdom, because the gospel is by definition the *testimony of God* (2:1). A *martyrion* is an action, statement, or circumstance adduced in court or in human affairs as a proof. Here it is the testimony God gives. It refers surely to the redeeming death of Jesus (1 Tim 2:6) and his resurrection, which is precisely the presentation of a fact to silence and convince the judgment of men. Such a testimony, given by God in the death-resurrection of Jesus, needs no embroidering of human eloquence, but rather the simple presentation of what has happened. It is this method—or lack of method—that was Paul's.

This is not to say that he ignored the importance of an approach psychologically adapted to his audience—see for example his speech at Lystra (Acts 14:14–16). But sizing up the Corinthians, so given to the spirit of dispute (1:20), he came to the firm and well-considered resolution (the Greek *ekrina*) that they must be met head on by the rude and brutal nudity of the Christian message. In preaching to the Thessalonians in Macedonia, Paul must have depicted Christ chiefly in his glorious title of returning Lord and in his role as eschatological judge. At Athens, he had begun with a compliment to the religious spirit of the city and worked from the insights of the philosophy of nature into the coming judgment of which the resurrection of Christ was the forecast (Acts 17:22–31). Little stress on Christ's redeeming death appears in the texts either of 1–2 Thessalonians or the Areopagus speech. But his words at Athens had little success in winning the Greeks, and this no doubt influenced Paul's decision to change his methods with these Corinthians who compounded the pretentions of Athenian wisdom with a native rusticity and, if we may judge from the remainder of the letter, a moral and social obtuseness. (That is also why the expression *among you* in v. 2 receives special stress.) The total object of Paul's kerygma is Jesus crucified.

Weakness, fear, and trepidation (1:3) describe the general physical and psychological state in which Paul found himself in the early days of his Corinthian ministry. He may have had an attack of illness (which he calls "weakness" in Gal 4:13). But even without that, his situation was enough to depress the noblest of souls: he had been forced to leave Macedonia after persecution in both Thessalonica and Boerea; he had had little success in Athens; he had arrived alone in Corinth without the support of his closest companions; he saw in the depravity of the city and the spirit of the Corinthians little hope for the call to holiness which he preached, and from his experience of the constant opposition of the Jews, he knew that he should expect no success in the synagogue. Whence the comforting vision of Christ (Acts 18:9) which seems to have been a turning point, teaching Paul that his weakness is the very sacrament of the manifestation of God's power (2 Cor 4:7).

The persuasive power of human wisdom is no match for the *convincing display of the Spirit's power* (1:4), literally the "demonstration of the spirit and of power"—the decisive manifestation, the public proof not merely "persuasive" but incontestable which accompanied Paul's preaching. It refers not to miracles worked by Paul, for he has been soft-pedaling their importance (v. 22), but rather to the action of the Holy Spirit in both preacher and hearer, which resulted in the abundant conversions that followed his preaching, and also doubtless to the charisms with which the Spirit filled the community (cf. 1 Cor 12, 14; Eph 1:17, 19; 1 Th 1:5).

The end or purpose of this kerygmatic approach is given in v. 5, which climaxes this section and forms an inclusion with 1:17. There, the motive for using this approach was to safeguard the content; here, it is to assure authentic faith. Now faith, if it is to be divine, cannot rest on human motives for its foundation; it is essentially an encounter with the power of God and a stable possession of that power. Here indeed is a "breakthrough" in the evolution of Paul's appreciation of his own gospel. Faith is something which no human appeal can create. His own experience, and that of the Corinthians, has been that it is born in the heart of a paradox that reverses all the human values cherished by both Jew and Greek. It is *totally other*. An important lesson: *reason cannot produce faith*. And much less can eloquence:

> For indeed the excess of folly is in these more than in any, these, I say, who commit unto reasoning things which cannot be ascertained except by faith. Thus, suppose the smith by means of the tongs drawing out the red-hot iron; if anyone should insist on doing it with his hand, we should vote him guilty of extreme folly (Chrysostom, *P.G.* 61:40).

6. The Gospel: Divine Wisdom: 1 Cor 2:6–3:4

6Wisdom indeed we do speak, but among those who are mature—not of course the wisdom of this world or of the rulers of this world, who are proving powerless. 7The wisdom we speak is of God; it is a wisdom in mystery, hidden, yet foreordained by God before all time for our glory. 8None of this world's rulers knew of it, for if they had known it they surely would not have crucified the Lord of glory. 9But, as it is written, "What no eye has seen, what no ear has heard, what no heart ever thought of, these are the things God has prepared for those who love him." 10For to us God has revealed them through his Spirit. For the Spirit fathoms all things, even the depths of God. 11Now what man knows the thoughts of a man, save the man's own spirit within him? Even so, the thoughts of God no one knows but the Spirit of God. 12Now we have not received the spirit of the world but the Spirit from God, that we may know the things that have been given us by God. 13These things we likewise express, not in words taught by human wisdom, but in words taught by the Spirit, interpreting spiritual matters for spiritual men. 14The natural man does not welcome what the Spirit of God imparts; it is stupidity to him and he cannot understand because it demands a spiritual judgment. 15The spiritual man, on the other hand, can bear a judgment on all things, while he himself is subject to no man's judgment. 16For "Who has known the mind of the Lord so as to be able to instruct him?" But we have the mind of Christ.

¹And I, brothers, could not speak to you as to spiritual men but only as to flesh-bound, as if to infants in Christ. ²I fed you milk, not solid food, for you were not strong enough for it. ³The pity is that you are still not strong enough for it, you are still flesh-bound. Surely if there is still jealousy and strife among you, are you not flesh-bound, are you not acting according to mere human standards? ⁴Certainly, whenever one says, "I am a follower of Paul" and another, "I am a follower of Apollos," are you anything else but men?

If the preceding section roundly skewered the pretentions of human thought and human eloquence to know the divine secret, the present passage balances that principle by another—namely that the gospel, rude in the elementary fact it preaches, becomes in reality the supreme wisdom and has an eloquence all its own. Paul here reflects the wisdom teaching of Israel, that rude beginnings bear fruit in joyful harvest:

> For discipline is like her name, she is not accessible to many. Listen, my son, and heed my advice; refuse not my counsel. Put your feet into her fetters, and your neck under her yoke. Stoop your shoulders and carry her and be not irked at her bonds. With all your soul draw close to her; with all your strength keep her ways. . . . Thus will you afterward find rest in her, and she will become your joy. Her fetters will be your throne of majesty; her bonds your purple cord. You will wear her as your robe of glory, bear her as your splendid crown (Sir 6:23–31; cf. 4:16–18).

This wisdom is not one that is preached, *kēryssein*, the verb used for the proclamation of the cross in v. 23, but one that is spoken, *lalein*, meaning rather a discussion, conversation. The fact of the cross demands acceptance and commitment, in short, the act of faith responding to the act of God. It will never be attained by a discussion whose preestablished horizons are limited to what the human mind alone can see. But once the act of faith is made, it becomes possible to receive and to communicate progressive insights into the faith.

This can be done, however, only among those who are mature in the faith. The word we here translate *mature* (2:6) is *teleois*, whose more common meaning is "perfect." The word appears very commonly in the language of Paul's day to describe one who has reached maturity and is thus endowed with or has acquired those qualities associated with it: strength, energy (Philo, *De Somn.*, II, 9–10), virtue (Philo, *Leg. All.*, III, 140, 144; Epictetus I, 4, 4; Strobaeus, *Floril.*, II, 198), wisdom (Seneca, *Ad Lucil.*, 4:2; Philo, *Leg. All.*, III, 144; *De Plant.*, 168), understanding (Philo, *De Plant.*, 168), instruction (Philo, *De Agric.*, 9), independence, liberty (Philo, *De Migr. Abr.*, 29), as opposed to the child who remains a minor, dependent on others (Philo, *Leg. All.* I, 94; Seneca, *Epist.*, 124, 10). This meaning fits perfectly Paul's thought here, that the Corinthians lack the understanding of the mature and show themselves so dependent on one preacher in preference to another that they are still infants, that is, those who cannot speak (*in-fans*) nor even understand the mature language of adults.

The "mature," then, are not a caste initiated into an esoteric wisdom of which other Christians are deprived—to speak of such would be to inflame rather than quench the Corinthians' snobbery—but rather those endowed with a deeper appreciation of the same truths, a wisdom open to all Christians who will have the courage to begin their quest in the humility of the cross. Of this type of wisdom the succeeding chapters of Paul's own letter will be a brilliant example, a true "theology of the event."

Again, however, Paul insists on the basic and incompatible difference of this wisdom from that of *this world* (2:6), used in its pejorative sense here, and of the *rulers of this world,* which in the light of v. 8 refers to the leaders of both the Jews and the pagans, conceived as instruments no doubt of Satan, the "prince of this world" (Jn 12:31). Worldly wisdom, in the light of what God has done, has proved itself bankrupt.

This explains the emphatic position of the word *God* in the next verse—*God's* wisdom, not man's, we speak (2:7). And God's wisdom is now no longer that merely which can be read in the open book of creation, but his wisdom in *mystery*. The word *mystērion*, derived from a word meaning "to close," particularly in the sense of closing the lips, means therefore something secret, or, as our text specifies, *hidden*. In our case it refers to something God alone knows, and this is his plan of salvation, or simply Christ, who is the mystery of God (Col 2:3). This wisdom, as Chrysostom already observed, is called a mystery and hidden not because it is *now* secret but because it can be known only by virtue of the revelation God has made (Lk 8:10; Col 1:26 f.), because it is attainable only through faith, and because it was contrary to all expectation (1 Cor 15:51). The roots of the Pauline *mysterion* are not Greek, wherein the mystery is attainable only by the select few, but Judaic. And in transferring the concept to Christ, Paul gives it a meaning even farther removed from Greek esoterism: "The idea of the 'hidden' leads, in the New Testament, not to esoterism, but to the universal mission" (A. Oepke, *Th. Woert.*, III, 798). Still, as Chrysostom likewise observed, "though everywhere preached, it is still a mystery," for it still exceeds the dimensions of human thought (St. Thomas). It is for this reason that Paul will later describe it in terms of richness and plenitude, as the source of endless growth in knowledge on the part of the believer (Col 1:26 f.; 2:3; Eph 3:18 f.). This very letter is an illustration of Paul's principle, for every page of it is a resolution of life and its problems in the light of union with Christ.

Thus the very content of the mystery involved a gift of God to man, and although there was a time when this was hidden in God, a time when man passed through the night brought on by his own sin, God from all eternity planned to dispense his mystery *foreordained before all time for our glory* (2:7).

> And this is what Paul is earnest to point out now—that God always loved us even from the beginning and when as yet we were not. For unless he had loved us, he would not have fore-ordained our riches. Consider not then the enmity which has come between; for more ancient than that was the friendship (Chrysostom, *P.G.* 61:56 f.).

V. 8 repeats the thought of v. 6. The *rulers of this world* refers here principally to the Jewish leaders and to Pilate, and behind them to the intellectual leaders who judged Christ according to the human standard of success. If they proved to be the instruments of Satan, it was really through a basic ignorance of the true identity of Jesus. After the pattern of the Master himself, who prayed that his executioners be forgiven because "they know not what they are doing" (Lk 23:34) and of Peter who attributed their tragic deed to ignorance (Acts 3:17), Paul says that had they known, had they possessed the secret of divine wisdom, they would never have sent to the gibbet their own God, Yahweh. For this is precisely who Jesus is. The title *Lord of glory* (2:8) is that of the Yahweh of the Old Testament, described by the psalmist as the "King of glory" (Ps 24:7, 9). It is a title used elsewhere only for the Father (Eph 1:17; Acts 7:2; cf. Rom 15:13, 33; 16:20). This text completes Phil 2:6–11 and confirms our interpretation of Phil 2:6, in which Christ was described as being "in the form of God from the start." As a matter of fact, Christ's nature as "Lord of glory," and therefore God, was not something that came to him merely at his resurrection. Even as he was being nailed to the cross in the weakness of his mortal flesh, he was "the Lord of Glory," namely God himself. The tragedy for those responsible for Jesus' death lay precisely in the fact that they did not realize his identity. They failed to receive the wisdom in paradox.

We should expect v. 9 to give the reason for their ignorance. But the strongly adversative *alla* (*but*) with which Paul chooses to introduce it marks the return of his thought to the revelation of the mystery to Christians. The citation is really a condensation of several Old Testament texts (Is 64:4; 65:17; Dt 29:3). Eye, ear, and heart simply represent all human faculties for knowing, the heart standing here, as it often does, for the intellect, the highest human faculty (cf. Lk 24:38; Acts 7:23), to which, in the literal words of the text, a thought "ascends." The *things* that God has prepared could be interpreted, in popular Jewish opinion even in the time of Paul, as the joys of heaven, which would follow the "days of the Messiah" (*Strack-Billerbeck*, 328–329). They refer here, as Theophylact observes, to the knowledge of Christ and to the mystery of salvation through the Incarnation and the Cross. It is important to notice that in citing the Greek text of Is 64:4 (Hebrew text 64:3), Paul substitutes the verb *love* for "wait for." His purpose is not merely to underline the superiority of love to hope, but to confirm what the whole context and particularly the following verse are saying, namely, that the goods God has prepared are now no longer merely *future,* they have begun in Christ and have been revealed in him. The Jews still "wait for" God's revelation. We *love* him *because* (*gar,* not *de* in v. 10) he has made these goods manifest to us here and now. The close link Paul intends between v. 10 and v. 9 amounts to a definition of Christians as "those who love God." Now it is precisely to all Christians—and not just to the Apostles—that God has *revealed them through his Spirit.*[4] It is the role of the Holy Spirit to give understanding of the mystery of Christ (12:3; Jn 14:26; 15:26; 16:13). He can do so because *he fathoms* (*eurana*) all things (2:10). The verb means to explore, examine, search out (Jn 7:52; 1 Pet 1:11). It is a technical term for the divine knowledge, not meant to indicate an acquiring of knowledge, but rather the comprehensive perfection of the knowledge, as "he who searches hearts" is he who knows perfectly the secret of all human hearts (Rom 8:27; cf. Apoc 2:23; Jn 5:39; Jer 17:10). Here the object is the *depths* of God (2:10). The word *bathos* is used in the Old Testament for the depths of the sea or the earth. It was easily therefore transferred to mean the obscurity, or better, the transcendent nature of an object surpassing man's power to encompass—and above all God (Rom 11:23). Here it is less the depths of the divine nature than those of God's secret plan to save the world through Christ. Note, in passing, how the Holy Spirit who gives knowledge is associated with love in the heart of Christians (v. 9). There is an implicit link here between love and knowledge, which is explicit in Phil 1:9 and will be fully developed in Col and Eph.

Paul buttresses his point by an argument *a fortiori.* The intimate thoughts of a man are known only by the man's own *spirit* (2:11). *Pneuma,* used here, is substantially equivalent to *nous* (mind) or *psyche*

---

[4]D. W. Martin, "Spirit in the Second Chapter of First Corinthians," *CBQ* 5 (1943), 381–395.

(soul), but it is chosen here to make easy the transfer to the Spirit of God. As it is only a man's "spirit" that knows man's thoughts, so it is only the Holy Spirit who knows (literally) "the things of God," that is, God's intimate thoughts (2:11).

This idea must not have been difficult for the Greeks to grasp, for it was commonly held that man cannot penetrate divine secrets: "It is not possible for the human mind, sprung from a mortal mother, to fathom the intentions of the gods" (Pindar, *Peans*, 13; cf. Philo, *De Fuga*, 165). Paul's statement here is an affirmation of the divine nature of the Holy Spirit, but not necessarily of his personal distinction from the Father and the Son (cf. Mt 11:27). Here the Holy Spirit possesses the divine consciousness. And it is this Spirit that we have *received* (v. 12). The Spirit has not replaced our natural powers but has been received into them as a principle of supernatural knowledge. It is a gift which demands receptivity and docility on the part of him who would know divine things. Contrasted with the spirit of the world and described as *"from* God," that is, imparted by God, the Spirit here means a participated principle of divine life, effected surely by the Holy Spirit, but now possessed in a real way which makes the creature share in the divine light. The first effect of this gift is to awaken the consciousness of the Christian to the divine grandeur of the things given him by God. "If you *knew* the gift of God!" (Jn 4:10). Here the "things given" are the glory spoken of in v. 7, the things no man has dreamed of (v. 9), and the mystery of our call to the divine sonship (Rom 8:16 f.). All of this is to be read in the mystery of the cross, divine paradox.

The gift of the Spirit goes beyond mere knowledge, however. It also imparts the power to speak of these things in a language appropriate to them. *Words taught by the Spirit* (2:13) is a clear affirmation that the wisdom of God is inspired even to the extent of the very words used—a vindication of the meditative theologizing done by the Church from its earliest hour. The wisdom of Christianity is not so transcendent that it may never escape the limit of a mystic incommunicability. It is communicable at least to some extent, and the Spirit indicates even the words which most aptly express it.

The following expression may simply be an explicitation of this same thought, for it may be translated "combining (or interpreting) spiritual truths in spiritual words" (taking *pneumatikois* as neuter). But it seems better to take it as returning to the theme to be developed in v. 14, namely, *interpreting spiritual matters for spiritual men* (2:13, taking *pneumatikois* as masculine). The only objection that could be made is that this would seem to introduce a special class among Christians, the "spiritual." But if we realize that "the spiritual" here is equivalent to the "mature" of v. 6, we shall see that the title is simply a challenge to grow up to what every Christian *should* be, namely one ruled by the Holy Spirit.

Unfortunately many a Corinthian Christian is still acting like the *natural man* of his pagan days (v. 14). This "psychic" man, as the Greek has it, means man endowed with his rational soul (*psyche*) but with nothing more. The *psyche* is good, and is meant to undergo the sanctifying action of the Holy Spirit (1 Th 5:23 f.) but as long as man does not open his *pneuma*, his spirit, to the Spirit of God, he will remain just a natural man. According to Pauline "psychology," man's *pneuma* is the point of contact with the divine *pneuma*, and when he opens this door welcoming the Spirit of God, not only his *pneuma*, but his whole being is renewed, sanctified and put on the road of endless spiritual progress (1 Th 5:23 f.). On the other hand, it is possible for a man to remain in the confines of the purely natural order; to such a one the wisdom of the Spirit will seem folly, for he does not possess the faculty for judging spiritual things. *The spiritual man* (v. 15), however, possesses a faculty by which he can bring a sure and superior judgment not only on the "things of the Spirit" but upon the entire universe (*panta*)—he has a totally new *Weltanschauung*. In turn, he is subject to judgment by no man. Not that the spiritual man is above criticism or community norms or authority. Paul is criticizing the Corinthians precisely for their lack of this essential of "spirituality." But the mature man is subject to the judgment of no *mere* man, certainly not the natural man with whom Paul is contrasting him:

> He that has sight himself sees all things that appertain to the man that has no sight; but no sightless person discerns what the other is about. So also in the case before us, we on our part know our own affairs and those of unbelievers; but they no longer have any knowledge of ours (*P.G.* 61:60).

Saint Thomas' theological commentary renders precision to this thought of Chrysostom:

> In all things he who is properly disposed has a right judgment of concrete cases. But he who in himself lacks some proper disposition, makes mistakes even in judging. The man awake rightly judges that he is awake and that another sleeps. But the sleeper does not have a right judgment either of himself or of the one awake. Thus things in reality are not what they appear to be to the sleeper, but such as they appear to him who is awake. And the same principle holds for the well and the ill concerning judgments of taste, and for the strong and the weak concerning judgments of weight, and for the virtuous and the vice-ridden concerning things to be done.... Thus the "spiritual man judges all

things" because a man whose intellect is enlightened and whose affections are set in order by the Holy Spirit, has a right judgment concerning the things which pertain to salvation.

The concluding v. 16 marks a double advance in thought. On the basis of a text from Isaiah (40:13), Paul shifts—quite deliberately— from "spirit" (*pneuma*) to "mind" (*nous*) and from the Holy Spirit to Christ. *Mind* here can stand either for the human faculty of thought or for the content of that thought (cf. Phil 2:5). In either case, the *nous* is the faculty of judgment, with its human activity of selecting, comparing, assessing, classifying, and ordering. Since this involves the formation of concepts and individual judgments, it makes possible an expression in human language; it is a wisdom therefore that is communicable, teachable. Paul in 14:4 will show its superiority to the incommunicable experience, and here in 2:16 he evidently wants to show that the Spirit does not bypass man's intellect and his power of speech but rather engages, directs, and transforms them. The gift of the Spirit has no other aim than to produce in the Christian the judgments (the power of judging and the acts) of Christ himself.

Why then did Paul not speak this refined wisdom to the Corinthians in the beginning? Not because of his inability but because of theirs. They were not *spiritual men* (3:1). The *pneumatikoi* here does not mean all Christians who have received the Holy Spirit but rather those in whom the progressive action of the Holy Spirit has made them achieve *in fact* what they are *by right*—just as those really deserve the title *sons of God* who are actually under the motion of the Spirit of God (Rom 8:14). The term is not contrasted with unbelievers, who are not "in Christ" at all, but with those who are *infants in Christ* (3:1).

Thus they are equivalent to the "mature" of 2:6. But "spiritual" here first suggests its antonym, "fleshly" or *flesh-bound* (3:1). There are two Greek words used in this passage (3:1–3) for "flesh-bound." The first to appear (v. 1) is *sarkinoi*, which is not pejorative and carries no sense of moral blame. It is easily associated with infants, whose newborn members are furnished with an abundance of soft and undeveloped flesh. It symbolizes the inability of the Corinthians at the beginning to assimilate the advanced nourishment of the adults or to speak as adults. Thus Paul could offer them only milk, that is, the basic essentials of the kerygma—faith in God's salvation, moral conversion, the necessity of Baptism, the means of sanctification, the resurrection, and the eternal judgment—detailed in Heb 5:12 f. in the same milk figure. The inability to go further at that time was understandable, as in all beginnings some distance is to be expected between the ideal and the reality—whence *sarkinoi*. But what is not understandable or excusable is that after so many years and so many instructors in the faith, they are still at the same stage. Now they are no longer *sarkinoi* but *sarkikoi* (v. 3), "flesh-bound" in its pejorative sense: they have not let the Spirit mature them, they have not been open to spiritual growth, which is the essential mark of the *pneumatikoi*, the men who are Spirit-moved. Proof positive of their stagnation is precisely their childish wrangling over parties. Whereas by now they should have achieved that unity which marks the mature and transforms them into the Son of God (Eph 4:13 ff.), they are still nothing else but men.

Significance of 1 Cor 1–3

The order of cosmic creation was, in God's original plan, destined to bring man to a personal and saving knowledge of his creator. However valid this may still be in theory, the experience of human history shows that an "objective" knowledge of the universe failed to bring man to personal union with God—man did not "know God" as a person—as would have been shown by "glorifying him" in a holy life. Instead, man fell into the grossest polytheism and immorality (Rom 1:21 ff.). In purely "objective" knowledge man is much more in control; he yields his convictions to rational evidence and risk is minimized. He is "wise" in his own conceits. Interpersonal knowledge, on the other hand, plunges one into mystery of infinitely greater proportions and evokes the whole range of human emotions—fear, love, trust—and leaves one with little or no control of the other. Understanding is not so much the condition of love as the result of it. Now to accept this way of relating to *God* is a supreme threat to the "psychic" man, the man who wants to be master of all he knows, including persons. At this point the divine initiative which went beyond cosmic self-revelation to enter human history in Jesus and the cross, presents a real stumbling-block, the scandal of weakness and stupidity, which makes sense only if man can accept it as an act of love addressed to him personally. But that would mean on man's part conversion and faith, the smashing of his self-made world that new life might be born (2 Tim 2:25). It is like dying. And only those capable of the risk of accepting the gift of love can enter this wholly new way of wisdom.

Once one has entered this new way of knowing, however, his mind sees the wisdom of it. If, looking back, he sees that the absolute break was essential, his mind, now possessed of the Spirit of God, the divine way of judging, finds joy in discovering the beauty and the reasonable —the divinely reasonable—harmony of God's plan. Thus his mind begins to evolve a theology, an understanding of what he now knows by faith.

Theology is therefore impossible without faith. To attempt to *prove* the truths of faith, the intimate wisdom of God, by reason is not only repugnant but impossible. And yet the man who believes uses his reason to the full, illustrating, comparing, striving to understand. Hence, there is a continuity with reason regained after the "new creation" of faith.

This new wisdom has likewise its own art. Because the mind now begins to express its new life in concepts, it needs to choose words of men if these thoughts are to be communicated to others. This too is possible to those who are moved by the Holy Spirit. As the Apostles possessed the fullness of that Spirit from the moment of Pentecost, they certainly spoke with words "taught by the Spirit." And it is in a similar way that the Church understands that the sacred writers were under the inspiration of the Spirit in making the judgments of words, texts, and sources as they set down Scripture which we call the Word of God. But there is an inspired penetration of the revealed riches available to all Christians, provided they attain their normal maturity and become "spiritual men," pneumatics, docile to the Holy Spirit and enlightened by charity.

THE BODY IS FOR THE LORD: 1 Cor 6:12–20

¹²All things are permissible to me, but not all are helpful. All things are permissible to me, but I shall not let myself be caught under the power of anything. ¹³Food is for the stomach and the stomach for food; yet God will put an end to the use of both the one and the other. The body, however, is not for fornication but for the Lord, and the Lord for the body. ¹⁴Now just as God raised the Lord, he will raise us up too by his power. ¹⁵Do you not realize that your bodies are members of Christ? Shall I then take the members of Christ and make them the members of a prostitute? Never! ¹⁶Do you not realize that whoever unites himself to a prostitute becomes one body with her? So says the Scripture, "The two shall become one flesh." ¹⁷But he who unites himself to the Lord becomes one spirit with him. ¹⁸Flee fornication. Every other sin a man commits is outside the body, but the fornicator sins against his own body. ¹⁹Do you not realize that your body is the temple of the Holy Spirit, who is in you, whom you have from God. You are not your own. You have been bought—and at a price! ²⁰So then glorify God in your body.

After treating with severity the case of incest (5:1–13) and discussing the scandal of Christian suing Christian before pagan courts (6:1–8), Paul rises to the principle of moral holiness in general: "Can it be that you are unaware that the unjust will not inherit the kingdom of God?

Make no mistake; no fornicator, no idolater, no adulterer, no pervert, no homosexual, no thief, no slave of avarice, no drunkard, no addict of abusive language, no miser, will inherit the Kingdom of God. That is precisely what some of you were. But you have been washed clean; you have been sanctified; you have been made holy in the name of our Lord Jesus Christ and in the Spirit of our God" (6:9–11).

It is striking that in Paul's catalog of vices such a preponderant place should be claimed by the sins of the flesh. Paul is preparing to discuss precisely that topic, but he is faithful to his practice of rooting his moral directives in dogmatic facts—if there is a *must* in Christian life, it is only because there is first an *is*, a new existence in the Trinitarian life of God (6:11) from which moral obligation flows as a natural consequence.

In this Paul was plowing new moral ground, at least for the Corinthians who had been Gentiles. For the pagan world had not censure for extramarital intercourse but even a positive rationale for it: "Mistresses we keep for pleasure, concubines for the sake of daily intercourse, wives to bear us legitimate children and to be our faithful housekeepers."[5] It would not therefore be immediately obvious that Christian initiation meant a change of this attitude, since the contemporary mystery religions made no such demand of their initiates. In the section we shall examine, Paul shows first that fornication is not an indifferent matter (6:12–14), and then that it is an outrage to Christ (6:15–17) and to the Holy Spirit (6:18–20) already named in v. 11.

In saying that *all things are permissible to me*, Paul is repeating a principle of Christian liberty he especially cherished (7:35; 10:23), one that he no doubt had given in regard to foods (cf. 8:8; 10:23). Some of the laxists of the community seem to have seized upon his statement and applied it to the use of sex. Without withdrawing the principle, Paul hastens to clarify it. The use of the principle should not lead to the absurdity of enslaving oneself under pretense of becoming free. One's new existence in Christ makes all things belong to the Christian (3:23), all things are "within his power," but for that very reason he should not fall under the power of anyone or anything. (In the Greek, there is a play on words, rendered here by *power*). The Cynic-Stoic ideal of "things for me, not me for things" Paul skillfully turns on these sophists, who, like the Cynics, were putting the sexual appetite into the same category as the nutritive: "What is natural is not shameful" (cf. *Diog. Laert.*, vi, 9 on Diogenes). But this equation is impossible, says

---

[5] Attributed to Demosthenes, c. Neaera 122, p. 1386. Cf. M. Enslin, *Reapproaching Paul* (Philadelphia: Westminster Press, 1972), 129.

Paul. The matter of sexual satisfaction is subject to another principle. It involves the whole body and thus the whole personality. Now the body is not for fornication in the way that the stomach is for food. It has a nobler end, a divine end. Whereas the nutritive power will cease to function—and even in the risen state will not be needed (1 Cor 15:50), the whole body, which is somehow involved in fornication, is *for the Lord* (6:13)—that is, it is not made for such transitory acts as eating and generation but is destined ultimately to be united and conformed to the glorious body of Christ now living in heaven (Phil 3:21). What is condemned is not marriage (cf. 7:7 and Eph 5:25–33) but its counterfeit. Yet Paul here combats fornication by an appeal not to the dignity of marriage but to the destiny of the Christian's individual body.

There is a wealth of theology in this body-Lord concept. First of all, the future life is conceived as necessarily involving the body. In this Paul reflects the Jewish conception of man as an animated body, unlike the Platonic idea in which man is rather an incarnated soul, whose destiny is ultimately to jettison the body. The latter philosophy could well be made to justify the moral indifference of any bodily action. But Paul goes beyond even the Jewish thought of the Apocrypha when he speaks of a spiritualized body independent of animal needs (1 Cor 15:40 ff.). The point here is that the body itself is called to eternal union with Christ. If it will not be subject to the needs of transitory animal acts, it will nevertheless be capable of those keenly spiritual sensible pleasures which derive from the total fulfillment of one's being in God. The body that has this destiny is not a different body but the very same body Christians now possess. It is precisely this that makes impurity horrendous. If this body is for the Lord, the Lord is also for the body—an added dignity. Christ's unique business, so to speak, now in his glorified state, is to be the principle of resurrection and life for the bodies of his members—as the sequence suggests, though it still relates the source to the Father. Fornication is the sabotaging of this divine work.[6]

The resurrection of Christians is here referred to the Father as its principle but Paul now goes on to explain—and for the first time with such clarity—how the Christians' bodies are already now intimately united with the body of Christ—they are the *members* of Christ (6:15). That what belongs to him so intimately should be snatched away

---

[6]Note in passing that when Paul says, *he will raise us*, he is putting himself in the category of those who will *need* resurrection, namely the dead. This association confirms what we said on 1 Th 4:15 concerning Paul's ignorance of the time of the Parousia, and his ability to place himself, for the sake of instruction, indifferently among the living or the dead at that hour.

through an act of violence is unthinkable. The verb for *shall I take* (6:15) is not the ordinary *lambanein* but *airein*, having here the connotation it frequently has of taking away by force or injustice (cf. Jn 19:15; Lk 6:29 f.; 11:22). But this is precisely what a Christian does who unites himself with a prostitute. He makes himself a *member*, that is, the *property* of the prostitute. And for one who has been freed by Christ through belonging to him, this is an enslavement, a "falling under the power of," of the type Paul excluded in v. 12. Union with a prostitute is not, of course, the only type of fornication, but Paul uses it here as the most typical and that which the city of Aphrodite presented as the most common temptation to the converts to the new faith.

Not only does the fornicator become the property of the prostitute, but he becomes *one body with her* (6:16). The act of sexual union, whether culpable or not, involves the whole personality of each partner—the libertines cannot say that in giving the body what it lusts for, the soul remains free and unengaged. The act is a fusion of persons—they become "one personality," as Gen 2:24 already stated. The nature of the act is total union—if this is not done in Christ, it disintegrates and vilifies the personality.

But not so *he who unites himself to the Lord . . .* (6:17). The expression, sometimes rendered "clinging to the Lord," is a technical term in the Septuagint for stable fidelity to Yahweh (Dt 10:20; 11:22; 2 Kg 18:6; Sir 2:3). But Jeremiah uses it in the starkly bold image of the loincloth, for the intimacy with which God has joined the people with himself: "For as close as the loincloth clings to a man's loins, so had I made the whole house of Israel and the whole house of Judah cling to me, says the Lord, to be my people . . ." (13:11). The reference is surely to the covenant-union, basis for that religious fidelity to which the other texts exhort. Paul transposes this Old Testament image to the Lord of the New Testament, Christ. The "clinging" refers surely to the act of Baptism, and to the life of fidelity to Christ which it enjoins. But it is remarkable that in Paul's text here the expression parallels the same expression just used for physical sexual union. Baptism and the life it engages thus involves a *physical union* with Christ (by it, after all, our bodies become Christ's members, v. 15). It was not therefore necessary to further parallel the expression of the preceding verse by "becomes one body with him," for this is already evident. Paul instead advances his thought by saying that this type of organic union—and it *is* organic—has a totally different effect upon man from that deriving from physical union with a prostitute. Whereas the latter makes man, body and soul, more "flesh," the organic union with the body of Christ makes man, body and soul, "spirit." This does not mean that the body vanishes, for in Hebrew thought, the antonym of "spirit" is not "body" but "flesh." Never does the Bible consider possible a "spiritual flesh"; but a "spiritual body" is not only possible, it is the destiny of Christians (1 Cor 15:44). The reason is that, already now, their bodies are united to the body of Christ, which in its risen state is "vivifying spirit" (1 Cor 15:44), and thus Christians in their very bodies become *one spirit* (6:17) with him.[7]

The only possible conclusion is *flee fornication* (6:18). Saint Thomas remarks that, unlike other vices which call for a tactic of resistance, fornication calls for the tactic of flight lest passion be enkindled by toying with the occasion.

The next sentence is difficult to interpret. Some commentators take it as meaning that whereas in other sins like theft or even gluttony and drunkenness, the body is merely the instrument by which a man sins, in fornication the body itself is the object of his sin. But it is hard to see in this case how intemperance is not a sin against the body too. A better solution is found in the typically Hebraic (and Pauline) manner of expression known as *comparative antithesis* (cf. Mt 12:31; 22:14; Rom 9:13—"loving Jacob and hating Esau" means preferring Jacob to Esau). No sin, even intemperance, so sins against the body as does fornication. For unlike intemperance, fornication is a gift of self to a person, and this means personal involvement and infidelity to him to whom one is already joined, Christ. By robbing Christ of the body, fornication despoils the body of that spiritualization which comes from Christ and which one day would end in the resurrection. Since the body united with Christ is already spiritualized, to animalize it by giving it to another as its owner is to *sin against one's own body* (6:18). No sin is more contrary to the sacred organic union with Christ which the Christian already enjoys.[8]

This sacred union has already been described as being "one spirit" with Christ. Paul now goes farther and concludes that this makes the

---

[7]B. M. Ahern, "The Christian's Union with the Body of Christ in Cor, Gal, and Rom," *CBQ* 23 (1961), 199–209; J. M. Lane, "The Body of Christ in 1 Corinthians," *TBT* 10 (Feb. 1964), 650–655; L. Cerfaux, *The Church in the Theology of St. Paul*, 262–286.

[8]That Paul conceives the union with Christ in a very real and even physical way is evident from: (1) v. 15: the body of each Christian is a member of Christ; (2) the meaning of *kollōmenos* in the context is something starkly physical; (3) the inhabitation in v. 19 is attributed to the Holy Spirit or to the Father, as is the case constantly in inhabitation texts involving the divine persons, whereas to Christ is reserved the "physical" role of foundation or point of contact with the divinity (1 Cor 3:11, 16, 17; 2 Cor 6:16–18; Rom 8:9–11; Col 2:7 ff.; Eph 2:20–22). There is only one exception to this rule, in Eph 3:17, where Christ is asked to indwell, but there is no case in which the Father or the Holy Spirit are depicted in the role of foundation. See G. T. Montague, "St. Paul and the Indwelling Christ," in *Lagrange and Biblical Renewal* (Chicago: Priory Press, 1966).

Christian share in Christ's own character as temple of the Holy Spirit. The very body of the Christian becomes then a temple of the Holy Spirit. Paul does not say that the soul is the temple. Philo, the Alexandrian Jew, speaks of the intelligence as being a temple, but he never applied the image to the body. But in the Christian synthesis, it is the body itself that enjoys union with the divine persons. In relation to Christ, the body is a member; in relation to the Holy Spirit, the body is a temple.

The Holy Spirit who thus indwells this body-temple is God in person. But he is also gift of God and truly possessed by the Christian. The text gives an emphatic position to the word *Holy*, implying that impurity takes on the character of sacrilege. This was something new in a city where in the temple of Aphrodite fornication was practiced as a rite of religious consecration. For the Christian it is a desecration of one's body made sacred by the indwelling Spirit of God.

The Christian may not dispose of his body as something of his own. He belongs to another, having been bought. The expression "to buy for a price" (6:19) was used for the purchase of slaves. We know of the ancient practice of freeing a slave by a rite in the temple of the gods. He was declared "servant of Apollo" and thus entered the state of freedom from slavery to men. Much was made of the price paid on this occasion, and the term used for slave was *sōma, body*. When we realize that two-thirds of the population of Corinth were slaves, that many of the Corinthian church were either slaves who still looked for their freedom, or slaves now freed, we can understand how meaningful would be the allusion to the liberating ransom of the redemption by Christ (1:30; Gal 4:5; 5:1). The ransom price was his blood (Eph 1:7; 1 Pet 1:19). Become now the servant and the property of Christ, the Christian is free from slavery to those passions which still tyrannize the pagans.

If the body of Christians is a temple, it is the place where God is worshiped and glorified (Ps 29:9). The very physical life of a Christian is then a liturgy (Rom 12:1) and chastity envelops him, body and soul, with a brilliance which reflects the glory of God (2 Cor 3:18; Phil 3:21).

When Paul wishes to correct moral deviations, he does not moralize. He theologizes. Our present passage indicates how he lifts the thoughts of the Corinthians from the morass of immorality to place them squarely in the life of the Trinity: members of Christ, temple of the Spirit of God. The whole passage echoes the Trinitarian dimension of v. 11. In 1 Cor 3:16–17, Paul had used the temple image for the sacred unity of the Christian community. Here he has used it of the body of each individual Christian. We shall see later (in 12:12–27 and in Col, Eph) how these two concepts are united in the term *Body of Christ* used for the Church.

MARRIAGE AND CELIBACY: 1 Cor 7:25–35

25As regards virgins, I have no precept of the Lord, but I have a counsel to give, as a man who by an act of God's mercy, is worthy of trust. 26I think that it is excellent, in view of the present distress, yes, that it is excellent for a man to remain thus. 27Are you bound to a wife? Do not seek to be free from her. Are you free? Do not seek a wife. 28Yet if you marry, you commit no sin, and if a virgin marries, she commits no sin. But the married will have their human trials, and I should like to spare you them.

29This I declare, brothers, that the allotted time has become very short. For what is left of it, those who have wives should live as though they had none, 30and those who weep should be as though they were not weeping, and those who rejoice as though they were not rejoicing, and those who buy as though they were not taking possession, 31and those who make use of this world, as though they were not using it up. For the stage-setting of this world is passing away.

32I would have you free from concern. He who is unmarried is concerned about the interests of the Lord, how he may please the Lord. 33But he who is married is concerned about worldly interests, how he may please his wife, 34and he is divided. The unmarried woman or the virgin is concerned with the Lord's interests, intent on being holy both in body and in spirit. But the married woman is concerned with worldly things, how she may please her husband. 35This I say to promote your good, not to constrain you but to further what is ideal, what would bring you closest to the Lord without distractions.

Starting with chapter 7, Paul takes up the matters concerning which the Corinthians had written him, and the first of these is marriage. Some exegetes like Lietzmann, Bultmann and Conzelmann, take this passage as expressing the view that marriage is an evil that frequently becomes necessary because of the weakness of the flesh. While not going that far, there was a long-prevailing view of marriage as a remedy for concupiscence, and this passage from Paul was invoked in support of it. However, recent scholarship has noted: (1) In 7:1 Paul is simply quoting the position of some highly ascetic Corinthians: "It is good for a man not to touch a woman." Paul does not accept the principle except within the qualifications which he now proceeds to give. (2) In 7:2 the exhortation to monogamy is addressed not to the unmarried but to those already married. (3) The "concession" Paul speaks of in 7:6 is not a concession for intercourse within marriage (as if that were necessary!) but rather for periodic abstinence within marriage. (4) The principle in 7:9 is addressed to professed celibates who are not *de facto* living celibately but are engaging in extramarital intercourse. It is better in this case to marry than to expose oneself to the fires of eschatological judgment.[9] Hence, Paul is not outlining a theology of marriage (for this one would do better to consult Eph 5) but is answering a specific question put by those who would take an overly ascetical view of Christian sexuality even within marriage.

Paul then develops his thoughts on the indissolubility of marriage (7:10–11 and under what conditions "departure" would be permissible (the "Pauline Privilege," 7:12–16). Then he addresses himself to the question of whether the call to be a Christian should of itself mean a call to leave the married state, on the one hand, or to enter it on the other. He answers negatively, introducing similar considerations about other states of life (7:17–24).

What then of the unmarried? The Corinthians had no doubt posed the question concerning their unmarried daughters, but Paul resolves it on a larger scale within the great principle of Christian liberty which he has just proclaimed (v. 23). Although the "virgins" in question did not refer to a group who professed virginity, the answer will enunciate the principle of celibacy for both men and women. *Parthenos* as applied to men was unheard of in pagan antiquity. The closest the word came was its use in the neuter for things not yet used—as today we say "a virgin forest." Its broader meaning in the Christian synthesis (used in Apoc 14:4 for both sexes) lies fundamentally in Jesus' recommendation of celibacy as a state preferable to marriage, for those "who can take it" (Mt 19:12). As to the practical application of that counsel, Jesus had given no specific directions, and Paul is concerned to point out that he thus has no normative *precept* (lit., *word*) *of the Lord* (7:25) by which the issue could be settled. Thus appears the important distinction, realized by the early Church and applied by Saint Paul, between the words of Jesus and those of the Apostles. This verse and others like it must be cited in any discussion of the transformation of the words and deeds of Jesus by the early Church in the process of preaching or teaching. The Apostles were more aware of the distinction than have been some of the extremists of the Formcritical school.

Nevertheless, the Apostle does act with authority, as one who not only had been unexpectedly called to be an Apostle on the Damascus

---

[9]To interpret "to burn" as to burn with passion or concupiscence is not justified by the Greek text. Cf. M. S. Barré, "To Marry or to Burn," *CBQ* 36 (April 1974).

road (God's act of mercy) but also as one having the Spirit of the Lord (7:40) and consequently is *worthy of trust* (7:25). At this point in the letter, Paul is no longer considering the states with their obligations but rather the perfection of the individual, goal of the Christian life. For this he has not a command but a counsel.

It is an excellent thing to remain thus (7:26)—that is, in the state of celibacy which he has just mentioned. The reason for Paul's preference for this state is *the present distress* (7:26). This term can be taken in two senses: (1) the difficulties to which any life in this world is subject—an interpretation which enjoyed the favor of the ancient commentators; or (2) the crisis of the final times preceding the Parousia. On the first interpretation, the expression would be equivalent to "tribulations of the flesh," the "human trials" of v. 29; on the second, it would be equivalent or parallel to the "allotted time" of v. 29. Both interpretations are possible, but the second seems preferable in that the term *anagke, distress*, takes on the character of a technical word for the sufferings characteristic of the final times in 1 Th 3:7; 2 Cor 6:4; 12:10. The life of virginity, already recommended by the word and example of Jesus, becomes particularly desirable because the meaning of time has been changed now that the Lord is on its horizon.

In v. 27, Paul speaks first of men not marrying, thus indicating that the principle of celibacy extends, beyond the question asked, to both sexes. This verse is not to be isolated from the context of vv. 2, 7, and 9, which take for granted that not all are called to absolute continence. Marriage is not sinful, but those who marry will have "tribulations of the flesh." These tribulations are not the eschatological ones but those anxieties, cares, difficulties, and sufferings inseparable from the married state. Unlike the tribulations suffered for the faith, these can be avoided without spiritual detriment. And it is for this reason that Paul for his part (the emphatic *egō* means "it is my personal intention") would like to spare them these *human trials* (7:28).

Paul, who is constantly preoccupied with time and eschatology, now declares in a solemn way that his recommendation is based on the nature of the life of any Christian in this world. The word *kairos*, which is translated *allotted time* (7:29) is not *chronos*, the succession of events, but rather a determined measure of time. Used frequently in the New Testament for time in the sense of opportunity, it is a technical term in Saint Paul for the interval between the two events of Christ—resurrection and Parousia (Rom 3:26; 8:18; 11:5; 2 Cor 8:13). Paul in no way specifies its exact duration, but like a sail gathered in as the boat approaches the shore (such is the figure evoked by the verb *systellō*), the Christian era is contracted; it is short. Its end has been forecast in its beginning, the Parousia of Christ in his resurrection (Acts 17:31). We are already living in the final times (1 Cor 10:11). It is not precisely on the brevity of one's individual life that Paul bases his instruction, but upon the brevity of the entire present age, marked for the Parousia. The individual judgment could then be merely the sight granted individuals after death of the solemn judgment that will close universal history.

This conception of existence throws new light on the Christian's life in the world, no matter what his state of life or his activity: marriage, mourning, joy, business, all are now temporary in a new sense. None of them bespeak lasting values; the danger is that one become absorbed or engrossed in them at the expense of what is meant to last—one's state as a Christian. This principle of interior liberty applies to all. The succession of paradoxes is climaxed by the play on words between *using* (*chrōmenoi*) and *using up* (*katachrōmenoi* 7:31), that is, making use of the things of the world but not pouncing upon them like a greedy child devouring the proffered sweets and grasping for more. The Christian holds his goods with a light grasp, not because he pursues a Stoic ideal of emotional serenity, but because he waits for his returning Lord. The text does not discourage human initiative (Paul had corrected the Thessalonians on this point, and of course the kingdom of God demands the best of one's efforts—*concerned about the interests of the Lord*, 7:32–34). But as to the vicissitudes of life, they are to be regarded more like pastimes that can be used or left unused until the Lord comes.

The *schēma* of this world is "figure," what is exterior, only appearance, as opposed to *morphē*, "form" in the sense of what is interior, genuine, and stable. Here the word is used in its Thespian meaning of *stage-setting* (7:31). The sane spectator knows that nothing is more changeable than the scene he witnesses on the stage. To make such a temporary setting the object of a total commitment to enjoyment is to live in a dream world.

Now it is this universal law of Christian liberty that inspires Paul's praise of virginity: *I would have you free from concern* (7:32). He who is unmarried is free to be concerned about the interests of the Lord, to *please him*, an expression used constantly for the aim of the Christian life (1 Th 2:15; 4:1; Rom 8:8; Col 1:10). Here it becomes clear that virginity has no superior value on the purely natural plane. Above all it must not be clung to out of selfish motives or because one wishes to avoid the responsibilities to partner, to family, or to society. The thought prepares Augustine's celebrated statement: "What we praise in virgins is not the fact of being virgins but of being consecrated to God by a religious continence" (*De virginitate*, ch. 11, *P.L.* 6, 401). Or, in the words of Saint Thomas, "The end which makes virginity a virtue is the liberty to occupy oneself with divine things" (II–II, q. 152, art. 5).

> The grandeur of virginity and of celibacy is wholly supernatural, and exists really only where this state is embraced out of a superabundant love for God, involving love of neighbor, love and service to which the one called fears he may not leave a place free enough and vast enough if he restricts his liberty, even by ties which are the most legitimate and the most necessary for the majority of men (E. B. Allo, *I Corinthiens, Etudes bibliques* series, ad loc.).

These recommendations Paul has made not with the intent of *constraining* the faithful (7:35)—literally "to throw a loop about you." Even in this matter there is freedom. He simply wishes to present what is *ideal (euschēmon* 7:35). This word radically means "what is beautiful in appearance," and in the moral sense, what is honorable, noble, hence ideal. The Christian life may be lived in any state, but no state comes closer to its ideal form than that of virginity. It was the state Jesus himself chose, as well as that of his mother and the beloved disciple.

A second advantage to virginity is that it places one *close to the Lord* (7:35). The expression *paredron* means "well placed" or "well situated," like those in the theater who would have the choice seats or those at a banquet who would be closest to the guest of honor. Paul is quite possibly thinking of the synoptic tradition in which Jesus vindicated the position of Mary, who, seated at his feet, had chosen the better part (Lk 10:39–42). Virginity makes possible a more intimate union with the Lord, it puts the soul totally at his disposition.

Thus virginity makes possible a service of the Lord which is *undistracted*, uninterrupted (*aperispastōs* 7:35). Unlike Martha who was engrossed (*periespato*) with her duties (Lk 10:40), the one totally given to God can give undivided attention to serving the Lord in the various ministries that build up the church.[10]

Conclusion

This passage, with Jesus' commendation of celibacy (Mt 19:12), forms the *magna charta* of the consecrated life. It is primarily a declaration of independence and freedom. The great good of charity, the love of God, which alone outlasts the changing scenery of this world, is worth immobilizing oneself in as a state of life. If Paul coincides with Plato in saying that the figure of this world is passing away, he does not make the philosophical principle of the changeableness of temporal things the main motive of his praise of virginity. Rather, we are living in a

---

[10]Cf. J. D. Quinn, "Celibacy and Ministry in Scripture," *TBT* 46 (1970), 3169 f.

segment of time cut at either end by the Christ-event. If we cannot see the Parousia end, we can see the resurrection end in which the Parousia is forecast and guaranteed. Thus we are living in a new kind of time. So radically has the meaning of time been changed that unnecessary involvement in essentially transitory states appears as a curtailment of freedom. Virginity, then, is the sacrament, the visible presence and symbol among men, of Christ's lordship of time. In the virgin, the Church proclaims that time is no longer secular but sacred. It is bathed already in the glory of the resurrection and the dawn of the Parousia. The virgin is the witness to this divine fact, much like the snowcapped peak that catches the first light of the sunrise and to a sleeping world heralds the day. Thus the virgin elevates even the state of marriage by being a continual reminder of the end of all Christian life.

THE EUCHARIST

1. The Table of the Lord: 1 Cor 10:14–22

> [14]*Therefore, my dearly beloved, flee from idol worship.* [15]*I address you as sensible people: judge for yourselves what I say.* [16]*The cup of blessing that we bless, is it not a communing with the blood of Christ? The bread we break, is it not a communing with the body of Christ?* [17]*Because the bread is one, we the many are one body, for we all partake of the one bread.*
>
> [18]*Consider the Israel according to the flesh. Do not those who eat the victims enter into communion with the altar?* [19]*What then am I saying? That an idol-offering amounts to anything, or that an idol is anything in reality?* [20]*No, but what the Gentiles sacrifice, they sacrifice to demons, to something that is not God. I do not want you to enter into communion with demons!* [21]*You cannot drink the cup of the Lord and the cup of demons; you cannot partake of the table of the Lord and the table of demons.* [22]*Are we going to provoke the Lord to jealousy? Are we stronger than he?*

In the long section preceding this (9:1–10:13), Paul had shown that liberty in Christ does not mean free-rein to selfishness; rather it inspires self-sacrifice. Paul himself renounces many privileges he could justly claim in the apostolate (9:1–18); he has made himself the servant of all (19–23). Christian prudence demands vigilance and sacrifice even of Paul himself (24–27), and the history of the Israelites shows that merely having been the beneficiaries of God's marvels does not guarantee salvation independently of one's personal dispositions and moral life (10:1–13). One of the desert marvels Paul is careful to point out was the common food and drink this people enjoyed (the manna, the spring), yet "with most of them God was not well pleased" (10:3–5). Paul is suggesting to his Christian readers that their own common spiritual food and drink, the Eucharist, is not a gift to be abused; it will not save them independent of their own dispositions.

With v. 14 Paul now turns to the practical question about meat that had been offered to idols. Two cases could present themselves: (1) participation in the cultic banquet, the sacrificial meal, whether this was held in a temple or in a private home; (2) partaking of such meats within a private meal with no cultic overtones. The Christians of Corinth must have quite often been faced with the latter problem, for the meats sold in the market had often previously been offered at the temple. (For convenience, the meat market was at times located near the temple, as the excavations of Pompeii have shown.) Whether in buying meat at the market or in accepting an invitation to dine at another's home, one would never know for sure whether the meat sold or served had been subjected to a pagan religious ceremony. Paul resolves this situation by setting the problem within the Christian conscience—buy meat or partake of it without scruple, being careful only to avoid scandal (10:23–11:1).

But concerning participating in the sacrificial meal Paul is categoric: *Flee from idol-worship!* (10:14). (The *from* in Greek makes the expression still more emphatic than the "flee fornication" of 6:18). Paul had already shown how prudence and charity demanded abstaining from such banquets (8:10), but here he shows that sharing in such a meal is an act of religious apostasy.

The Corinthians probably did not look upon it in this way, and many of them would find it painful to give up practices ingrained by years of custom. These anticipated psychological difficulties on the part of his readers are suggested by the tact and affectionate appeal Paul uses in this passage: the address *dearly beloved* (10:14), the appeal to their good sense (10:15), and the evoking of their union with the immolated Christ (10:16).

Why must Christians flee from the banquets of idol-worship? Because they have a banquet of their own which achieves what the pagan sacrificial meals only pretend to achieve—union with God. Vv. 16 and 17 are of dense doctrinal import and bear careful analysis.

The *cup of blessing* (10:16) may be interpreted, with Chrysostom, as meaning the cup that obtains and imparts all blessings. The more obvious meaning, however, is that of the Hebrew and Aramaic equivalent designating the "cup of blessing," the third ceremonial cup of the Paschal meal, poured after the eating of the Paschal lamb, over which the father of the family would pronounce a thanksgiving and before drinking say, "Blessed art thou, Lord, our God, King of the universe, who dost create the fruit of the vine." But Paul, saying in a pleonasm, "the cup of blessing that we *bless*," surely puts a Christian meaning to this expression. It could refer to prayers of blessing and thanksgiving with which the early Christian liturgy celebrated the Lord's supper. The *Didache* (chs. 9, 10) as a matter of fact gives examples of such prayer accompanying the communion (using the verb *eucharistein*, however, instead of *eulogein* which Paul uses here). On the other hand, the verb is used in 1 Sam 9:13 for the act of *consecrating* a victim done by a priest in the name of the people, and the expression here is parallel to "breaking bread," which is surely the action of the one presiding. Hence it is more likely that *we bless* (10:16) refers to the act of consecration which sets the Christian liturgy apart from both pagan and Jewish rites, but which would be performed by the one presiding. The cup is mentioned first, either because Paul wishes to draw the Christian contrast with the pagan sacrifices which began with a libation, or, more probably, because Paul wishes to develop further his thoughts on the bread. The *Didache* (ch. 9) nevertheless gives us a prayer of thanksgiving over the chalice first.

The union effected with the blood and the body of Christ is described as a *communing, koinōnia* (10:16). This term has a richness of meaning difficult to express in a single word. Some translate it *participation* or *partaking*, a sense justified by the verb, "we partake," in v. 17. Others translate it by "fellowship," or "communion." In documents contemporary to Paul it is a favorite expression for the marital relationship as being the most intimate between human beings (Isocrates 3, 40; 3 Mac 4:6; Josephus, *Ant.* 1, 304; and the papyri). Followed by the genitive of person, it means a union with that person, as Paul has already in this letter spoken of a *koinōnia* with the Son of God (1:9). Followed by a genitive of the thing, it means a common sharing in that thing, for example, in the faith (Phm 6), or in sufferings (Phil 3:10), or in a work of service (2 Cor 8:4). It is in this sense too that most exegetes understand the "fellowship of the Holy Spirit" of 2 Cor 13:13—a common participation of Christians in the Holy Spirit. Hence we have the convergence of all these meanings, and there is no need to exclude any of them. The Eucharist is: (1) a common sharing or participation in the body and blood of Christ; (2) an intimate union with the person of Christ; (3) a union or "community" effected by the Eucharist—as will be specified in v. 17.

It is significant that Paul says the chalice *is* and the bread *is* this union, indicating Christ's real presence in or under these elements.

The *body* and *blood* (10:16–17) are treated separately in a repetition that suggests the importance of the distinction or the separate consecration (union with the blood, union with the body). It is difficult to imagine, then, how Paul could be conceiving the Eucharist otherwise than as a sacrificial banquet, a union with Christ in his state of victim reproduced by the double consecration commemorating the separation of his body and blood on the cross. The point of Saint Paul's reasoning here is that the common and ceremonial partaking of the thing sacrificed is a participation in the sacrificial act and in all that it implies. The sacrificial nature of the Eucharist will become even clearer in ch. 11.

V. 17 is translated by some in the sense of an explanatory clause, bread and body being paralleled, "because we the many are one bread, one body." But most moderns understand it as we have translated it above, the unity of the body being rooted causally in the unity of the bread. In what sense is this meant? The unity made of a group partaking in a common meal is easiest to understand, and it seems that the primitive community found in the gesture of Christ breaking a single loaf and distributing it, now liturgically repeated (Acts 2:42, 46; 20:7, 11; Lk 24:35), a symbol of its own new oneness. The *Didache*, followed by Augustine, sees in the very constitution of the bread itself a symbol of the unity of the Church: "As this broken bread, once scattered upon the mountains, was gathered to make one whole, may your Church be thus gathered from the extremities of the earth into your kingdom" (9:4). But neither of these interpretations does justice to Paul's thought: *Because* the bread is one, we are one (10:17). *We* applies to all Christians and not just to those of Corinth who would be symbolically united by sharing in one "loaf," even granted the possibility of a single loaf large enough for the whole community. For Paul to be able to say that all Christians, whether of Corinth or Ephesus or Jerusalem, all partake of *one* and the *same* bread, there must be a *numerical* unity to it transcending the mere oneness of a single loaf and even the specific unity of "bread." Bread here then clearly stands for the real *body* of Christ. Paul sees the unity of the Church as going beyond the external gesture of breaking a common bread. He attaches himself to the words of consecration. "This is my *body*" to show that the unity of the Church is made by a sacramental union with the *body* of Christ. And hence if we partake of that one "bread" we *become* what we partake in, namely the body of Christ. We are really an extension of that same body to which we are joined in the Eucharist.

This text is a capital one in understanding Paul's concept of the "Mystical Body." Already he has spoken of the Christian's individual body as being "for the Lord," as being the "members of Christ" (1 Cor 6:13–17). Here he speaks of the whole Church as being this body, becoming its extension by the sacramental union. Whether in Baptism or Eucharist, it is always the physical Christ who makes the unity of Christians: we become, in the words of St. John Damascene, *concorporeal* with Christ (*De fide orth.*, IV, 13; *P.G.*, 94:1153).

The Apostle now buttresses his point with proof from the Jews' notion of sacrifice, which Paul as a Jew had subscribed to and which was still current when he wrote this letter. *The Israel according to the flesh* (10:18) is simply the old Israel, to be contrasted with the "Israel of God" (Gal 6:16), the Christian Church, the true descendants of Abraham (Rom 9:6 ff.). Now it was a commonplace of Jewish theology that to partake of the victim sacrificed was to become involved in the sacrifice itself ("the altar"—cf. Philo, *De spec. leg.*, I, 221), and since the altar was conceived as a figure and substitute for Yahweh (Dt 12:11, 12; 18:1–4; Heb 13:10), eating the sacrificial meal was a union with Yahweh. This does not mean, Paul hastens to say, that he considers the pagan idols of Corinth as being anything similar, as having any intrinsic power (v. 19), or the sacrificial meals as having any inherent efficacy. Though nothing in themselves, these idols and rites are the instruments of demons, whom the Old Testament presents as the influence behind idols and the ultimate beneficiaries of idol worship (Dt 32:17; Ps 96:5; Bar 4:7). The point is the significance of the act. Among the pagans as well as among the Jews, the purpose of the sacred banquet (the "banquet of God," *Pap. Oxy.*, 1:10; 3:523; 14:1755) was to unite oneself with the divinity, who was thought to preside at the meal and even to take his place among the guests (cf. *Ael. Arist.*, or. 8; A-J. Festugière, *Notules d'exégèse*, in *Revue des sciences philosophiques et théologiques*, 1934, 359–362; *Le monde gréco-romain au temps de Notre Seigneur*, vol II, 172). Though such divinities are nothing in reality, to sacrifice to them is to enter into communion with demons. Now the incompatibility of this sacrificial meal with the supper of the Lord is absolute: whence the contrast of the *cup of the Lord* and the *cup of demons*, the *table of the Lord* and the *table of demons* (10:21). Here "table" (*trapeza*) has replaced "altar" (*thysiastērion*), but this is no way impairs the sacrificial nature of the Christian meal, for "table" is used frequently as a synonym for *altar* in the Old Testament (Mal 1:7–12; Ezek 41:22; 44:16; Is 55:11) and in profane Greek, where the inscription "the table of God" occurs frequently as a term for altar. The Council of Trent had good reason for declaring that in this text Paul is comparing altars (Sess. 22, *De sacrif. Missae*).

Finally, using the Deuteronomistic theme of God's jealousy (Dt 32:21; Rom 10:19), Paul points out that such association in pagan sacrifices is an infidelity to Christ and then skewers those Corinthian Christians who under pretense of Christian liberty thought themselves "strong" enough to engage indiscriminately in any kind of pagan activity. To do so is to pretend to be *stronger than Christ* (10:22).

*   *   *

Conclusion

This text shows the nature of the Eucharist as "communion" in the triple sense described above. But it also shows that the Eucharist is a sacrificial meal. This becomes apparent from: (1) The double mention of body and blood in the sacrificial context, (2) the contrast of cup and table, and particularly, (3) the *point* of the whole contrast. Any contrast must have some basis of comparison to start with, so that the point of distinction may come to light. Now the point of contrast is *not* the sacrificial nature of the pagan meal as against the nonsacrificial nature of the Christian meal but rather the *union* which is effected, on the one hand with Christ, on the other with demons. In this light the common basis of comparison would be the sacrificial nature of each meal, Paul forbidding Christians to partake in pagan sacrifice "because we have our own."

2. The Lord's Supper Is a Covenant-Meal: 1 Cor 11:17-34

[17]*In giving these instructions I find nothing to praise, for your meeting together is not for better but for worse.* [18]*First of all, I hear that when you gather in assembly, there are actually divisions among you, and to some extent I believe it.* [19]*(Divisions are bound to arise among you, so as to show who are the tried and true.)* [20]*When you come together in the same place, it really can no longer be called the Lord's Supper.* [21]*For each one goes ahead and takes his own supper; and one has an empty stomach, while another gets drunk.* [22]*Do you not have houses for eating and drinking? Or do you despise the assembly of God and embarrass those who have not? What shall I say to you? Shall I praise you? Not on this point.* [23]*For I received as coming from the Lord himself, what I transmitted to you, namely that the Lord Jesus, on the night he was betrayed, took bread, and giving thanks broke it and said:* [24]*"This is my body for your sake. Do this in memory of me."* [25]*Likewise the cup, when he had finished the supper, saying, "This cup is the new covenant in my blood. Do this, whenever you drink it, in memory of me."* [26]*As often, then, as you eat this bread and drink the cup, you proclaim the death of the Lord until he comes.* [27]*It follows from this that anyone who eats the bread or drinks the cup of the Lord unworthily, is guilty of the body and of the blood of the Lord.* [28]*But let a man examine himself and only thus eat the bread and drink the cup.* [29]*Otherwise he who eats and drinks, eats and drinks judgment upon himself, since he does not discern the body.* [30]*That is why there*

are among you many infirm and ill and many falling asleep. [31]*If we judged ourselves, we should not be judged. But when we are judged by the Lord, we are brought to correction, that we may not be condemned with the world.* [32]*Therefore, my brothers, when you assemble to eat, wait for one another.* [33]*If anyone is that hungry, let him eat at home, so that your assembling be not a cause of your own condemnation.* [34]*The rest I shall put in order when I come.*

This passage forms an integral part of the larger section which began with 11:2 and extends through chapter 14, all of which is concerned with putting order and propriety into the worship of the Christian assembly. Each of the successive topics under this heading is developed by its own theological arguments, but one theme is common to them all—Paul's concern that the *traditions* received and held in other Christian assemblies be followed in Corinth too (11:2, 16; 14:37). The term *traditions* (*paradoseis*) was one consecrated by rabbinic usage (cf. Gal 1:14). It stresses that the content of the teaching or practice is not the whim of Paul's personal fancy (1 Cor 11:2, even though the Apostle himself could legislate with full authority did he so desire) but a sacred deposit (1 Tim 6:20) received from the Lord (1 Cor 11:23) or the first Apostles (1 Cor 15:3), to which Paul himself felt bound (Gal 2:2). Such traditions were to be received and transmitted in their integrity, and, surprisingly enough for the Apostle of liberty, they had the force of law. The "traditions" were universal Christian customs (1 Cor 11:2 ff.; 14:34), or liturgical rites such as the Eucharist (1 Cor 11:23–24), or dogmatic or moral teachings (Rom 6:17; 2 Th 3:6; 1 Cor 7:10, 12, 25; 9:14; 15:3 f.).

Although Paul opened this section by praising the Corinthians for holding to the traditions he had given them (11:2), there are some areas of their conduct which call for censure (v. 17). First among these is the divisions that appear, paradoxically, at the very moment that the Christians are coming together in assembly (*ekklēsia*, church). The divisions over personalities cited by those of Chloe's household are now overshadowed by the report of divisions in the very celebration of the sacrament of unity. The Corinthians seem to have no concept of the real communal nature of this meal. Paul mitigates his judgment (as if the real situation could not be as bad as reported), but he is not surprised, since it is the divine wisdom that allows divisions to occur; in them the genuine members of Christ become manifest.[11]

---

[11]Chrysostom already remarked that the Greek *hina* ("so as to . . .") need not imply purpose but rather result, just as when Paul says "The Law intervened that the offense might abound" (Rom 5:20). Hence this text cannot be used to show that the good because of which God permits evil is the consequent good that can result from it.

The early Christians gathered, obviously not in a church building but in a home, like that of Gaius (Rom 16:23). Their purpose was ostensibly to eat the Lord's Supper. Saint Paul speaks of the meal here as the Lord's Supper because it obviously refers to the Last Supper of Jesus which the disciples now commemorated and relived. From the context it is evident that to the Eucharistic celebration was joined a meal, later called *agapē*, which was meant to symbolize and effect a solidarity in the community joined at a common table, and in so doing to care for the poor. As a matter of fact, however, the opposite was taking place, so that the meal had the appearance not of a banquet but of a series of picnicking circles or individual dinner groups such as might be found in today's restaurants or cafeterias. There was no spirit of sharing or equality; the first arrivals did not wait for the others but plunged into the food or drink they had brought and that even to excess—while the poor were left to go hungry. This could not be called The Lord's Supper: "The Lord's Supper, i.e., the Master's, ought to be common. For the property of the Master belongs not to this servant without belonging to that, but is common to all" (Chrysostom, *P.G.* 61:227).

Once again Paul struggles to bring these new converts to the sense of community. Their action shows a real contempt for the assembly of God, or really no realization at all of the notion of *ekklēsia*, assembly or church. "For it was made a church (*ekklēsia*, assembly), not that we who come together might be divided, but that they who are divided might be joined; and this the act of assembling shows" (Chrysostom, *P.G.* 61:228).

To show the sacredness and sobriety demanded by this meal, Paul now recalls in what sense it is the *Lord's* supper. What Paul has handed on to them (and they know it already) is a tradition going back to the Lord himself—and that on the very eve of his death.

The text of v. 23 literally begins, "For I received from the Lord what I also handed on to you." At first sight it would seem that Paul, in reciting this *paradosis*, this tradition, is telling the Corinthians of something he had as a direct revelation from the Lord. Three considerations, however, make this highly improbable: (1) The Greek verbs for "I received" and "I transmitted" are the normal terms used for the process of handing on a tradition in a human way; they correspond exactly to the rabbinical terms *gibbêl* and *mâsar*. When Paul wishes to speak of revelation, he uses nouns like "revelation" or "mystery" (1 Cor 15:51), or the verb "appear" (Rom 16:26; 1 Cor 4:5, etc.) and these generally refer to truths concerning the universal message of salvation, which it is Paul's mission to proclaim, or the future events of the Parousia. The things that concern the earthly life of Christ would more naturally be part of the "traditions" Paul received from the Apostles of Galilee. In the same vein (2) one might ask *when* this revelation could have taken place. Three days after his conversion, Paul was in full contact with the community at Damascus; he was instructed and even preached the new faith in the synagogue. It is hardly conceivable that his brethren would not have instructed him on the "breaking of the bread." On the view of a direct revelation, we are forced to conclude that it took place during the three days of his blindness before Ananias came to cure and baptize him. (3) The Greek preposition *apo* (from) in "from the Lord" does not necessarily imply a direct communication, as would *para*, which Paul precisely omits, contrary to his custom with the verb *paralambanein*. The sense then is that given in the translation: "a tradition going back to the Lord himself."

What follows is the first historical witness in the New Testament to the institution of the Eucharist, antedating Mark by some five to ten years. But Paul already affirms that it is well anchored tradition, even in the details, the first of which was that it was the night on which Jesus was *betrayed* (11:23) a point which should immediately alert the Corinthians to the sobriety and gravity of the occasion:

> For even if one be a very stone, yet when he considers that night, how he was with his disciples, "very heavy," how he was betrayed, how he was bound, how he was led away, how he was judged, how he suffered all the rest in order; one becomes softer than wax and is withdrawn from earth and all the pomp of this world. Therefore Paul leads us to recall all those things . . . putting us to shame and saying, "Your Master gave even his own self for you: and you do not even share a little food with your brother for your own sake" (Chrysostom, *P.G.* 61:229).

He broke it . . . (11:23). The "breaking of bread" was the essential act of Christian worship from the earliest times.

Paul's version of the words of institution are more than Mark's and Matthew's which lack *for your sake*, and less than Luke's, which has "*given* for your sake." The words taken alone could mean that the body is given for the benefit of the disciples, although this would seem a belaboring of the obvious in a text where every word counts. The parallelism with the blood of the covenant demands, however, taking *for your sake* seriously as an affirmation of the sacrificial nature of this body which brings salvation to his disciples. The death of Christ has this significance in the synoptics (Mk 10:45; Mt 20:28) and repeatedly in Saint Paul (Rom 5:6–8; 8:32; 14:15; 1 Cor 1:13; 15:3; Gal 2:20; 3:13; Eph 5:25; 1 Th 5:10; Tit 2:14). Here, then, the body of Christ is identified with the body immolated on the cross (so likewise Jn 6:51).

In a still more important way Paul's version differs from that of the synoptics.[12] The words *Do this in memory of me* (11:24) do not appear in Mk and Mt, and appear only once in Lk, whereas Paul has them twice. Obviously the Apostle is concerned with the iteration of the rite, which is precisely his point with the Corinthians—that the Eucharistic meal of Christians by Christ's own will is identical with the Lord's sacrificial meal the night he was betrayed. The memorial *(anamnēsis)* is not the faculty of memory but the act of bringing to mind, of observing a memorial service. Paul's insistence on the recalling and repetition reflects his conception of the Eucharist as the Christian fulfillment of the Passover feast of the Jews, in which the recollection and repetition of the original Passover meal was minutely prescribed (Ex 12; 13:9). (Paul seems to have written 1 Cor shortly before the Jewish Passover in spring of A.D. 57.) Jewish tradition elaborated on the thought:

"Now even though all of us were wise, all of us of great understanding, all of us familiar with Scripture, it would still be our duty to tell again the story of the Exodus from Egypt" (Passover Haggadah; cf. Dt 16:3).

What in the Passover Haggadah was "in remembrance of the day you came forth from Egypt" is now "in remembrance *of me*."

The sequence over the cup (v. 25) confirms the paschal image. Whereas Mt and Mk have "This is my blood of the covenant," Paul (and Lk) have *This cup is the new covenant in my blood.* The image evoked is Ex 24:3–8, which should be carefully reread at this point, along with some explanation of the meaning of covenant in the ancient Near East and in the Old Testament.[13] Paul's use of the word *new* evokes Jeremiah's prophecy of the new covenant (Jer 31:31; cf. Heb 8:8–12), and Jesus' words about the new wine he brings (Mk 2:22; Mt 9:17; 5:38; Jn 2). Jesus brings a new teaching (Mk 1:27), a new commandment (Jn 13:34; 1 Jn 2:7; 2 Jn 5); he gives a new life (Rom 6:4); in him man becomes a new creation (2 Cor 5:17). For Paul, however, all of this is viewed from the vantage point of his Jewish and rabbinical formation, in which the covenant and the formation of a covenant-community is foremost.[14] It is precisely the Corinthians' need to become aware of their identity as the new covenant community that made it necessary to discuss the Supper at all. What better motive for solidarity could they have than to realize that at the Lord's Supper, the

---

[12]G. Sloyan, " 'Primitive' and 'Pauline' Concepts of the Eucharist," *CBQ* 23 (1961), 1–13.

[13]Such as G. E. Mendenhall, *Law and Covenant in Ancient Israel and in the Near East* (Pittsburgh: The Presbyterian Board of Colportage of Western Pennsylvania, 1955). Reprinted from *The Biblical Archaeologist* 17 (1954), 26–46, 49–76.

[14]W. E. Lynch, "The Eucharist: A Covenant Meal," *TBT* 5 (March 1963), 318–323; J. H. O'Rourke, "The Passover in the Old Testament," *TBT* 5 (March 1963), 302–309; G. Wood, "The Eucharist—The New Passover Meal," *TBT* 5 (March 1963), 310–317.

new covenant and its people are ratified and formed anew? To this principal idea two subsidiary ones may be noted: (1) Paul does not say that the blood is "shed" or "given," but the sacrificial character is sufficiently implied in the idea of covenant blood, especially in the light of Ex 24:5–8, so that the meaning may be rendered with J. Weiss, "This chalice is the new covenant because it contains my blood." (2) The covenant, in Greek *diathēkē*, also means "testament," and in this sense the covenant has, by the death of the Testator, taken on an unbreakable character (Gal 3:15 f.; Heb 9:16). Whence it is impossible to change the nature of the Lord's Supper or caricature it as the Corinthians are doing.

V. 26 is the Apostle's conclusion from the tradition, *paradosis*, he has just recited: whenever you celebrate the Eucharist, you are proclaiming the *death* of the Lord. The Eucharist is not merely the presence of the body and blood of Christ; it is the solemn reenactment of his death. The verb, *proclaim* (*kataggelō*) has the general sense of making a solemn and public proclamation of some new order of things now in effect (1 Cor 9:14; Acts 3:24; 4:2; 13:5; 15:36; 16:21). In the Eucharist it is the death of Jesus that is so proclaimed; it is the sign and sacrament of his sacrifice.

The Lord's Supper thus calls for sentiments of bereavement or at least contrition and humility; this is why "I do not praise you." But more than that, as v. 27 now concludes, anyone who communicates unworthily is guilty of the body and blood of the Lord. The closeness of "death of the Lord" and the lingering force of "the night he was betrayed" suggest that the unworthy communicant is another Judas, who instead of bereaving and sharing the fruits of the tragic sacrifice, makes himself an accomplice in the very death of the Lord. Hardly could a more vivid statement of the real presence be asked for.

The unworthiness in this case is of course caused by their violation of charity, union, and sobriety:

> How can it be other than unworthily when it is he who neglects the hungry? Who besides overlooking him, puts him to shame? For if failing to give to the poor casts one out of the kingdom, even though one should be a virgin—or rather, not giving liberally . . . consider how great the evil will prove, to have done so many sacrileges? . . . You have partaken of such a Table, and when you should be kinder than any and like the angels, you have become more cruel than any. You have tasted the blood of the Lord, and not even at that moment do you acknowledge your brother. Of what forgiveness then are you worthy? For even if before this you had not known him, you should have come to know him from the Table; for he has been deemed worthy to partake of it—and you do not even judge him worthy of your food! (Chrysostom, *P.G.* 61:230).

An examination and purification of conscience must precede a worthy communion (cf. 2 Cor 13:5), just as at the Last Supper, each of the disciples asked, "Is it I, Lord?" (Mt 26:12). Receiving communion otherwise, one swallows his own judgment—*krima*, not the act of judging but the sentence received. It is spiritual poison; the reason is that such a person does not appreciate the sacrament for what it truly is: *the Body*. One will note that the single term *sōma* (body) here replaces both "the bread" and "the cup." In the context it is obvious that the "body" here can only mean the Eucharistic body just mentioned, and not the Church. Chrysostom explains again the stark realism of the real presence:

> "Not discerning the Lord's body," i.e. not searching, not bearing in mind, as he ought, the greatness of the things set before him; not estimating the value of the gift. For if you should come to know who it is that is before you, and who he is who gives himself, and to whom, you will need no other argument, but this is enough for you to use all vigilance (*P.G.* 61:233).

To this disrespect for the Eucharist Paul attributes the multiplication of afflictions in the Corinthian community, especially an apparently unusual incidence of sickness and death (*falling asleep*, 11:30). Not that all sickness and death would cease if order were restored, but Paul tells them that these temporal afflictions are one way in which God's judgment is already manifest, yet the purpose of them is medicinal, as corrections are given a child for his education (cf. Heb 12:5 f.; 1 Pet 4:7).

Paul hopes they learn the lesson, and lest they miss the point he concludes by stating it in the form of a precept, 11:33: Wait for one another before you begin eating. This obviously refers to the meal taken before the Eucharistic celebration, or in connection with it, and it does not imply Paul's intention here to separate the two meals completely, as will be done by the Church later precisely because of abuses of the type Paul here describes. Nevertheless the Apostle does tell them that if one cannot have the self-discipline to wait for the full assembly, let him eat at home, for the Christian's assembly should never present the contradiction of coming together "for judgment."

To sum up Paul's Eucharistic doctrine here: (1) The Christian Eucharist is a repetition of the Lord's own supper, according to the ritual he prescribed. (2) It is a proclamation of his death; and hence, (3) like the body and blood immolated on the cross, it is sacrificial in nature; (4) it is the covenant meal of the new dispensation, the Paschal Meal of the Christian passover. (5) So real is his presence in the cup and the bread that the unworthy communicant commits sacrilege not only in that he performs a perjurious religious act, but in that he dishonors the very body of the Lord. (6) Finally, the Eucharist belongs to the sacramental order, the span of time between the Lord's resurrection and final reunion with him ("until he comes"). It is through the Eucharist, the Passover meal of the New Covenant, that the deliverance by the Savior is made a contemporary reality and the covenant renewed until it is consummated at his final coming.

Notes on 1 Cor 12–14

This section of 1 Cor, while always claiming interest because of the hymn to eternal charity in chapter 13, has taken on added importance in recent years because of increased discussion of gift and charism in the church, and especially because the charismatic movement has over-flowed the confines of classical Pentecostalism and become widespread in many of the Christian churches. While the student may be referred to more extensive studies than are possible here,[15] some comments of a general nature will hopefully put these three chapters in focus.

The primitive church described its unique experience as the Holy Spirit. Among the effects of the gift of the Holy Spirit to the church were the experience of God as Father expressed in the acclamation, "Abba!" (Rom 8:15; Gal 4:6; the very name Jesus had used to address his Father, Mk 14:36), the enthusiastic acclamation of Jesus as Lord (1 Cor 12:3; Rom 10:9), and a new life marked by love, joy, peace, purity (Gal 5:22; 1 Cor 6:19). But the Holy Spirit also had an overwhelming effect on individuals and community, endowing them with various gifts which Paul here calls either *pneumatika* ("spirituals") or *charismata* (gifts) or *phanerōsis* (manifestation) of the Spirit. The most novel of these gifts is described in Acts 2 as the first effect of the coming of the Spirit upon the community: speaking in tongues. Though the passage in Acts seems to imply an endowment with unlearned human languages, the other passages in Acts and those in Paul indicate that the gift was basically a nonrational or preconceptual kind of praise (1 Cor 14:14–16), or, in some cases perhaps petition (as in Romans 8:26–27). In any case it is a gift of prayer, prayer that is vocalized but not verbalized. Its nonconcep-tual nature made it appropriate as a mystery-language for communing personally with God in private prayer (1 Cor 14:2). But it was also apparently used by some individuals in the public assembly, and then it had the character of oracular speech requiring interpretation (14:5–13). Interpretation is not the recognition of a known language by someone in the audience; rather it too is a gift of the Spirit (14:13) and therefore

---

[15]See especially George T. Montague, *The Spirit and His Gifts* (New York: Paulist Press, 1974); a critical biblical study with bibliography, *The Holy Spirit: Growth of a Biblical Tradition* (New York: Paulist Press, 1976); and, in a more popular and spiritual vein, by the same author, *Riding the Wind* (Ann Arbor: Charismatic Renewal Services, 1974).

seems best understood as a conceptualizing of the preconceptual prayer of the tongue-speaker.

Prophecy appears similarly as a gift of the Spirit (and not the effect of study or human experience, but rather of inspiration). It is a word-gift prized by Paul as the highest of the gifts because it combines both inspiration and intelligibility (12:31; 14:1) and is directly effective in building up, encouraging and consoling the community (14:3).

Other gifts mentioned here are: the word of wisdom (probably a counsel on Christian living), the word of knowledge (perhaps a specially inspired insight into the Christian mystery or even an unusual knowledge of some hidden fact), faith (a special manifestation of the kind of faith that wins miracles), healing and miraculous powers (12:8–10). In 12:28 there is a list that looks less like passing movements of the Spirit and more like a series of offices set in order: apostles, prophets, teachers, miracle-workers, healers, assistants, administrators, tongue-speakers. The first three of these *were* considered offices in the church from a very early time (Eph 4:11). Other lists of gifts and/or offices appear in Rom 12:6–8; Eph 4:11.

One way to understand the variety of these gifts and offices is to see them as expressing and fostering the various elements that are essential to the community's life. The community is essentially one of cult and praise (whence the function of tongues), one in which the word of God comes alive with a *now* meaning (whence the gifts of prophecy, interpretation, wisdom, knowledge). It needs to integrate these fresh insights with the traditional (whence, teachers). It is a community that administers wholeness and integration to its members (whence, healing) and builds up their faith through constantly fresh surprises of the Spirit (whence, miraculous powers). It also as a human community needs many services, including administration. It is a community that reaches out to those who have not yet heard the good news (evangelists). Finally, it seeks the unity of the Spirit (Eph 4:3), and that means a continuity not only with the larger community of the church throughout the world but also with the community of the past, going back to the authentic tradition that stems from the risen Christ and the primitive Jerusalem community. The apostle fulfills this function; he is the visible link between the community of believers and the risen Christ (1 Cor 9:1; Acts 1:22; compare John 20:29) and the assurer of continuity in the tradition (1 Cor 14:36).

Unhappily for him but happily for our instruction, Paul had difficulty with nearly every one of these dimensions of the life of the Corinthian community. His own authority as an apostle was challenged (cf. 1 Cor 3–4; 2 Cor). The gifts of tongues and prophecy were being used in a disorderly way more for the benefit of the user than for the upbuilding of the community. In chapters 12–14 Paul sets about to clarify the meaning of the gifts and especially to direct their use to the upbuilding of the community.

He begins by pointing out that while the movement of the Spirit may have a certain nonrationality about it, mere impulse is not a sign of the Holy Spirit. The Spirit can be discerned by his confirming and promoting the basic Christian faith in Jesus (12:1–3). Then Paul stresses that while there is a variety of gifts (12:8–10), there is a unity both in their source (12:4–6, 11) and in their purpose, the common good (12:7). This principle is illustrated by the analogy of the body (12:12–30).

In 12:31a Paul urges his community to seek after the greater gifts, a thought which he picks up and develops in 14:1, but he interrupts his treatment of the *gifts* to discuss the *way* which surpasses everything else (12:31b). This is the way of love, without which none of the service-gifts make any sense (13:1–3). It is the fundamental attitude, the universal power directing the whole Christian life (13:4–7). It will outlast all the service-gifts (13:8–13).

In chapter 14 Paul then gives practical applications for the use of the gifts. It is obvious that Paul condemns none of the gifts themselves, not even tongues about which he has so much to say (14:39). He himself says that he speaks in tongues more than any in the community (14:18); but he is concerned that all the activity be directed toward the common good (14:40), that is, for building up the community (14:5). This means that the preconceptual activity of tongues should be brought to a suitable term through conceptualization in interpretation or prophecy (14:1–5), and this is important both for the sake of those within the community (14:6–19) and for the sake of outsiders who may be present (14:23–25). Hence, some rules of order are laid down (14:26–36). He notes that the Spirit is not so overwhelming that he removes rational control and freedom from the individual (14:31–33). Hence, the individual has the responsibility for judging the appropriateness of his contribution. The gift of prophecy is not a gift of infallibility, for it must be subject to discernment of others in the community (14:29). The kind of speaking which Paul denies to women in 14:34 is not the use of the gifts of tongues or prophecy (he assumes that women pray and prophesy in 11:5), but, as is suggested by the Greek verb, the kind of talking and discussion that has no place in a prayer meeting.

Finally, Paul insists that what he has written is not just another nice idea to throw into the pot of bubbling enthusiasm at Corinth but an authoritative decision backed by the Lord himself (14:37).

We have here then a program providing an amazing blend of freedom to be moved by the Spirit, even enthusiasm for seeking such movement through the gifts, and a call for order backed with full apostolic authority. And squarely centered in the midst of the whole discussion is the reminder that love is the heart of the matter.

THE RESURRECTION: 1 COR 15

Death has always been a mystery to man, and his history could be written as a struggle to come to terms with it. Early cave drawings and burial accoutrements attest to man's desire and belief that he could somehow survive death. Plato gave a philosophical rationale for survival by his doctrine of the immortality of the soul. Modern medicine, on the other hand, has made a dent in death's kingdom by prolonging the average span of this life, but its success has only been in delaying the inevitable. Even philosophers who hold that man's life ends with the grave, struggle to remove the pall of futility cast over life by the spectre of certain death.

The Bible struggles with the same question, and from the viewpoint of man's natural constitution comes up with surprisingly negative answers: man will return to the dust from which he comes (Gen 3:19), his end appears no better than that of animals (Qoh 3:18–21), and what abode of the dead there is, Sheol, is a shadowy half-life at best (Job 10:20 f.; Ps 94:17; 115:17).

But within its own history Israel had an experience of *life* that opened up new and unheard-of possibilities. Her own existence as a people had been made by the intervention of a God of historical action, Yahweh, who had not only delivered her once from slavery in Egypt but also bound her to himself in covenant, thus making her future his own. A faithful God, he promised fullness to life to those who would remain faithful to him. Though "fullness of life" was first understood to mean land and descendants and material blessings (Gen 15:1–7; Deut 28), it was inevitable that the question of its bearing on personal survival of death should ultimately be raised. There were growing doubts about the equity of reward and punishment in this life (best stated by Job and Qoh). But the covenant theology met its moment of truth when it was confronted by the death of its martyrs—those who died precisely in order to remain faithful to the covenant. Could the covenant union and its promise be thwarted by the very act of fidelity to it? The problem thus raised in its most acute form triggered a development of the tradition that took various paths. The image of resurrection which earlier texts had used in a purely figurative way for the restoration of the nation after exile (Is 26:19; Ezek 37) Daniel took literally as a promise of bodily resurrection for those who had died for their faith (Dan 12:1–3). Later texts like 2 Mac 7 would graphically depict the martyrs' repossession of the body. But if vindication beyond death was granted to the martyrs, why should not God also vindicate the man whose *life* is an unjust suffering, even though he may die a natural death? The author of Enoch 102–104 used previous O.T. motifs to affirm the belief in God's vindication of the righteous poor, though he did not seem to think bodily resurrection necessary for it. The Psalms of Solomon (specifically Psalm 3) promises resurrection simply to the righteous irrespective of their lot in life. The book of Wisdom further interiorizes the transcendence of death by using the Greek notion of immortality not for the natural immortality of the soul but rather for the state of immortality which the righteous enter already in this life. "Death" for Wisdom is not the event of physical death but the persistent state of the ungodly experienced already while they seem to live; similarly immortality is experienced by the righteous even now, since "righteousness is immortal" (1:15), and the righteous man does not really die but only seems to die (3:2), for he enters God's presence (3:6). Wisdom thus does not talk about the resurrection of the body as such, and in this respect is similar to the Qumran Scrolls, which minimize physical death and transfer the focus to the existential decision man makes in this life.

The common thread in all these variants is the belief in the vindication of the just man, as Habakkuk had already written: "The just man because of his fidelity, will live" (Hab 2:4) and as the Psalmist had sung: "With you I shall always be ... in the end you will receive me in glory. . . . And when I am with you the earth delights me not. Though my flesh and my heart waste away, God is the rock of my heart and my portion forever" (Ps 73:23–26). This vindication of the just man was seen necessarily to encompass the transcendence of death, whether this be by repossession of the body (2 Mac 7), glorious transformation of the resurrected body (Dan 12:1–3), a resurrection of man's spirit while his bones remained in the earth (Jubilees 23:31), or the experience of immortality even in this life (Wisdom).[16]

Paul's vision of the risen Christ locked him squarely into the faith and the tradition of the primitive disciples that bodily resurrection was indeed a viable category for understanding the vindication of the Just One (Acts 3:14; 7:52), for it had actually happened in the case of Jesus (Acts 4:2), making him moreover Messiah and Lord (Acts 2:36). But for some reason at Corinth the implications of this event for Christians had come into question, perhaps because of the persistence of the Platonic

---

[16]Cf. G. W. E. Nickelsburg, Jr. *Resurrection, Immortality and the Eternal Life in Intertestamental Judaism* (Cambridge: Harvard U. Press, 1972). J. J. Collins, "Apocalyptic Eschatology as the Transcendence of Death," *CBQ* 36 (1974), 21–43.

view of the body that could see it happily jettisoned by the soul at death. Thus a tendency seems to have arisen to interpret the resurrection of Jesus as a mere symbol for the immortality or the spiritual resurrection of souls.

In answer to this tendency to a false gnosis, Paul writes a veritable "Wisdom discourse" which forms the climax of the entire letter. He had begun with a long consideration on Christ crucified (chs. 1–2). At 13:12 he had announced the Beatific Vision. But not even this is a sufficient culmination of the Christian life here below. Chapter 15 affirms and explains the real bodily resurrection of those in Christ.

1. Christ's Resurrection: A Fact: 1 Cor 15:1–11

> [1]*Now I recall to your minds, brothers, the Good News I preached to you—you also received it, you stand in it,* [2]*through it you are being saved if you continue to cling firmly to it in the form I preached it to you—otherwise your act of faith has all been for nothing!*
>
> [3]*The first thing I handed on to you was what I also received, namely that Christ died for our sins according to the Scriptures,* [4]*and that he was buried, and that he rose the third day according to the Scriptures,* [5]*and that he appeared to Cephas, and after that to the twelve.* [6]*Then he was seen by more than five hundred of the brothers at one time, the majority of whom are still with us, although some of them have fallen asleep.* [7]*Then he was seen by James, then by all the Apostles.* [8]*Last of all, as by one born out of due time, he was seen also by me.* [9]*For I am the least of the Apostles, not worthy to bear the name Apostle, because I persecuted the church of God.* [10]*But by the grace of God I am what I am, and his grace which entered me has not been fruitless—in fact, I have worn myself out in toil more than any of them. No, not I, but the grace of God working with me.* [11]*Whether, then, it is I or they, this is the message we preach, and this is what you believed.*

This first section is, like 1:18–25, a recalling of the essence of the kerygmy—the fact of the resurrection. The theological thought proper to Paul in the subsequent sections is all rooted in an historical fact which forms the basis of both the proclamation and the faith that saves. Paul is concerned that the essence of the kerygma be held in the very form and meaning in which he transmitted it. The *form* (*logos*) of v. 2 means a body of doctrinal elements in didactic form, a kind of creed, involving dogma and its definitive formulation. The series of statements each headed by "that . . ." comes like the recitation of a formula already well established. Paul has in this matter *handed on* what he has *received*—and received, not merely from his vision of the risen Christ, but from the Apostles of Jerusalem. This was the *first* apostolic action of Paul to the Corinthians.

The epistles preserve for us little of the Pauline kerygma (they are mostly concerned with his *didachē,* the subsequent elaboration on the kerygma), but it is important to remember that there is a wealth of Pauline preaching which has not come down to us. In it, as we have a precious indication here, he followed strictly the *logos,* the pattern or form, of the Palestinian kerygma. In that primitive proclamation, Jesus' death was an atonement for sin; his burial was confirmation of his death and a necessary preamble to the fact, important for early apologetics, of the incorruption of his body (Acts 2:24–31; 13:34–37). *According to the Scriptures* referred primarily to the Suffering Servant of Isaiah 53, who after giving his life for us, is rewarded with life. The listing of those who saw the Lord is obviously not meant to be exhaustive but "official," and the order is not necessarily chronological. "The Twelve" has become such a technical term for the collegial group that it can stand for them even in the absence of Judas and Thomas. Paul himself enjoys the rank of an apostle but one whose birth into the faith and into the apostolic college was abnormal, unexpected, and violent—he refers to Christ's "seizing" him (Phil 3:12) on the Damascus road.

His place among the Apostles is last not only because of time but also because he persecuted the *Church of God.* Canon Cerfaux believes that Paul refers here to the church of Jerusalem itself, the first to give itself the title "church of God," a title later assumed by other Christian communities.[17] Nevertheless it is true that Paul's persecution was not limited to the Jerusalem Church—in fact, his "seizure" by Christ occurred on his way to Damascus to round up the Christians there.

Whatever Paul *had been*, he now enjoys equal authority with the Apostles and he will feel obliged to expound the principle at more length in 2 Cor 11:5, 23 ff.; 12:9–10. The concluding v. 11 stresses once again that what he told them of the resurrection of Christ is the *common* tradition of the apostolic college, and the universal foundation of Christian faith.

2. The Resurrection of Christians, an Equal Certainty: 1 Cor 15:12–19

[12]If Christ is preached as raised from the dead, how is it that some among you say there is no resurrection of the dead? [13]But if there is no resurrection of the dead, then neither has Christ been raised. [14]But if Christ was not raised, there is nothing to our preaching, and there is nothing to your faith. [15]We are caught in being false witnesses to God, in that we have testified that God raised Christ, whereas he did not raise him, if the dead are not raised. [16]If the dead are not raised,

---

[17]Cf. L. Cerfaux, *The Church in the Theology of Saint Paul,* 110.

*neither has Christ been raised, *[17]*but if Christ has not been raised, your faith is groundless—you are still in your sins. *[18]*It follows also that those who have fallen asleep in Christ have perished. *[19]*If in this life in Christ we have been hopers only and only that, we are of all men the most to be pitied.*

The tendency to put in doubt the resurrection of Christians does not appear well organized, nor explicitly taught by some group, for Paul, without resorting to violent polemic, merely clarifies the doctrine—though this he does vigorously and lucidly. The tendency really comes from a lack of logic—the presumed principle of "no resurrection of the dead" is proved invalid by the resurrection of Christ. In the apostolic kerygma the resurrection of Christ announces the resurrection of the dead. James and John "were proclaiming in *Jesus* the resurrection from the dead" (Acts 4:2). The solidarity between the two resurrections is, in our case, not in that Jesus is a member of the race, as if the one instance shows the possibility of all men rising. The resurrection of pagans is not envisaged in this passage, but only the resurrection of those in Christ. The solidarity is not in human nature, but in the divine will or intention, made manifest in Jesus' resurrection, to raise Christians. The thought is exactly the same as that which Paul expressed in 1 Th 4:14, "If we believe that Jesus died and rose again, so with him God will also bring those who have fallen asleep through Jesus." Hence, at this point Paul has not yet revealed, as he will in vv. 20–22, what is the intrinsic link between the resurrection of Jesus and that of Christians, but he explains it in terms merely of its unique extrinsic cause, God's will.

If Christ has not been raised from the dead, the apostles' kerygma, i.e., the sum of their preaching, is *vain* (15:14). This term means not only that the kerygma lacks any historical foundation, but that its very object has vanished. For Paul and the apostles, to preach at all was to preach the resurrection of Jesus—and to accept this divine deed was to become a Christian: "If you confess with your tongue that Jesus is the Lord, and believe in your heart that God raised him from the dead, you shall be saved" (Rom 10:9).

The Lordship of Christ in this text is explained by the parallel "God raised him from the dead." This point is capital for an understanding of Pauline (or, for that matter, Christian) theology. There are certainly many other truths which the Christian is expected to know—he will learn them in a very detailed catachesis. But all of them are known through the resurrection of Jesus. For Saint Paul, the resurrection of Jesus is *a revelation of God.* It is the single light that opens to man the whole world of the supernatural—God's true nature (Rom 1:4) and the mystery of his plan for men (Acts 17:31; 1 Th 1:10). Among the truths which the resurrection of Jesus reveals is the future resurrection of Christians. To deny this is to deny the Light itself, Jesus' own resurrection. Paul will tell us why in vv. 20–22.

More than that, the Apostles, who by definition are witnesses (Acts 1:22; 5:32; 1 Cor 3:5), and witnesses primarily to the resurrection (Acts 10:42), would be perjurers, either witnessing "against God," or better, calling God to witness to a lie. This would be seeking to glorify God by saying he has done something he has not done and thus also to deceive others. But already Job had exclaimed that God does not need lies (Job 13:7–9). Certainly this text affirms that the resurrection was no hallucination—the Apostles themselves thought of that possibility long before their rationalist critics (Lk 24:11).

Vv. 16 and 17 repeat the same thought, but conclude with an important addition: If Christ is not risen, then you are still in your sins. Catechetics of the past has so insisted that we are saved by Christ's death, that the capital importance of the resurrection for our salvation has often been obscured. For Paul, the death of Christ was a transitory event whose value for us was made definite only by the resurrection. "He was delivered up for our sins, and was raised up for our justification" (Rom 4:25). Not only was the resurrection the Father's personal reward to Christ for his obedience and sacrifice (Phil 2:6–11), not only was it God's warranty to us of the true saving value of Christ's death, but it puts Christ in the condition of "life-giving Spirit" for the new creation (v. 45, which we shall examine more thoroughly below).

In the context of the Corinthian problem, it is important to recall the intrinsic connection the Jewish mind always held between death and sin. Death is the negation of life, the greatest of God's gifts; death's presence in the world cannot be ascribed directly to the creator but to man's sin, his violation of God's plan. For the Platonic mind of the Greek, schooled to think of the soul happily jettisoning the body at death, this theology was difficult to grasp. For Paul, the Judeo-Christian, however, the soul's separation from the body is not a release—it is the principal punishment of sin! Consequently, if Christ came to vanquish sin and himself remained a definitive victim of death (sin's principal victory), he would not have destroyed sin, the cause of death. And that is why if Christ is not risen *you are still in your sins* (v. 17), and moreover (v. 18) the dead in Christ are lost. Paul does not even consider here the possibility of an afterlife of the soul in Sheol.

The last line pushes the argument to its logical conclusion: then we are of all men the most to be pitied. The sacrifices the Christian life imposes, even though they produce a virtuous life and bring joy and peace of conscience, are not worth it. Paul shudders at the thought of the kerygma being a "beneficent deception." The protasis of the sentence may be read "If with only this life in view we have hoped in Christ" (i.e., if only for temporal goods) or, better, in the sense in which we have translated it, "If all we are in this life is 'hopers' in Christ, without real issue to our hope. . . ." Of the essence of both kerygma and faith is the certainty of the future resurrection of those in Christ.

3. Christ the Firstfruits: 1 Cor 15:20–28

> [20]But the fact is, Christ has been raised from the dead, the first-fruits of those who have fallen asleep. [21]Since death came by a man, by a man will come resurrection of the dead. [22]For just as in Adam all die, so in Christ all will be brought to life. [23]But each in his proper order: Christ the first-fruits, then Christ's own, at his coming. [24]Then the end, when he will hand the kingdom over to God the Father, once he has reduced to nothing every other principality and authority and power. [25]For he must exercise his reign until "he has put all his enemies under his feet." [26]The last enemy to be destroyed is death. [27]For "he has put all things under his feet." Of course when it is said that he subjected everything, he obviously is excepted who subjected everything to him. [28]Once everything has been brought into subjection under him, then the Son himself will be subject to him who subjected all things to him, that God may be everything to everyone and everything.

After detailing the sombre and radical nothingness to which the Christian faith would be reduced without the resurrection of the faithful, Paul undertakes the positive theology of the Christ-event. He begins (v. 20) with an expression of belief which restates: (1) the fact of Christ's resurrection, already affirmed in 3–11, and (2) the fact that it is an anticipation of the resurrection of Christians. At once we sense a solidarity of Christ with the faithful—it is from among the dead that he has been raised; and of those who have fallen asleep he is the *firstfruits*. This biblical term has no real counterpart in our modern industrialized society. Among the Jews, the offering of the first sheaves of grain at harvest, or a cake from the first batch of new dough was the prescribed way of manifesting that the entire land and its produce were the Lord's, and the consecration of this part was really a consecration of the whole (Lev 23:10–14; Nm 15:18–21; Rom 1:16). The sixteenth day of Nisan was the prescribed occasion for offering the firstfruits to Yahweh in the temple. This was precisely the day of Jesus' resurrection, and the coincidence of these events may have suggested to Paul the application of the metaphor to the risen Christ. At any event, the image suggests in what relation the risen Christ stands to believers—he is the first of the harvest, meaning the rest will follow, the "firstborn of the dead" (Col

1:18; Apoc 1:5). This last expression squares with the preaching of Christ's resurrection in terms of a birth (Acts 13:33; Heb 1:5) and the risen Christ as the firstborn of a multitude of brothers (Rom 8:29).

This incipient statement of Christ's instrumentality is now reaffirmed and explained in v. 21: Just as a man was the source of death—in its total sense of physical death and the spiritual and "eschatological" death which for a Jew meant separation from the God of Israel—so a man is now the source of resurrection and life. Here for the first time Paul introduces the Adam-Christ contrast. There is no convincing evidence that Paul drew his doctrine from Philo's Platonic distinction between a heavenly and an earthly Man or from the Iranian conception of the *Urmensch*, the primordial man who was thought to be the prototype of mankind and to be connected in some way with its origin and continued existence. The use of the definite articles with both Adam and Christ indicates that Paul is thinking of historical persons who have influenced history. In saying that in Adam, all have died, Paul is supposing a real solidarity of men with Adam, who causally effects their death. So *in Christ* affirms a solidarity of Christians with Christ who will effectually cause their resurrection. The resurrection of infidels is elsewhere affirmed by Paul (6:2; 11:32; Rom 2:5 f.; cf. Jn 5:29) but it is not in the scope of his consideration here, as v. 23 indicates. Likewise at this point Paul's conception of Christ as the new Adam is from the aspect of *communicating* the new risen *life* he now possesses. The antithesis in the matter of obedience and suffering will be affirmed only in Rom 5, where the death of all Adam's descendants will be explained by men's participation in his sin.

Christ precedes as *firstfruits;* then, after a considerable interval (since Christ is already risen), the resurrection of his members at his coming (15:23). On the meaning of the *Parousia,* see above on 1 and 2 Th.

Then the end (15:24). The word *telos,* here translated *end,* is explained by some as "the rest," i.e., the reprobate (Theodoret, Oecumenius, Cajetan), or the just who died before the incarnation (Cyril of Alexandria), or the non-Christian just who would rise only at the end of a period of messianic wars or a thousand-year reign of Christ, the millennium of Apoc 20:1–10 (Lietzmann, Bachmann, Loisy). The "rest" theory, implying two resurrections of the dead, has been adequately refuted, especially in the last form, among others by Père Allo in a long excursus in his commentary.[18] The "end" follows at once, in a sequence that is logical rather than chronological. V. 25 is an adaptation of Ps

---

[18]*Etudes Bibliques*, Paris, 1934. Cf. also W. D. Davies, *Paul and Rabbinic Judaism*, 2 ed. (London, 1955), 285–298.

110:1, which the Jews of Jesus' time already interpreted messianically, "Sit at my right hand until I make your enemies your footstool." Christ, enthroned as Royal Messiah in the resurrection, has already begun to reign. The Parousia is the consummation, not the beginning, of his reign. The present age is a progressive conquest of the rebellious powers, of which the last, death, is destroyed by the resurrection of the dead (cf. v. 54–55; Apoc 20:14; 21:4).

V. 27 is an adaptation of Ps 8:7, in which it is said that God has put all things under the feet of man (called the "son of man" in v. 5). The Talmud applied this to Moses and to Abraham, the intimate friends of God; Paul applies it with all the more reason to Christ, whose favorite title was "the Son of Man."

What is the meaning of this "handing over" of the kingdom and of the subjection of the Son to the Father (15:24)? It cannot quite mean the abandoning of the kingdom, for elsewhere the kingdom of Christ is identical with the kingdom of God (Rom 5:17; cf. 14:17; Eph 5:5; 2 Tim 2:12), and just as in the Apocalypse the Lamb shares the divine throne (Apoc 7:17; 22:1, 3), so also in Eph 1:1–8, Christ never ceases to reign. The thought therefore must rather be that the present age is a militant one, in which Christ, enthroned as king by his resurrection, now sets about the conquest of the kingdom that is already his by right. He is now a king at war. When he wins the final battle, destroying death itself by raising the "dead in Christ," he will bring his trophies, a new creation crowned by the triumph of his risen members, to do homage to his Father, who sent him on this mission of love and renewal. Cosmic history, made anew by resurrection, ends in the sharing of the intimate life of the Trinity, where God will be (literally) "all in all" (15:28), that is, total source of life, immediate presence, and object of direct contemplation. It is the new Jerusalem enlightened by God and the Lamb (Apoc 21:22–27).

4. Resurrection Faith in Practice: 1 Cor 15:29–34

²⁹*Otherwise, what are they to do who have themselves baptized because of the dead? If the dead do not rise at all, why do people receive baptism because of them?* ³⁰*Why do we at every moment expose ourselves to danger?* ³¹*I am exposed to death every single day—so much are you a source of glory for me in Christ Jesus our Lord.* ³²*If for human motives I fought wild beasts at Ephesus, what use was it to me? If the dead do not rise, let us eat and drink, for tomorrow we die.*

³³*Don't fool yourselves: "Bad company corrupts good morals."* ³⁴*Return, as is proper, to your senses, and do not go on sinning. For some men are ignorant of God. I so speak to move you to shame.*

Here the emotion that underlay the preceding section now comes to the surface in a series of reflections, not all related. Vv. 29–33 nevertheless are a supporting argument from a common practice among the Corinthians and from Paul's own example. The "baptism for the dead" has been a *crux interpretum* and still remains so. One thing is certain: Paul does not reprimand it, but uses it as a valid argument to buttress faith in the resurrection of the dead. (1) Some say that the practice was a rebaptism of Christians as a kind of vicarious baptism for their deceased relations or catechumens who died without baptism; hence, it was not the sacrament but a kind of sacramental by which Christians expressed their prayer for the non-Christian deceased and their desire to see them incorporated into Christ. This would take the preposition *hyper* in the sense of *anti,* "in place of." (2) A slight variation of the preceding: the catechumen receiving baptism would do so with an intention that the grace of his baptism be also applied to his deceased unbaptized relatives with whom he hopes to be rejoined at the resurrection. Both these hypotheses suppose a kind of suspended state of the dead in the afterlife before the final judgment. (3) The third solution, winning more support today, is that which takes *hyper* in its most common final meaning, "for the sake of" or "because of," and "the dead" as referring to deceased Christians (which is, after all, the sense in which Paul is using it throughout this chapter), and "baptized" in the genuine sense of receiving the sacrament, so that it refers to those who come to the faith and seek baptism because of the certainty they are thereby given of being joined to their beloved dead in the final resurrection. It must not have been an unusual thing, for example, that a pagan whose Christian fiancée or wife died, should, under the impact of his grief at her loss and the Church's faith in her resurrection, desire to become a Christian in order to be reunited with her at the final resurrection.[19] Paul argues to the existence of a doctrine from a worthy traditional practice of the Church, a method which the Church has used ever since.

Paul's own life and vigorous apostolate illustrate his hope in the resurrection. Otherwise, there is no reason why the Christian's daily life should be guided by any other principle than the mocking line of Is 22:13. (The conflict with wild beasts is probably a metaphor for the great struggles Paul engaged in at Ephesus.)

The last two lines are an appeal to Christians not to allow the purity of their faith to become corrupted by the influence of pagans who make a

---

[19]Cf. J. Jeremias, "Flesh and Blood Cannot Inherit the Kingdom of God," *New Testament Studies* 2 (1955/56), 155 f.

show of *knowledge* (*gnōsis*) but in reality do not know (i.e., have never experienced the reality and power of) the true God. Stop sinning—i.e., deviating from the true doctrine of the resurrection.

5. How the Resurrection Can Take Place: 1 Cor 15:35–49

[35]*But someone will ask: How can the dead be raised? With what kind of body will they come back?* [36]*Senseless man! What you sow is not brought to life unless it dies.* [37]*And what you sow is not the body that is to be, but a bare grain, perhaps of wheat or something else.* [38]*But God gives it a body such as he wills, and to each kind of seed the body proper to it.* [39]*Not all flesh is the same flesh, but men have one kind of flesh, beasts another, birds another, and fish still another kind.* [40]*And there are heavenly bodies and earthly bodies, but the splendor of the heavenly bodies differs from that of the earthly bodies.* [41]*The sun has its own splendor, the moon its own, the stars their own. Star indeed differs from star in splendor.* [42]*So it is with the resurrection of the dead.*

What is sown in corruption rises in incorruption.
[43]*What is sown in humiliation, rises in glory.*
What is sown in weakness, rises in power.
[44]*A natural body is sown, it rises a spiritual body.*
If there is a natural body, there is also a spiritual body. [45]*Thus also it is written,*
"The first man, Adam, became a soul having life."
The last Adam became a spirit imparting life.
[46]*But first came not the spiritual organism,*
    but the natural and then the spiritual.
[47]*The first man was from the dust of earth,*
    The second man from heaven.
[48]*As was the man of dust,*
    So are they who are of the dust.
And as is the Heavenly Man
    So are those who are heavenly.
[49]*And just as we have borne the likeness of the man*
        of dust,
    So let us bear the likeness of the Heavenly One.

Having reaffirmed the fact of Christ's resurrection (1–11) and the certainty of the resurrection of the faithful in union with him (12–35), Paul now takes up two theological questions which had no doubt been part of the discussion among the Corinthians: (1) How is it possible that a body, corrupted by death and the grave, should rise? (2) What kind of body will it be? Both these questions are stated in v. 35, and answered in the pericope 35–49.

If the Corinthians converted from Hellenism were exposed to the Platonic extreme of minimizing the body and even excluding it from final bliss, the converts from Judaism would have been influenced by various views of the mode of resurrection. Many of them even prior to their conversion doubtless believed in the resurrection of the dead, though in the first century this was a controverted point between the Pharisees on the one hand and the Sadducees and Samaritans on the other. Rabbinical teaching had not reached great precision on the condition of the elect at the resurrection, and hence it was easy for popular conceptions to be formed, according to which the future life would simply be the revival of present human existence. On the other hand, if we may believe the testimony of Josephus (*Jewish Wars*, 2, 10, 11), even such an ardently Jewish sect as the Essenes came under the influence of Platonism to the extent of seeking escape from the body for their immortal souls. Even the resurrection of the body might therefore be explained in such a way that the body might no longer really be corporeal. Whence the significance of Paul's two questions.[20]

In the style of the diatribe, common in the Stoic literature of his day, Paul raises the question (*but someone will ask*, 15:35) and proceeds to answer it (*Senseless man!*). The "death" of seed is only the condition of its passing into a more perfect existence. The image is not an allegory, in which every detail can be transferred, but a simple comparison which anyone can understand; it was a common symbol in the ancient world for survival and resurrection, both in the mystery religions and in rabbinic Judaism. Paul's immediate source is probably a saying of Jesus which we find reflected in Jn 12:24, "Unless the grain falling into the ground die . . ." It is not the Apostle's intention to teach that death is an absolute condition for the glorious life to come (cf. below, v. 51), and certainly not to say that resurrection is the *natural* outcome of death, but simply to illustrate by an example that death and corruption of the tomb in no way weaken what he has said about the certainty of the resurrection, nor in any way limit the omnipotence of God. The grain that is sown is not what it is to become, but a simple grain. There is, however, a marvelous transformation that takes place, and an identity of the risen sprout with the buried grain.[21] Saint Thomas adds the theological precision, when transferring the image to the resurrection, that the risen body is not only of the same species but is the same individual body. This

---

[20]H. Cornelis, J. Guillet, et al., *The Resurrection of the Body*, trans. M. Joselyn (Notre Dame: Fides, 1964), 11–122.

[21]On the question of the identity of the risen body, see the thorough discussion by M. E. Dahl, *The Resurrection of the Body, A Study in Corinthians 15* (London: SCM Press, 1962).

is Paul's point, and while he uses the rabbinic image of the seed, he does not trifle with the speculation of the rabbis about the just rising clothed.[22]

Even so, the body will not have the same qualities as it had here below. But neither is this transformation of the identical body impossible to God. If there is such variety already observable in creation, why should God's power be limited to the kind of bodies we can see? It is important to observe that Paul reduces the whole question to the first cause. He does not of course say that the transformation of the grain is miraculous; but it is an effect of God's will, his *gift*. So, too, the body may be entirely corrupt; God can not only restore it but elevate it to a superior state. The heavenly bodies are the stars, which the ancients thought to be incorruptible; there is no ground for supposing Paul thought them to be angelic bodies. To interpret the line *star differs from star in splendor* (cf. Dan 12:3) of the varying degrees of glory within the company of the elect, is to read into the text more than Paul put there. He is concerned to show only how the elect can have, in common, a glory all their own in the vast gamut of God's creation.

So it is (v. 42) with the resurrection of the dead—the comparison bears on vv. 37–38, the transformation of bare grain into a more perfect reality. Now follow four parallel antitheses, in which there is internal rhyme in the Greek between *what is sown* (*speiretai*) and "is raised" or *rises* (*egeiretai*). The corruption in which man is sown refers to the corruption of the grave, but this is merely the culmination of man's whole existential condition, in which the flesh weighs him down and pulls him away from God (Rom 8:21; Gal 6:8; Col 2:22; 2 Pet 2:12). The incorruption of the risen state means imperishability. *Incorruption* is a type of existence that belongs properly to God (Wis 2:23; Rom 1:23; 2 Tim 1:10). Now communicated to the elect, it is the equivalent of immortality (1 Tim 1:17).

Second trait: from a state of dishonor, humiliation, sordidness, the body rises in *glory* (*doxa*), which here is not just honor, but a quasi-physical splendor, light, brilliance. As Jesus at the Transfiguration appeared *in glory* (Lk 9:31), so "the just shall shine like the sun in the kingdom of their Father" (Mt 13:43). The bodies of Christians at the final resurrection will be made conformable to Christ's glorious body (Phil 3:21).

Third trait: from weakness to power. To say man's whole present condition is one of *weakness* is equivalent to saying it is *flesh*. The flesh is, by definition, weak (Mt 26:41). This condition involves ignorance of

---

[22]*Pirke Rabbi Eliezer* XXXIII, 245; b. Sanh. 90b.; cf. W. D. Davies, *Paul and Rabbinic Judaism*, 305.

divine things (Rom 8:26), moral weakness (Mt 26:41), and vulnerability to suffering, temptation (2 Cor 12:7–12), and death (2 Cor 13:4). As the antonym of weakness is *strength*, so the antonym of *flesh* is *spirit*, so that "power" (*dynamis*) and "spirit" (*pneuma*) are often equivalents (cf. Lk 1:35; 4:14, 36 etc.). The Christian here below already is indwelt by the Spirit as firstfruits or "downpayment" (Rom 8:11, 23), but the full effect of the Spirit's action takes place, as it did in Christ (Rom 1:4) at the resurrection of the body. If the power of the Spirit is already experienced in the Christian's present life (Rom 7:6; 8:14, 26; 15:13, 19; Gal 5:22, 6:8 ff.), in the future life the remaining encumbrances of the flesh will be totally removed. This is, in part, what the speculative theologians have called the property of *agility* in the glorified body.

The fourth trait is really a summary of the others: From being a *natural* (*psychichon*) body, it becomes a *spiritual* (*pneumatikon*) body. We use the term "natural" here to describe this body animated by a human soul (*psyche*), i.e., a principle of life proper to it, yet still for all that quite limited to merely human horizons. This very same body (as will be affirmed in v. 53) at the resurrection will be animated and totally penetrated by a new principle of life, the pneuma or Spirit, which will not, of course, replace or destroy the natural soul (any more than it destroys the human intelligence, 1 Cor 14:14) but perfect and elevate it, as it does even now to a limited extent (Rom 8:11, 23). The transformation then, however, will flow over completely into the physical, transforming it.

Whether we like to admit it or not, our modern mind still thinks in Platonic categories. So accustomed are we to think of what is material, bodily, or corporeal, as opposed to what is spiritual, that the term "spiritual body" sounds as much a contradiction in terms as a "square circle." Teilhard de Chardin's intiution represents a happy break with this incompatibility, but really the insight was in the Jewish tradition already in the Old Testament, and Paul possessed it totally. *Spirit* means the active creative power of God, or creation inasmuch as it is given being, movement and life by God. Hence a spiritualized matter, or a "spiritual body" means a body in which the creative and life-giving power of God has become totally operative.[23] In the case of the first creation, it was by God's breath, his *pneuma* or spirit, that man became a living being (Gen 2:7). His same divine power now exerted upon the deceased person (the Hebrew idea of *body* implies the integrity of being which we call person) not only restores the natural life but charges it with

---

[23]Cf. R. North, "Separated Spiritual Substances in the O.T.," *CBQ* 29 (1967), 419–449. B. V. Schneider, "The Corporate Meaning and Background of 1 Cor 15:45b," *CBQ* 29 (1967), 450–467.

a new and divine vitality which the first creation did not know. The risen body is not a ghost; it is real matter enjoying a superior and definitive state of being. This state Paul calls *pneumatic*, or "spiritual," packing into that term all that two thousand years of Hebrew tradition knew of the life-giving power of *Yahweh-Elohim*, and all that the Apostles and Paul himself knew of the risen Christ whom they had seen and with whom the twelve ate and drank (Acts 1:3 f.), plus thirty years of experience of the Spirit of God mightily at work in the Church.

The superiority of the new creation over the old is illustrated in v. 45 by a reference to Gen 2:7. At God's breath (*pneuma*), Adam became a living soul (*psyche*). But the last Adam, Paul now adds, not only had life from God, he became a *life-giving spirit*—that is, sharing in the way the first Adam did not in God's own creative power, his *pneuma*. The humanity of Christ, glorified in the resurrection, became at that moment the *principle* of resurrection for the new humanity. True, this "spirit of holiness" was his from the moment of the incarnation, but it was the resurrection that made it manifest (Rom 1:4) and available to men. Paul has moved into a much more intrinsic causal relationship between Christ and his members; the way is now laid for the whole development on justification in Romans 5:12 ff.

"The natural body" came first, then the spiritual (v. 46). This could refer to the body of Christ or even of Christians in its natural state before the resurrection; but the context invites us to understand it of the two Adams—the Adam of Genesis came first; the Adam of Easter morning did not in his glorious human nature exist in heaven before the creation of Adam; he is himself a descendant of Adam; and so likewise it is the existential lot of men to pass through Adamic existence and even death before attaining the risen state—as indeed Christ himself did.

With v. 47 begins a second series of our lyric parallels, betraying the emotion Paul feels as he sings the superiority of the Last Adam over the first. The heavenly origin of the "second man" is understood by some to refer to the resurrection, when the Spirit, a "heavenly principle," raised Jesus. We think this is too restrictive a sense and would understand it as referring to the preexistent divinity of Christ, in the sense of Phil 2:6. Surely, it was the resurrection that made this manifest (Rom 1:4).

In the second and third of the parallel statements (v. 48), the contrast is continued as to the effects of the two "Adams" in the kind of existence they communicate to men. Adam not only was taken from dust, but the punishment of his sin was that he should return to dust (Gen 3:19), and this lot fell to all those descended from him. The solidarity of all men in Adam is here affirmed, and it is experienced in suffering and death. But the elect have an equal solidarity with the Heavenly Man. They are "the heavenly" and will (barring some catastrophic apostasy, which Paul is not considering here) inevitably share the lot of their risen Lord.

The fourth parallel draws the conclusion. Adam begot Seth in his own image and likeness (Gen 5:3), and thus the descendants of Adam all bear his resemblance, which, concretely, is his same corruptible nature. Christians too have borne that likeness. But they are destined to be conformed to another likeness, that of their glorified Lord.[24]

There is a disputed reading of the verb *bear* in 49b. A great number of critics adopt the manuscript reading "we shall bear," even though it is less well attested by the texts, for the alleged reason that Paul's concern here is with the *future* lot of Christians and not with their present state. The more difficult reading "let us bear" which we have adopted, is much better attested by the manuscripts (including the latest Chester Beatty papyrus). It enriches the thought by presenting this destiny as something that must be *won* by conforming one's present life to it and thus beginning even now to reflect that image. We have not yet reached the explicit affirmation that we are *presently being transformed* into that image by Christ's power (2 Cor 3:18), but the idea of the challenge that the glorious destiny presents prepares the moral reminder to follow immediately in v. 50.

The final explanation of how the resurrection can take place is then this: it has already taken place in Christ, who is not just one man among others, but the new Adam of a new humanity, endowed with creative power (spirit) which the first Adam did not have. Paul affirms the solidarity of Christians with Christ, but he does not tell us *how* they are united with him so that his risen power may be communicated to them. For this we must await the sublime sacramental theology of Romans (see ch. 6).

6. The Final Victory: 1 Cor 15:50–58

> [50]*But I affirm this, brothers, that flesh and blood cannot inherit the kingdom of God; neither can what is corruptible inherit what is incorruptible.*
> [51]*Look, I am telling you a mystery:*
> *We shall not all fall asleep,*
> *But we shall all be changed.*
> [52]*In an instant, in the twinkling of an eye,*
> *At the last trumpet,*
> *When the trumpet sounds,*
> *Then the dead will be raised incorrupt,*
> *And we shall be changed.*

---

[24]J. de Fraine, "Adam and Christ as Corporate Personalities," *TD* 10 (1962).

> [53]*For this corruptible nature of ours is destined to be*
> *   clothed with incorruptibility,*
> *And this mortal nature of ours to be clothed with im-*
> *   mortality.*
> [54]*When this corruptible nature is clothed with incor-*
> *   ruptibility,*
> *And this mortal nature with immortality,*
> *Then will be realized the words of Scripture:*
> *"Death is swallowed up in victory!*
> [55]*O Death, where is your victory?*
> *O Death, where is your sting?"*
> [56]*Death's sting comes from sin*
> *And sin's rampant power comes from the Law.*
> [57]*But thanks be to God, who gives us the victory*
> *Through our Lord Jesus Christ.*
> [58]*In this conviction, my beloved brothers, be steadfast, immovable,*
> *pouring yourselves out in the Lord's work, realizing that your toil is not*
> *in vain, done as it is in the Lord.*

Verse 50 can be viewed as the conclusion of the preceding pericope, as well as the beginning of the present one. At any rate, the idea is expressed as a formal pronouncement. *Flesh and blood* is a Semitism to express human nature in contrast to the divine (or what today we call the *supernatural*), particularly the native inability of man to penetrate the divine sphere or to suspect the plans of God (cf. Mt 16:17; Gal 1:16; Eph 6:12; Heb 2:14). If this is true of what originates in God's counsel (Mt 16:17), it is especially true of the destiny God has planned for his elect (cf. 1 Cor 2:9). It is not possible to the natural powers of man; what is more, that destiny itself is not a mere revival of natural life. The *kingdom of God* in Paul is identical with eschatological glory (1 Th 2:12) or, here, with the state of incorruptibility. He has already affirmed that the unjust will not have any share in that kingdom (1 Cor 6:9; cf. Eph 5:5); here he affirms that even man's natural powers cannot attain it, much less produce it (cf. also Rom 14:17).

What then, of those living at the Parousia? What more do they need to be partakers in the imperishable glory of Christ? Must they first die? Here Paul reveals the divine secret, *mystērion* (for the meaning of this term see 1 Cor 2:7 above). It is not necessary that all die, nor is it God's plan that those living at the final moment should pass through death before being glorified. The point is, however, that they too will be changed, made to be "heavenly men" like the heavenly Man whose image they are to bear. Both dead and living will be transformed; here explicitly Paul states that the resurrection of the dead is more than revival of natural life: all shall not die, but all shall be changed. To dramatize the event, Paul calls on the apocalyptic terminology which we have already discussed in the Thessalonian letters (1 Th 4:16). He uses especially those symbols which express suddenness of the event, and indicates that both resurrection and transformation of living and dead are simultaneous. The resurrection-transformation will occur at the time appointed by God as a brilliant manifestation of his omnipotence. For the sake of his instruction, Paul associates himself with those alive at the Parousia (v. 52, *we* emphatic). Since Paul elsewhere considers as possible his death before that moment (1 Th 5:9 f.; Rom 8:11, 14:8; Phil 1:20–23; 2:17), we must not draw the conclusion (which some have mistakenly drawn) that he was certain of being among the living (see above on 1 Th 4:17).

No really new thought is added by v. 53 and 54a, except a very clear affirmation that the glorified body is the very *same* body as that now possessed (the pronoun *touto* "this" used four times in two verses).[25] The state of glory does not destroy personal integrity but restores it.

When this happens, there is nothing more to do except to sing the victory song as Paul here does, combining a very free citation of Is 25:8 and Hos 13:14.

Whence comes the assurance of this victory? Death is really the sting, i.e., the venomous poison and the pain, caused by sin. The advent of the Law did not reduce sin's power over man but rather increased it, not in the sense that the Law itself was bad, but, revealing as it did the commandment of God without of itself giving the power to keep it, it occasioned the multiplication of transgressions and made man's responsibility for sin all the graver. (This whole theology is soon to be developed when Paul writes to the Romans.) But this pitiable state is now over and gone. Grace has supplied what the Law could not, and Christ has destroyed sin. Death's defeat (the "mop-up" operation of Christ's victory) is therefore already a certainty, and the Christian lives in a spirit of thanksgiving to the God who *is giving* him this victory constantly in Jesus Christ, the risen Lord.

It is this joyous certainty that makes the present life worth living. The concluding verse is the positive echo of 29–32. Two attitudes are then the natural consequence: (1) firmness and stability in the faith, rooted in the living, life-giving Christ; and (2) commitment of all one's energies to the "work of the Lord," that is, a deepening of personal faith (1 Th 1:3; Jn 6:29), and the expansion of the Church.

The expression *in the Lord* is the grand finale not only of the whole chapter 15, but really of the entire epistle (chapter 16 has the character

---

[25]See above, note 21.

of an epilogue or postscript). Union with Christ here and hereafter is the principle to which all the issues of this letter have been reduced. In concluding with these words, Paul recalls that Christ is not only the firstfruits, the one who is returning, who will preside over the final resurrection; he is already present to the community as it wends its toilsome pilgrimage to the heavenly Jerusalem.

SECOND CORINTHIANS

What is now our second canonincal letter to the Corinthians lacks the unity we saw in 1 Cor. Chapter 1, 2 (to verse 13) and 7 look back on a struggle with Paul's opponents which led to complete reconciliation. But chapters 10–13 depict the highpoint of conflict. Because of this striking and unexplained return to controversy after reconciliation, many authors think that these last chapters are really nothing else than the substance of the "painful letter" Paul refers to in 2 Cor 2:4 and 7:8, and were therefore originally written before chapters 1–2 and 7 and were later tacked on to the Pauline correspondence. There is a similar discontinuity visible at 2:14. If the section 2:14–7:4 is excised, the train of thought follows smoothly from 2:13 ("So I said goodbye and went off to Macedonia") immediately to 7:5 ("When I arrived in Macedonia . . .") while the intervening section is another defense of Paul's apostolate, though much more pacific than 10–13. This defense, many scholars think, belongs to an earlier stage of the conflict and represents still another, earlier letter of Paul written when he still counted on the church's insight and loyalty to back him (6:11 f.; 7:4). Chapters 8 and 9 have to do with the collection made for the church in Jerusalem but from different viewpoints, chapter 8 being a personal letter of recommendation for Titus for the work, chapter 9 Paul's final word on the matter. Consequently, it seems that 2 Cor is really a collection of Paul's later correspondence with the Corinthian community. This hypothesis finds support in the fact that 1 Clement, Ignatius and Polycarp, at the end of the first century or the beginning of the second, frequently quote from 1 Cor but never from 2 Cor. The suggestion is plausibly made then that the Pauline correspondence having largely to do with a defense of his apostolic authority at Corinth was assembled as a single letter toward the end of the first century, at a time when, on the evidence of 1 Clement, the Corinthian church was again threatened with rebellion.[26] It is recommended accordingly that the student read the parts of the letter according to the outline given below.

---

[26]Cf. G. Bornkamm, *Paul* (New York: Harper & Row, 1971), 244–246.

A Word about 2 Cor 5:1–10

Since most of 2 Cor is concerned with Paul's defense of his apostolate, there are not weighty dogmatic issues at stake here. One passage, however, 2 Cor 5:1–10, does concern his theology of the resurrection and immortality, and it significantly complements his earlier teachings in 1 Cor 15. There Paul envisaged the resurrection from the viewpoint of the final consummation of all things at the Parousia. But the Christian communities had had to deal with the fact that while awaiting the Parousia many of their members had died, and if the question of their bodily resurrection for the Parousia had been settled in 1 Th 4:13–18, the question of their lot in the meantime continued to arise. Paul himself in this letter confesses that he was himself at death's gate on one occasion in Ephesus (2 Cor 1:8–10). These events led him to elaborate his resurrection theology in terms of the interim: (1) He bears the message of the New Covenant of glory shining on the face of Christ (2:14–4:6). (2) Though suffering and persecution seem to be wearing away the "outward man," the power and life of the risen Christ is renewing the "inward man" day by day. (3) Finally, death itself neither severs nor delays his union with Christ but achieves it in a new way. This is the thought developed in 5:1–10. Using the image of the tent to portray the transitoriness of the "body" of this present life (an image that is Jewish as much as it is Greek),[27] Paul introduces the vertical dimension to the eschatology he had previously treated horizontally. Jewish thought considered the "age to come" in two ways. On the one hand, it is to appear at the end of the present age to replace it. On the other hand, it also exists already *now* in heaven (1 Enoch 71:14 ff.) and into it, according to rabbinic thought, the souls of the just enter at death.[28] Paul uses this "vertical" understanding to describe how union with Christ, already begun here below, transcends physical death for the individual. He will be "with the Lord" (5:8). Does this mean an immediate bodily resurrection after death? Some scholars think so, and for them the final resurrection at the end of time will simply be the *revelation* of the sons of God already risen (on the basis of Rom 8:19; Col 3:4). However, a word of caution is in order. For Paul, the risen life is already begun here and now through the Holy Spirit (3:18; 5:5). The final transformation is clearly described in 1 Cor 15 as a resurrection for those Christians who have experienced death. What the intermediate event of physical death means for the Christian in this process is the removal of the limitations experienced by the non-resurrected body (this is the aspect from which

[27]Cf. W. D. Davies, *Paul and Rabbinic Judaism* (London: S.P.C.K., 1958), 312–314.
[28]Cf. Davies, 315–316.

Paul considers "body" in 2 Cor 5:6) so that he may not only be *in* the Lord but *with* him (5:8–9). The nakedness which the Christian hopes to avoid at death is not the absence of his body but the absence of righteousness (5:3). Consequently, the union with Christ attained by the believer after physical death, while superior to the present ("a lot by far the better," Phil 1:23), is not the last word about the Christian's glorification. But neither is it the first, since the process of glorification is already at work here and now (4:16–17).

OUTLINE

(On letters A and B, see introduction to 1 Cor.)

LETTER C: PAUL'S APOSTOLATE: CONCILIATORY DEFENSE	2:14–7:4
LETTER D: PAUL'S APOSTOLATE: VIGOROUS, POLEMICAL DEFENSE	10:1–13:14
LETTER E: RECONCILIATION	1:1–2:13; 7:5–16
LETTER F: RECOMMENDATION OF TITUS AND THE COLLECTION	8:1–24
LETTER G: FINAL WORD ON THE COLLECTION	9:1–27

CHAPTER FIVE

Galatians

A central section of Asia Minor received the name Galatia from Celtic (or Gallic) tribes that originally invaded the area in the third century B.C., and eventually grouped around the cities of Tavium, Pessinus, and Ancyra (modern Ankara, capital of Turkey). Under the Romans, Galatia was made a province, and the official Roman name included also the regions south of Galatia proper, with cities well known to us from Acts: Antioch of Pisidia, Lystra, Derbe, Iconium, all of them evangelized by Paul. The question has therefore been debated whether it is to these latter churches that Paul addresses his letter (Gal. 1:2) or to the churches of Galatia properly so called, the northern section originally settled by the tribes. In either case, it is certain that Paul is addressing a restricted group of closely knit communities, so that the possibility of his including *all* the churches of the vast Roman province is excluded.

It can be reasonably concluded from Acts that Paul also evangelized the northern cities (Acts 16:6; 18:23). That the letter was directed to these churches, rather than to those of the south, is supported by the following reasons: (1) The name *Galatia* in contemporary usage, even official, ordinarily designated the country of the three Gallic tribes. (2) Even though *Galatia* was at times understood to include the southern regions, the term "Galatians," designating the people themselves as an ethnic group, would have fit much better those of the north, who long retained their original unity. It is much less likely that Paul would have addressed the Lacaonians and Pisidians with the odious title "Foolish Galatians" (3:1), but the fickle temperament Paul describes (1:6) matches perfectly Caesar's description of the temperament of the Celts in his *Gallic Wars* IV, 5. (3) The letter treats the judaizing problem as a totally new issue. But for the churches of South Galatia, the issue had already been settled, in principle at least, by the decree of the council of Jerusalem, which the Apostle delivered to them (Acts 16:4).

There are no explicit indications in the epistle to the date or place of its composition. In all likelihood, it is to be placed close to the time of 2 Cor and shortly before Romans. Hence it may have been written shortly before Paul left Ephesus for Troas, or during his journey, or shortly after his arrival in Corinth, where he would write the letter to the Romans in early 57 or 58.

Galatians is the most violent and polemical of all Paul's epistles. His adversaries are Jewish Christians who are proclaiming that salvation is impossible without the observance of the Mosaic Law. What they are promoting is not just supererogatory practices, but really a doctrine of salvation, *another gospel* (1:6), which distorts the gospel of Christ (1:7). For in preaching to them, Paul had left completely aside the observance of the Jewish law. The letter will urge them not to sacrifice their faith in Christ, who is the new Torah, in order to fall back into the slavery of the old Law. In Christ they are free!

To achieve this end, Paul sets about: (1) to prove that the gospel he has preached is the authentic gospel; hence he gives an *apologia* in which he documents his "accreditation" as an apostle (1:1–2:21); (2) to show how senseless it is to add to this gospel the practice of the Jewish Law, which would amount to denying the really new order of things begun by Christ (3:1–5:12; cf. 6:15); (3) to show that the genuine gospel, far from being license, is the source of all virtues (5:12 ff.), and hence of everlasting life (6:8).

The sections chosen here for commentary cannot be understood without a careful reading of the entire epistle. Because the theme of justification by faith will be developed at greater length in Romans, we shall limit our selection to those texts which present the point of view most characteristic of Galatians: liberty.

OUTLINE

---

1. From Slavery to Sonship, From the Law to Freedom: Gal 3:23–4:7

[23]*Before the faith came, we were in the custody of the Law, held captive while waiting for the faith to be revealed.* [24]*In this way the law has been our attendant on the way to Christ, that we might attain justification by faith.* [25]*But now that the faith has come, we are no longer under the care of the attendant.* [26]*You are, in fact, all children of God through faith in Christ Jesus;* [27]*yes, all you who have been baptized into Christ, have put on Christ.* [28]*No longer is there reason to distinguish Jew and Greek, slave and freeman, male or female. For you are all one in Christ Jesus.* [29]*And if you are Christ's, then you are the offspring of Abraham; heirs according to the promise.*

¹Now I say, as long as the heir is a child, he differs in no way from a slave, though he is master of the entire estate, ²but he is under tutors and guardians until the time set by his father. ³In the same way, we too, when we were children, were in a state of slavery under the control of the elements of the world. ⁴But when the fullness of time came, God sent forth his son, born of a woman, born under the Law, ⁵that he might purchase those under the Law, that we might receive the adoption as sons. ⁶And because you are sons, God has sent the spirit of his Son into our hearts, crying: Abba, Father! ⁷You are then no longer a slave but a son; and if a son, an heir also through God's grace.

The entire chapter 3 has been devoted to showing that faith, not the observance of the Judaic law, brings justification. It was because of their faith that they have had an experience of the Holy Spirit at work in their midst (3:1–6); just as it was because of his faith that Abraham was blessed (7–9). Man by his unaided powers cannot fulfill the Law and thus it becomes for him a curse; only through faith is the Spirit received who gives the necessary power (10–14). The right to inherit comes from God's promise to Abraham, and this situation is nowise altered by the Law given later to Moses (15–18). What role, then, did the Law have? Not to impart life (19–21), but rather to "shut up" everything under sin, "in view of realizing the promise by faith in Jesus Christ in favor of those who believe" (22). This complicated image will be clarified in Romans (cf. 11:32). If we had this text alone, the purpose of the Law would seem to have been highly negative. But there are other images that will complete the Pauline picture of the Law, and several of them are used here: attendant (*paidagōgos*, 3:24, 25); guardian (*epitropos*, 4:2); steward (*oikonomos*, 4:2); elements (*stoicheia*) of the world (4:3).

The meaning of the bondage spoken of in v. 22 is probed in v. 23. The Law kept the Israelites in custody. The verb here is not used in a pejorative sense, but rather in the sense in which a person would be guarded for his own protection. The Law, with its many severe restrictions, did hold the people together; it fused the motley tribes of escapees from Egypt into a community in which alone the hope for a Messiah might arise. During the Exile, in the absence of the temple, it was the only bond of unity for the Israelites; and on their return, it was the basis for the reconstitution of the people (Neh 10:29). The Law was a beneficent bondage, but a bondage nonetheless, like dungeon darkness compared to the light now revealed. Note here how "the faith," contrasted with "the Law," has become a term to describe the whole present order of things. It now plays, too, the unitive and communitarian role once played by the Law, so that Paul can contrast two communities, those "of the Law" (Rom 4:14; Gal 3:10) and those "of the faith" (Rom 4:14, 16; Gal 3:7, 9).

The Law has thus fulfilled the role of a *paidagōgos*, which we translate *attendant* (3:24) for want of a better word. In the Greek custom of education, a child's first years were spent under the vigilance of his mother and/or a nurse. At the age of seven, he was given a partial emancipation from this feminine influence and committed to a *paidagōgos*. This was not a teacher; he was a slave whose function it was to accompany the child outside the house, to supervise his conduct and deportment, and most importantly, to escort him to school, carrying whatever equipment was needed. If ideally the one chosen for this office should have been a person of high character and education, the contrary often proved to be the case, and frequently it was a crippled or decrepit slave who was judged no good for anything else. At any rate, the child in these years practically lived with slaves; certainly he was under their authority and discipline. The child in antiquity was not considered a person whose life was his own. Though exercising authority, the "attendant" really had only a temporary function; he did not teach but led to the teacher; and when the child reached the fullness of age, the attendant had nothing more to do.

Paul makes the application to the Law, whose function was to lead to Christ, either as to the teacher, or, better simply to exercise authority until the "coming of age," which means the advent of faith in Christ. Note again how "the faith" is presented here as a thing existing in itself, autonomous, as it were. It is more than a virtue; it is a new order of existence.

In v. 26 a strong contrast is intended between what has preceded and the word *sons* (or children). The child enters truly the status of sonship at the "coming of age" ritual, which Paul surely has in mind here. This Roman-Hellenistic rite was celebrated with great solemnity on a public feast day, usually that of the "Liberalia" or feast of Bacchus, March 16. The day began with a morning sacrifice offered to the household gods, at which time the youth laid aside his *toga praetexta*, decorated in red, to take on the *toga virilis*, the toga of manhood, also called "pure" because it was completely white, or "right" or "free," because it signified the beginning of his life of freedom. Then the youth was taken solemnly to the forum as an act of presentation to the citizenry which now must regard him as one of its members.

It is faith that has accomplished this access to sonship (cf. Jn 1:12); faith implies baptism. *Through faith in Christ Jesus* of v. 26 finds an exact parallel in *baptized into Christ* in v. 27 (cf. Rom 6:3; Mk 16:16). We have discussed above (on 1 Cor 1:13) the meaning of the expression "baptized into," with the idea it conveys of making the person the property of Christ. In 1 Cor 10:2, Paul spoke of the Israelites of the Exodus being "baptized into Moses." We might have expected "in the sea" were Paul bent on showing the crossing of the sea as a type of Christian baptism; but he chooses to accentuate the personal commitment of the Israelites to God's accredited representative. Moses is their leader and redeemer (Acts 7:35), and in accepting him as such, the people have thrown in their lot completely with him. In this, Moses is a type of Christ, "into" whom Christians are baptized.

Baptism "into Christ" has meant "putting on" Christ. This verb was already used in an ethical sense in the Old Testament (putting on virtue, strength), and Paul uses it frequently this way (1 Th 5:8; Col 3:12; Eph 4:24; 6:11, 14). In the context here, however, he is obviously suggesting that Christ is the toga of manhood, the one who puts us in a new relationship with God our Father and makes us citizens of the heavenly commonwealth (Phil 3:20). See the important place given to white vesture in the Apocalypse (3:5, 18; 4:4; 6:11; 7:9, 13 f.; 19:14; 22:14; cf. Acts 1:10).

This interpretation of the corporate or social dimension of the figure is confirmed by the description Paul gives of what the investiture with Christ involves (v. 28). It is not the putting on of a better ethical spirit, but the entrance into a corporate personality, the *whole* Christ, head and members. And here the walls of distinction of race or class or sex dissolve. All are equally members; the only distinction that can be tolerated is the apportionment of services which can be rendered to the same body (1 Cor 12). Paul has already enunciated the principle to be stressed in the captivity epistles, that putting on the new man means that we are members *of one another* (Eph 4:24 f.), and human distinctions have no significance (Col 3:10 f.). It would be too much to say that in this line Paul is calling for a reform of the society of his day. But he has laid down the principle of the dignity of the human person as the child of God and the basic equality of all men in that spiritual union of the divine sonship.

V. 29 now draws a conclusion. If you are *of Christ*, i.e., forming one corporate being with him, then you are what he is, the offspring promised to Abraham, and with him you are heirs. The sense is not heirs "to the promise" or "of the promise," but heirs *just* as promised.

The promise made to Abraham was that he should have posterity; that promise was fulfilled by Isaac in type, by Christ in reality. But faith and baptism made Christians one with Christ; hence they are with him the offspring and heirs promised to Abraham.

In the sequence (4:1 ff.) Paul merely elaborates the ideas already expressed. Resuming the image of the child who lives like a slave until the appointed time (*tutors* and *guardians* here replace the *attendant* but without any substantial shift in sense), Paul applies this to the state of man before the coming of Christ. Man was under the *elements of the world*. The expression is a difficult one to make out. *Stoicheia* was already used in classical times for the elementary principles of learning, the "ABC's" as we would say today, and some authorities take it in that sense here, as if Paul were speaking of the elementary forms of religion, both Jewish and Gentile, which were eventually superseded. The difficulty of this interpretation is that it does not sufficiently account for "the world." Other scholars have consequently sought the meaning along the sense in which the word stands for the elementary substances, the basic elements of which the world is composed, or heavenly bodies, which in ancient times were regarded as personal beings and given divine honors. Paul as a Jew of course would not share this polytheistic conception; but the Jews of Paul's time did firmly believe in the existence of angels. It was a widespread conception (witnessed by the rabbis and the apocryphal books) that the angels are in charge of the elements of the world—stars, wind, rain, and so forth—and, in harmony with many biblical texts, the angels were conceived as having important roles of intervention in the sacred history of God's people. In particular, the promulgation of the Law was done through the ministry of angels, a tradition mentioned not only in Stephen's discourse (Acts 7:38), but also a few lines previously in our present text (Gal 3:19).[1] Consequently Paul here seems to be referring, by metonymy, to the guardian angels of the Law (cf. Col 2:8, 20), who held man in a state of servitude, just as the attendants, tutors and guardians did for the discipline of the immature child.

But when the fullness of time came, i.e., the time appointed by the Father (v. 2), God, desiring to promote men from slavery to sonship, sent forth his own son. Though the mere semantics of the verb "send forth" may not imply the preexistence of the Son, in the light of Paul's doctrine elsewhere we may rightly infer that here it does. However, what is here emphasized is, like Phil 2:6–11, the abasement or, better, the utter solidarity with man which the incarnation accomplished. *Born of a woman* (4:4) is simply a Semitic way of saying "a man like any other" (Job 14:1; Mt 11:11). Nothing can be drawn from *this* text either for or against the virgin birth. Christ has taken on the state of man in all its tragic history; a real solidarity of man with him (3:28) is made possible by his first sharing totally their present state—a state of slavery, for he too was *born under the Law*. The divine plan was therefore that he should save the world *from within—that he might purchase those under the Law* (4:5). The verb *exagora-zein* never means "to buy back," nor to "redeem." It simply means "to

---

[1] See J. Bonsirven, *Palestinian Judaism in the Time of Jesus Christ*, tr. W. Wolf (New York: Holt, Rinehart & Winston, 1964), 35 f.

buy, acquire." It evokes Ex 19:5, "If you harken to my voice and keep my covenant, you shall be *my special possession*, dearer to me than all other people." By his act of deliverance God has acquired a right over his people, they are his own, and this forms the basis for the suzerainty covenant he gives them. So likewise Christ by his saving death now acquires as his own those until now under the Law. A transfer of ownership and loyalty is thereby effected from the Law to Christ.

In further qualifying this liberation as an *adoption* Paul introduces a new idea. The term *hyiothesia* occurs neither in the Septuagint nor elsewhere in the New Testament outside of Paul (Rom 8:15, 23; 9:14; Eph 1:5). He has evidently picked it up from the juridical world of Rome and Hellenism. To a man who had no natural offspring (or had legitimately disowned them), adoption was a recourse offered by both law and religion for three purposes: (1) to perpetuate his name and descendants; (2) to assure the continuity of domestic worship; (3) to transmit his goods.

If one possessed natural offspring, and yet wished to adopt another, it was necessary first to disown the natural offspring legitimately and discharge them from the household. To a limited extent, this element too underlies Paul's thought, in that the Father gave up his own son or abandoned him (cf. Mt 27:47; Mk 15:34) that the inheritance might pass to us (Rom 8:32). The image limps, of course, in that far from losing his inheritance, Christ won it for both himself and us. But the cycle of the *kenōsis* of Phil 2:6–11 is still preserved with emphasis now on the corporate effect—from the state of Son to that of Slave, that the slaves might become sons and heirs.

Promotion to the status of divine sonship, however, means more than the transfer of a title. It involves the communication of God's own Spirit, the Spirit of his Son (note a reference to the Trinity) to the hearts of Christians. In this the divine adoption infinitely outstrips human adoption, for it communicates the interior principle of divine life, from which now springs an entirely new moral life, as will be shown in 5:13–26. For the moment, Paul is content with showing the Spirit's relation to cult: He cries (or makes Christians cry, Rom 8:15), *Abba, Father* (4:6). It has been rightly observed that the formula "Abba, Father" expresses the official prayer of the community, the Lord's prayer, which very early was incorporated as an integral element of Christian worship (*Didache*, 8). This thought may have been suggested to Paul in part by the lingering image of *adoption*, one of the purposes of which was to assure the continuance of domestic worship.[2]

---

[2] M. W. Schoenberg, "Saint Paul's Notion on the Adoptive Sonship of Christians," *The Thomist* 28 (1964), 51–75; R. Sargent, "The Spirit of Sons in Galatians 4," *TBT*, 656–659.

The third purpose of adoption was to make sure that the estate passed to a definite heir. It is with this thought that the passage concludes—if you are now a son, you are also an heir. The inheritance is the divine glory to be possessed on the final day. Paul, theologian of grace, cannot terminate without adding that the right of inheritance, like the adoption in which it is founded, comes not from personal merit but only from the loving-kindness and free initiative of the Father.

The section which now follows (4:8 ff.) simply draws the practical conclusions from the above.

2. The Meaning of Freedom and Slavery: Gal 5:1

¹It was for a state of freedom that Christ has set us free. Stand fast, then, and do not be caught again under the yoke of slavery.

The opening line of Chapter 5 is joined by some texts to the preceding verse, "by that freedom wherewith Christ has set us free." However, the better Greek manuscripts indicate that a new idea starts here. Even so, the apparent redundancy has given rise to all kinds of attempts to improve the text, as the many variant readings attest. K. H. Rengstorf has discovered in the rabbinic literature a passage which has brought considerable light to our present verse.[3] According to *Mishna Gittin* (IV, 4), when a slave is imprisoned and then is released, if the release means he is to continue to be a slave, he must continue to be a slave; but if he is released as a freeman, then he must not continue in slavery.

If Paul is thinking along the same line, as the movement of his thought indicates, then there is no redundancy whatever in the expression: The release by Christ is a real emancipation and we must not return to the state of slavery.

By this time the sense in which Paul is using slavery and freedom should be clear. Slavery for Paul is subjection to the Law of Moses—*not* because law itself is bad, not because Paul is proclaiming release from any type of moral restraint, but for this reason: man in his native existential condition has not the power to fulfill the Law in its integrity. Alone, without grace, he cannot measure up to the divine demands; he is helpless. In this state of impotence before the Law, man is in a state of slavery.

As to the Pauline notion of freedom:

The "free man" is the man in Christ, he who has received grace and has been endowed with the resources proper to a "son," so that with them he can realize the existential plenitude toward which he anxiously strains.

[3] K. H. Rengstorf, *Theol. Literaturzeitung*, 1951, 659–652.

Paul does not mean by "liberty" the psychic faculty of choosing between two opposites, even less does he mean a juridic or moral autodeterminism. For him "liberty" is the state of "sons of God" which involves possession of the "spirit of God" (3:6) by which they are now intrinsically empowered to overcome their great alienations: sin and death.[4]

It is, in fact, sin and death that make man belong to something other than himself, that truly enslave him. The Law simply makes the slavery more poignantly evident. For Paul the two enemies are intimately connected. Christ's salvific death destroyed them both, and the gift of the Spirit conveys the power to live holily and to attain resurrection. Christ and his Spirit have therefore removed the "external accuser" of man's sinfulness by empowering him to virtue from within. Under these circumstances, to expect to find life and salvation in which is essentially passé and decaying is to fall into slavery again after being freed.[5]

3. The Life of Liberty in the Spirit: Gal 5:13–26

[13]*Yes, brothers, you have been called to liberty; only do not use your liberty as a pretext for gratifying the flesh, but through love put yourselves at the service of one another.* [14]*For the entire Law is fulfilled by the observance of one precept: "You shall love your neighbor as yourself."* [15]*But if you bite and devour one another, take heed, or you will be consumed by one another.* [16]*But I say, walk by the Spirit, and you will not yield to the tendencies of the flesh.* [17]*For the flesh has tendencies that oppose the spirit, and the spirit has tendencies that oppose the flesh. There is an implacable antagonism between the two, so that you do not succeed in doing what you would like.* [18]*But if you let yourselves be led by the spirit, you are no longer under the power of the Law.* [19]*Now the deeds of the flesh are manifest: fornication, impurity, licentiousness,* [20]*idolatry, witchcraft, enmity, contention, jealousy, outbursts of anger, quarrels, factions, schisms,* [21]*envy, drunkenness, carousings, and other vices similar to these. I warn you beforehand, as I have already said, that those who do such things will not inherit the Kingdom of God.* [22]*But the fruit of the spirit is charity, joy, peace, long-suffering, affability, goodness, fidelity,* [23]*gentleness, self-control. Against these the Law has nothing to say.* [24]*And those that are of Christ Jesus have crucified their flesh with its passionate cravings.* [25]*If we live by the spirit, by the spirit let us also walk.* [26]*Let us not become desirous of vainglory, provoking one another, envying one another.*

---

[4] J. M. González-Ruiz, *Epístola a los Gálatas* (Madrid, 1964), p. 232.

[5] S. Lyonnet, "Saint Paul: Liberty and Law," *TD* 11 (1963), 12–20. See also R. N. Longenecker, *Paul, Apostle of Liberty* (New York: Harper & Row, 1964), and the review of this work in *CBQ* 27 (1965), 170 f.; A. Güemes, "La *eleutheria* en las Epístolas Paulinas. Examen de textos," in *Estudios Bíblicos* 21 (1962), 37–63; J. Cambier, "La liberté-chrétienne selon saint Paul," *Lumière et Vie* 12 (1963), 5–40.

This section contains an important complement to the preceding one because it defines more precisely what Paul means by liberty. Using as his point of departure the principle that the Christian life is as much a call to liberty as it is to holiness or anything else, Paul shows that the new state is not one which automatically puts the Christian in the possession of absolute perfection. It rather *enables* him to act in a way to attain it. Consequently, liberty itself is a good that must be used. It is not the license to gratify every personal whim or taste (*for gratifying the flesh*); rather it impels to a new kind of service—that of one's brothers. Thus we begin to divine that Christian liberty itself is equivalent to Christian love, both of them resulting immediately from the gift and presence of the Holy Spirit (Rom 5:5; 2 Cor 3:17). Poured forth from God, charity enjoys the freedom of God because it seeks the interests of God which are primarily the good of the community.

As for the Law, it must indeed be fulfilled. It is a false simplification to say that Paul did away with all law or even with the essential requirements of Old Testament Law. The enslaving effect of the Law came from man's native inability to accomplish its demands. The emancipation comes in a twofold sense: (1) By the gift of the Spirit man now has the power to fulfill the Law; (2) By the fact the whole Law with its voluminous prescriptions and rituals can be reduced to one essential: love. In this Paul is no innovator. The Synoptic tradition is unanimous in tracing this thought back to Jesus himself—that it is on the command of love that all the Law and the prophets are based (Lk 10:25–37; Mt 22:35–40; 25:31–46; Mk 12:28–34). If Paul speaks here only of fraternal love, he means that the fulfillment of any divine precept implies an act of love of neighbor; and, inversely that he who truly loves his neighbor will fulfill the commands of the Law. Or, as he says in Rom 13:8: "He who loves his neighbor has fulfilled the Law. . . . If there is any other commandment, it is summed up in this saying: 'You shall love your neighbor as yourself.' Love does no evil to a neighbor. Love therefore is the complete fulfillment of the Law." The Law is to be fulfilled, not abandoned. But the Law is essentially love. Since, then, we are now empowered by the Spirit to love, we are freed from the "binding" or "accusing" effect of the Law, for we are able to fulfill it perfectly. To love is to be free (v. 18).

Not only is love the fulfillment of the Law; the very existence of the community depends upon it. Its absence will eventually destroy the community (v. 15). But this will not happen if they *walk by the Spirit* (v. 16). The imperative here implies that the new life is a power that must be used; it is not a magical transformation absolving the Christian from acting. The opposition between "flesh" and "spirit," as already discussed, does not imply a Platonic dualism in Paul; "flesh" is what man can and will do by himself, without God; "spirit" is what he can do by God's grace. The opposite "pulls" of these two forces in man are dramatized in Rom 7. In v. 19 the various and plural "deeds" of the flesh are listed—not exhaustively, but to show how manifest they are in the world. The *deeds of the flesh* include not only sins of sexual excess and intemperance, but irreligion and especially vices against fraternal charity and union among brothers. Those who do these will not inherit the kingdom of God, that is, as we know already from 1 Cor 15:50, 52, the state of incorruption at the resurrection. Against these "deeds" is contrasted the *fruit* (singular) of the Spirit (5:22). Charity heads the list here, suggesting that it is the single fruit that contains the rest. Against these the Law *has nothing to say.* Once again (as in v. 18), the thought is that man, who as "flesh" was condemned by the Law in that he could not fulfill it, now is out of its overpowering force, now can only be praised by it, because by the grace of God he can achieve all that God demands.

The flesh has already been crucified in the death of Christ and in the baptism of the Christian (Rom 5, 6); it is now a matter of really living the new life of the Spirit (vv. 24, 25). The last verse simply draws a specific application to the Galatian community.

CHAPTER SIX

Romans

All indications are that Romans was written from Corinth during Paul's three-month stay there during the third missionary journey, shortly before his departure for Jerusalem with the alms for the poor (15:25). This would place it before the Passover (Acts 20:6) of the year 57 or 58.

What led Paul to write this, the lengthiest and most systematic of all his epistles? He had never been to Rome, and hence he was not writing *back* to any community he had founded, as was the case with his previous letters. Moreover, the problems particular to the Roman community seem to occupy him little—there is not even an allusion to the community as such in the whole body of the epistle! However, Paul is planning to begin his ministry in the west, using Rome as a springboard to Spain (15:28). The letter will introduce him to the Roman community by giving them an illustration of his doctrine. Really, though, Paul seems to use this as a good occasion for working out the problems that have been fermenting in his own mind, and to give some systematic structure to the insights which heretofore had been stimulated by inquiries or by the needs of polemic to wage or abuse to correct. The greatest thorn in the Apostle's side was the Judaizers, Jews or Jewish Christians who dogged Paul everywhere and sought to "bring back" these ultraliberals to a practice of the Jewish law. He may well expect to find them at Rome too. Every community founded by Paul was a mixture of Jews and Gentiles, and the problem of integrating these two vastly dissimilar cultures was an agonizing one. Recall Paul's repeated exhortations to unity and charity and peace. One of the great gestures by which he sought to seal the unity of the churches was the collection he took among the Gentile churches to succor the impoverished church of Jerusalem. At the time of writing Romans he had most of the collection gathered; and for Paul it surely symbolized the fundamental unity of the universal Church.

Consequently it is not surprising that he should compose at this time a "theological treatise" in which he seeks to define what the gospel really is: God's plan and method to save Jew and Gentile. Around this axis are grouped many other subordinate themes, of which a great number have already been sketched in previous epistles.[1]

OUTLINE

---

[1] On the occasion for writing this letter, cf. R. J. Karris, "Rom 14:1–15:13 and the Occasion of Romans," *CBQ* 35 (1973), 155–178.

---

1. Definition of the Gospel: Rom 1:16–17

[16]*I am not ashamed of the Gospel. For it is the power of God unto
salvation for everyone who believes, to Jew first and then to Greek.*
[17]*For in it the justice of God is revealed from faith to faith, as it is
written: "The just man will have life by faith."*

These two verses, if not the most important of all the Pauline corpus,
are certainly the most important for understanding the theology of
Romans, for in them he announces the theme of the entire epistle. Paul
has declared, in his introduction to Romans, his intention of coming to
preach at Rome; the prestige of this city, capital of the empire and, by
the same token, seat of the imperial worship, might make any missionary
think twice before attempting such a venture. Paul in particular had
experienced at Athens how "foolish" his gospel looked to the "wise" of
the city who gathered to hear him. He is, however, not ashamed of his
message because, as Paul writes from Corinth, he cannot erase the
memory of his own brilliant success there, shortly after the "men of
Athens" turned a deaf ear: the gospel is the *power of God* (1 Cor 1:24).
Paul does not here define the gospel in terms of its content but in terms
of what it can do. To call it the *power* of God is to evoke all of sacred

history, which progressively schooled the Jews to an understanding of Yahweh through an ever greater appreciation of his power.

Among the Semitic tribes, the supreme God was designated precisely as *El*, "Power." The Hebrews took over this designation of the divinity, and its original meaning must be understood when found in the early patriarchal traditions. Thus, when Hagar, saved from death in the desert, exclaims "You are *El roi*," she means "You are the *Power* that sees" (Gen 16:13). For the Yahwist, the God of Israel created the world not by winning a battle with the primeval elements (as did Marduk the creator-god of the Babylonians), but by exercising, at his good pleasure, his power to *make* (Gen 2:4, 7). He works a marvel of creative power for the sterile Sarah (Gen 18:10, 14), and deeds of power "in a strong hand and arm" to deliver from slavery the people he has chosen (Ex 3:19–20; 6:1; 9:16; 34:10, 13). He promises to continue his saving power as long as the people remain faithful, but the *refusal to believe* suffices to suspend it (Nm 13:30–33; 14:11–12). Nevertheless at the faith and prayer of one person, he restores what was lost (Nm 14:13–20).

The prophets, beginning with Amos (6:13–14), teach that Yahweh's power extends to the armies of Israel's enemies. Isaiah, possessed with the notion of God's holiness, stresses his twofold power—to punish (1:24, 25) and to save (28:28–29). He insists that true strength will come to the nation not by reliance on the horses of Egypt (31:1; 30:15) but by *faith* in the Holy One of Israel (7:9; 28:16). His words were confirmed in Jerusalem's deliverance from the Assyrian army in 701 B.C. (36:1–37:9; 37:10–36). Isaiah knew well that it was through "natural" causes (the plague) that Yahweh had acted (10:6, 18), just as he had in the Exodus (Ex 14:21)—the important thing to Israel's faith is that what happened was a manifestation of Yahweh's personal interest and power to save. Jeremiah, in an anguished prayer for guidance, summarizes Yahweh's titles of power (32:17–25), and hears Yahweh's response that his previous marvels of power will be superseded by a greater one—the giving of a new heart to his people, and the sealing of a new covenant (32:37–40; 24:7; 31:27–33), and this will really be a new creation: Yahweh creates again on the earth; the spouse, Israel, seeks her spouse, Yahweh (31:22).

In the priestly tradition during the exile the idea developed that the greatest of God's works is the holiness he gives to men (Lev 19:2; Ezr 20:12; Ex 31:13). Second Isaiah, in describing the return from exile, sees in it a marvelous manifestation of Yahweh's power to save (Is 50:2); it is the power of the creator (40:25–26) that revives his people (40:28–31; 41:17–20; 44:24; 45:13; 48:13–14). Yet an even purer, more spiritual notion of God's omnipotence appears in the Songs of the Servant of

Yahweh, this mysterious personage whose triumph and glory, after passing through an ignominious death that brought life to the multitudes, is the supreme revelation of the *arm* of Yahweh (49:4–5; 53:1). In the Maccabean period, and at the time the Book of Wisdom was written, Israel began to perceive that the great work of God's power was the resurrection of those who had remained faithful to him until death. Jesus reflects the belief of many Jews of his day when he says that to deny the resurrection of the dead is to be ignorant of the power of God (Mt 22:19; Mk 12:24).

With this background, and knowing how the divine power was manifested in the works of Jesus (Mt 13:54; Lk 6:19) and especially in his death and resurrection (Rom 1:4) and communication of the Spirit (Lk 24:49; Acts 1:8), we can easily understand the capital role it would have in the theology of Paul, the Jew. *Dynamis* stands for the divine power itself as manifested in the works of God, not only in the death (1 Cor 1:18, 24) and resurrection of Christ (Phil 3:10; Rom 1:4; 2 Cor 13:4) and of Christians (1 Cor 6:14), but also in the very proclamation of those facts (1 Cor 1:18; 2:5; 2 Cor 6:7) and in the hearts of those who believe (1 Th 2:13; Eph 1:19).

The gospel then is the power of God that leads to *salvation*. "Salvation" has a progressive history similar to the "power of God."[2] In earliest times it meant deliverance from enemies (e.g., Jg 6:37; 15; 18): the prophet Zephaniah is the first to apply the term to a future restoration by Yahweh after he has chastised his people (Zeph 3:14–20), a hope given precision by Jeremiah—personal salvation (Jer 15:20; 17:14) or deliverance from drought (8:20; 14:8 f.), repelling an invasion (4:14 f.), but notably the establishment of the messianic kingdom (23:6–33:16), the salvation of the remnant (31:7), and eventual liberation from exile (30:10 f.–46:27 f.). Ezekiel describes salvation in terms of a deliverance of the people from their sins, which are the real oppressor (Ezek 36:29; 37:23). In Second Isaiah, in addition to the political sense, salvation means the establishment of God's kingdom, which includes knowledge of his Law (51:4), a salvation that is universal (45:22; 49:6; 51:5) and everlasting (45:17; 51:6, 8).

It is above all in the Psalms that the Old Testament notion of salvation reaches its heights—the goods hoped for are related to a purification from sin, which must precede their bestowal. In the New Testament, salvation is chiefly a matter of being released from sin (Lk 1:77; 7:49 f.), or from God's final wrath or condemnation (Rom 5:9; Jn 12:47). But for Paul salvation is not merely being saved *from* something; it is being saved

---

[2]See "Salvation" in *EDB* 2101–2107, and bibliography given there.

for something. The first place where Paul gives Christ the title *Savior* is Phil 3:20 where the Savior's return will mean the transforming of the bodies of Christians into his glorious body. The Pauline notion of salvation is then primarily future or eschatological—and this is his preferred view in Romans: whereas justification is something God has already done for us (5:9 f.) "as yet our *salvation* is a matter of hope" (8:24).

This salvation is open to *everyone* who believes. But the Jews enjoy the privilege of being its first hearers. "Jew" and "Greek" are not thought of here in the same categories as 1 Cor 1:22, "The Jews demand signs and the Greeks look for wisdom," although one might be led to infer this from vv. 14 and 16. In Romans, however, there is a definitely privileged place given to the Jews (2:9 f.; 3:1, 2, 9, 29; 9:4–6; and all chapter 11); it was Paul's principle to preach to them first (Acts 13:46). "Greek" here, then, stands for "the rest, the Gentiles." The blessing that comes to them in Christ is the realization of the promise to Abraham that *in him* all the nations would be blessed (Gal 3:14), and in Eph 3:6, the salvation of the Gentiles is depicted as a "letting them in" on the promise made to the Jewish people first of all—and still standing.

The expression *from faith to faith* (1:17) has been variously interpreted: (1) Many of the early interpreters took it as contrasting the faith of the Old Testament with that of the New. (2) Ambrosiaster took it as meaning "from the faith (fidelity) of God promising to the faith of man believing." (3) Some moderns take it as meaning that God's justice demands a life of faith from beginning to end. (4) Finally, others, alluding to Ps 83:8, think Paul is saying that the life of faith grows ever more perfect. The last two interpretations are the more probable, and are not mutually exclusive.

We now come to the critical term, the *justice of God* (1:17). This term here and especially in 3:21–26, is the most celebrated for theological controversy since the time of the Reformation. Before discussing the various things that have been read into the text, or out of it, we shall try to examine it within the senses suggested by the Bible, the Pauline corpus and especially the letter to the Romans itself.

If for some reason the word "justice" in 1:17 were illegible and we were obliged to guess at its meaning from the context (that is what happens when fragments of manuscripts or inscriptions are found), what would we suppose the word meant? We would first observe that there is a perceptible parallel in vv. 16 and 17.

> [16]*The power of God unto salvation for everyone who believes.* . . .
> [17]*For in it the X of God is revealed from faith to faith.*

The importance of faith in man is stressed in both lines (and additionally supported by the quotation from Habakkuk 2:4 "the just man lives by faith"). The conjunction *for* at the beginning of v. 17 indicates that the thought *continues* that just expressed in v. 16, and certainly is not introducing an opposition or contrast with it. The unknown X of God therefore must be similar in meaning to the "power of God unto salvation" of the preceding line. This discovery alerts us not to assume automatically that "justice" here means what it means in our modern language. Had the nominalist theologians whom Luther read in his early days been better biblical scholars, they would not have made the error of identifying the "Justice of God" here with his vindictive punishment of sinners. The crushing effect this teaching had on Luther is well known.[3] If Paul constantly reveals the patterns of Jewish thought and Old Testament theology, a second lead, and a better one, will be to discover what the Old Testament meant by the "Justice of God."

Consultation of the passages where the words *sedeq* ("just") or *sedaqah* ("justice") occur in the Old Testament reveals surprisingly how often it is associated with *salvation*. E.g.: "There is no *just* and *saving* God besides me" (Is 45:21). "I am bringing on my justice, it is not far off, my *salvation* shall not tarry" (Is 46:13)—here "justice" and "salvation" are synonymous, as also in Is 51:5. In Is 56:1. "My *salvation* is about to come, my *justice* about to be revealed," the Septuagint translated "justice" by *eleos* "mercy," just as it also frequently used the Greek *dikaiosynē* (justice) to render the Hebrew *hesed* (loving-kindness). The Psalms abound in examples: "The Lord has made his *salvation* known: in the sight of the nations he has revealed his *justice*. He has remembered his faithfulness toward the house of Israel . . ." (Ps 98:2 f.; see also Ps 40:10; 22:23, 28, 31, 32; 36:7). In Ps 69:25–28, the Psalmist prays that his enemy may have no share in God's justice! Of the many times *sedeq* (just) and *sedaqah* (justice) are used in the Psalms, not once is God's justice presented as punishing his own chosen people as sinners, even though the infidelity of Israel is often noted.

Certainly God's justice is not to be equated with his wrath—frequently it is expressly contrasted with it (Ex 15:7, 8, 13; Mic 7:9; Ps 85:5, 6, 12, 14; Dan 9:7–18). The same sense of God's justice is found in the later extracanonical documents such as the Book of Jubilees (1:5 f., 15; 10:3; 31:25) and Qumran's *Manual of Discipline* (11:13–15; 1:21; 10:23).

The "Justice of God" in the biblical sense then is *salvific*: it is the trait by which God delivers or restores his people, frees them from slavery to sin, and brings them back to himself. Now this equation of God's justice

---

[3]"I hated this word 'Justice of God,' which by the use and custom of all doctors I had been taught to understand philosophically as they say, as that formal and active justice whereby God is just and punishes unjust sinners." (*Works of Luther*, Weimarer Ausgabe, 54:179 ff.)

with his power to save is precisely what we had been led to suspect by the context of Rom 1:17.

One question remains: why did the Jews call it justice; why did not the word *salvation* or some other suffice? The word "just" evoked to the Jews the idea of rectitude, of measuring up to a norm, or of impartial judgment, just as it does to us today. When God is called "just," is there not some norm to which he is said to measure up? Yes; but obviously the norm is not a human one; it can only be *God as he has revealed himself*. And to the Jew this could only mean the God of the Exodus who had chosen his people and bound himself to them in covenant: "You shall be my special possession, dearer to me than all other people" (Ex 19:5; cf. Jer 31:31 ff.). God is just in that he fulfills his promises, whether these be to Abraham, to Moses, or to David. The whole idea of God's justice is then *theocentric*. The point hard for our modern mentality to grasp is this: We would think that if man kept his part of the covenant, God would be just in rewarding him. Since man broke the covenant, God would be just, we should think, in punishing him. But the amazing thing is that after man had failed to keep his part, God intervened to *save* man—and it is precisely *this* that is called God's justice! The norm of justice is not therefore man, but God himself.

From all that has been said, one should not conclude that God never punishes sin, nor that there is no vindictive punishment, no hell. Precisely because man is exposed to sin and its penalties, the most obvious of which is death, God's justice (= his salvific activity) will be directed to delivering man from this, the most fundamental of his alienations. And hence the "Justice of God" means that he *justifies men*.[4] This effect in man of the justice of God we shall examine next.

First read carefully the intervening section, 1:18–3:20, which intends to show that the revelation of God's saving justice announced in 1:17 is radically needed by man, whether he is pagan or Jew. This state of need on man's part is described as his being under God's *wrath*, a concept easily misunderstood if taken with all the modern psychological weight the term carries today. (1) The concept, we have seen, is distinct from the saving justice of God. It is that *from which* man is saved. (2) But viewed from the human side, it is a state which results from deliberately turning from the God who has revealed himself in the created universe (1:18–23).[5] The results of this culpable turning away, though described in the biblical language of "God delivering them up," are in reality only the natural effects of their action—moral chaos (1:24–32) and perversion of the moral conscience (1:23–32). Thus the wrath of God is really nothing

---

[4] S. Lyonnet, "The Saving Justice of God," *TD* 8 (1960).

[5] J. J. O'Rourke, "Romans 1:20 and Natural Revelation," *CBQ* 23 (1961), 301–306.

else than man's self-imposed alienation from a good God. As long as he clings to his sin, man can experience God only as *wrath*. That is what Paul means in 1:18: what reveals the *wrath* of God is the disastrous effects of man's turning from him. Here Paul is thoroughly reflecting O.T. tradition: "At the wrath of the Lord of hosts the land quakes, and the people are like fuel for the fire," cries Isaiah. Then he describes concretely what this means. The wrath is not really some natural catastrophe but the very sinfulness of the people: "No man spares his brother, each devours the flesh of his neighbor" (Is 9:18). Even clearer is the text of Job 4:8–9: "Those who plow for mischief and sow trouble, reap the same. By the breath of God they perish, and by the blast of his *wrath* they are consumed." This view agrees with the broader biblical teaching that sin is its own punishment and that the evil God brings on sinners is nothing else than the fruits of their own schemes (Jer 2:19; 6:19; Hos 11:6; Prov 1:31; 26:27; Wis 11:16; 12:23, 27; Sir 27:25–27).

Paul's description applies first to the pagan. But the Jew is no better off (2:1–3:20). Despite his condemning the pagan (2:1–11) and his possessing God's superior revelation in the Law (2:12–16), he will be condemned like the pagan (2:17–24). Repeating and developing the same idea, Paul says that despite circumcision (2:25–29) and the promises of God to Israel (3:1–7), the Jew, like the pagan, is a sinner, and Scripture attests to the fact (3:8–20). Whether then man's state be described as the wrath of God or the sinfulness of man, his experience of it is meant to lead him to yearn to get out of his situation and accept the gift of God's saving justice. To that revelation Paul now turns.

2. *The Justice of God Justifies the Believer: Rom 3:21–26*

[21]*But in the present dispensation independently of law the justice of God has been definitively manifested, attested by the Law and the prophets,* [22]*the justice of God that is given through faith in Jesus Christ to all who believe—for there is no difference:* [23]*all have sinned and need the glory of God—*[24]*and they are justified by his gratuitous gift in virtue of the redemption accomplished in Christ Jesus.* [25]*In the shedding of his blood God has publicly exhibited him as the propitiatory available to those who believe. God's purpose in so doing was to demonstrate his justice, to remit the sins committed formerly* [26]*in the period of God's patience so that he might demonstrate his justice in the present time—in short, God's purpose was to be just and to justify him who has faith in Jesus.*

In v. 20 Paul concluded the section on the Jews' need for justification by a quotation from Ps 143:1 f., the full text of which is: "O Lord, hear my prayer; hearken to my pleading in your *faithfulness*; in your *justice* answer me. And enter not into judgment with your servant, for before you no living man is *just*." The citation is in perfect context, for the psalmist invokes God's *salvific justice*, proclaiming the lack of justice that is his own lot and that of all men.

The stage has now adequately been set for Paul to introduce God's answer to man's predicament. *Now* (meaning the present, final times, as in Heb 1:2), *apart from the Law*, that is, without the observance of the Mosaic Law being the instrument of an efficacious salvation, the justice of God has been *manifested*. The verb suggests that this justice was somehow always there, in God's wisdom, waiting to be made known to men (cf. Rom 16:26; and compare Col 3:3 f.) at a time when there was no longer any human hope of salvation (1:18–3:20). The placing of the mystery in God alerts us not to interpret the distinction between the Christian and the pre-Christian era in merely chronological terms. Paul never says that no one in the Old Testament was justified or saved; the point he will make (using Abraham as an example) is that those who were saved in the Old Testament were not saved by a mere mechanical observance of the Law but by faith in the promises of God. The *Law and the Prophets*, that is, the whole Old Testament, bears witness to this justice of God which transcends the Law.

This justice of God is available to men on one condition: that they believe (v. 22). Addressed as it is to creatures who retain their freedom, it is a gift which, to be efficacious, must be accepted and allowed to explode dynamically in the life of its recipient. The faith that justifies has Jesus Christ for its object, affirming that the divine promises are realized in him. Since it is faith and nothing else that justifies, there is no distinction between Jew and Gentile (this was the point Paul labored to establish above, 1:18–3:20). All have sinned—obviously not original sin here, but the sins of which Paul accused the Gentiles and Jews above. All therefore *need* the glory of God. Various interpretations are given of this last expression: (1) To simply call the "glory of God" sanctifying grace is to take it for a technical theological term, which is too restricted. (2) The term *doxa* in Greek means honor, good reputation, esteem. Some exegetes have taken the term in this way, as meaning that all men need to be reinstated in God's good esteem. Paul, however, is not thinking in Greek patterns here but in Jewish. Hence (3) others have thought that he is using rabbinical ideas concerning the "glory" of Adam and Eve, which they lost through their sin. According to the *Assumption of Moses*, the glory of the first parents was an emanation of the divine glory; it enveloped their bodies and served as a garment. The realization of their nakedness indicated that they had lost this glory. The luminous nature of it was symbolic; glory represented justice, as may be seen from Eve's way of speaking in the apocryphal work, "Immediately my eyes opened and I knew that I was stripped of the *justice* with which I had been clothed, and I wept, saying: Why have you done that to me? I have been stripped of the *glory* with which I was clothed" (ch. XX; see also *Manual of Discipline*, 4:12 f.; *Damascus Document*, 3:20). This glory was to be restored in messianic times. The difficulty with this interpretation of our Pauline passage is that it gives no greater glory to the Messiah than to Adam (which contradicts the view of 1 Cor 15:45 f.); furthermore, the verb used here, translated "need," does not of itself imply privation of something originally possessed. (4) Consequently, the best interpretation is to take the "glory of God" here as referring to God himself inasmuch as he makes himself present to his people and unites them with himself (Ex 24:16; 40:34 f.; 1 Kg 8:10 f.). The absence of this glory is characteristic of the time before the Messiah (Ezek 9:3; 10:4); its presence marks the messianic times (Ezek 43:2 ff.; Ps 85:10; Is 40:5; Hag 2:7). For Paul, of course, Christ is the source of this divine glory which transforms men (2 Cor 4:6; 3:18).

After the parenthetical thought of v. 23, the next verse picks up the thought of v. 22 on the communication of God's justice, but whereas v. 22 stressed the importance of personal responsibility, v. 24 stresses the utter gratuitousness of the gift—literally, "justified by the gift of his favor." This "justification"—for we are now concerned with the effect produced in man by God's justice—is accomplished in virtue of the *redemption* in Christ Jesus. The word here is not the same as "purchase" of Gal 4:5, but the meaning is not greatly different.[6] Used repeatedly in the Septuagint for the deliverance from Egypt at the Exodus (Ex 6:6; 15:13; Dt 7:8; 9:26; 13:5), the verb does not of itself imply the payment of ransom money (in Ex 21:8 it is used simply for the release of a slave by her master); in the context of the covenant, the stress is upon the ownership that God acquires over his people (Ex 19:4 f.). The new covenant foretold by Jeremiah would perfect the people's belonging to Yahweh (Jer 31:33). The covenantal imagery passed into the New Testament: Christ "delivered" the new Israel from the slavery of sin (Col 1:14; Eph 1:7); he "acquired" the Church by shedding his own blood (Acts 20:28); he "redeemed" the new people of God by giving himself up for their sake (Tit 2:14); he "purchased" them (Gal 3:13; 4:5; 1 Cor 6:20; 7:23). This act has already been done in the passion of Jesus, but it will

---

[6] F. R. Swallow, " 'Redemption' in St. Paul," *Scripture* 10 (1958), 21–27; S. Lyonnet, "Saint Paul and a Mystical Redemption," *TD* 8 (1960), 83–88.

be consummated at the Parousia (Lk 21:28) by the resurrection of the body (Rom 8:23; cf. Eph 4:30; 1 Cor 1:30), when the acquisition will be total (Eph 1:14). There is no doubt that Scripture uses the figure of redemption to stress: (1) God's possession of his people; and (2) the *cost* of that acquisition. Although Jesus does say he will give his life as a *ransom* (Mk 10:45; cf 1 Tim 2:6), nowhere is there a hint of the one to *whom* the price is paid, certainly not to the devil; but the New Testament does not even say it is paid to God. Christ did indeed offer himself to the Father (Eph 5:2), and in him men return to God. But the shedding of blood is never considered properly as an offering to God. The reserve of Scripture in this matter was not observed by later theologians who tried to extend the figure beyond its biblical limits by speculating about the one to whom the price was paid. Scripture affirms only the mysterious necessity of the tragic death of Christ and its beneficial and liberating effects for the world.

Some key to the mystery is given by v. 25. The deliverance is evidently a deliverance from sin. For in the passion and death of Jesus (in the shedding of his blood) God has publicly exhibited him as the real *propitiatory*. This *hilastērion*, as it is read in the Greek Bible, was the golden covering for the ark, mounted by two golden cherubim, serving as the place of the divine presence (Ex 25:17–22) or the very throne of Yahweh (1 Sam 4:4). From this sacred spot, Yahweh was understood not only to make known his will (Ex 25:22) but also, on the feast of the Atonement, when the priest in a liturgical rite sprinkled blood on and in front of the "propitiatory," to pardon the sins of the people (Lev 16:1–19). A similar rite was called for to expiate a fault which had implicated the whole community in guilt (Lev 4:3, 13, 17). Done in the secret of the Holy of Holies, this rite is now publicly manifested in Christ—the veil has been torn away (Mt 27:51) and the blood of Christ has shown him to be the instrument of propitiation absolving all believers from their sins and bringing back the divine presence which, according to the Old Testament conceptions, the sins of the people had caused to be withdrawn.[7]

God's purpose in bringing sacred history to this consummation was to show, by the irrefutable evidence of a concrete deed, his justice (3:25). *Justice* here must not be ripped from the context—it means still the fulfillment of God's promise to save, or, as the sequence states, *to remit the*

---

[7]On the biblical background of propitiation, expiation, and atonement, see E. J. Joyce, "But Christ Lives in Me," *TBT* 11 (March 1964), 714–720; S. Lyonnet, "Scriptural Meaning of 'Expiation,' " *TD* 10 (1962), 227–232; L. Morris, "The Meaning of *Hilasterion* in Rom 3:25," *New Testament Studies* 2 (1955–1956), 33–43.

sins committed formerly in the period of God's patience. This curious phrase has been variously translated by the commentators. From the seventeenth century on, it became common to translate the Greek *paresis* as a "passing over" or "tolerance" of sins instead of "remission" of them. Today this interpretation is gradually being abandoned, for the term *paresis* never means *neglect* but always has the notion of remission (as all the early commentators held), and the meaning would go patently against the context. God's salvific justice could not be satisfied with a mere "looking through his fingers" at men's sins. He was determined truly to *remit* them. If there was a period of time in which sins were punished (the era of God's wrath, 1:18 ff.), God did have the intention not merely of punishing but of truly forgiving them. From this point of view the pre-Christian period may be viewed not as a period of wrath but as one of God's long-suffering and patience. Like a Father who metes out medicinal punishment toward a wayward child, God has vented his wrath upon Jew and Gentile alike, but with the purpose of achieving ultimately their total conversion and the bestowal of genuine pardon. It took the cross of Christ to achieve both the grace of man's conversion and God's pardon. This deed, which has ushered in a wholly new period in salvation history (v. 26), is the consummate manifestation of God's justice, his promise to save. It was not merely that men might *come to know* the justice of God, but that God might *be just* (= saving according to promise) and might *justify* (= make truly righteous, pleasing to God) him who has faith in Jesus. The point in this: God would not be just and truly saving did he not save man from enslavement to sin.

The natural law condemns the pagan; the revealed Law condemns the Jew. The ritual sacrifices of the Old Law did not of themselves achieve man's liberation from guilt (Hebrews shows how the very repetition of the rites testified to their own insufficiency), but the sacrifice of God's own Son has illumined their meaning and fulfilled their symbolism. In Christ, God makes the believer *just*, that is, measuring up wholly to what God expects of him. "The sacrifice of Christ has satisfied once for all the demand for exterior justice which God had deposited in the Law, and at the same time it brought the positive gift of life and interior justice which the Law was radically incapable of producing."[8] Or, to conclude with the precision of Saint Thomas, "Paul shows that through the remission of sins the justice of God is shown, whether God's justice be taken as that by which he is just or that by which he makes other just. . . . By the remission of sins God is shown to be just in himself both because he remits sins *as he had promised*, and because it pertains to God's justice to *destroy* sin by incorporating men into the justice of God."

[8] P. Benoit, "La loi et la Croix d'après Saint Paul," *Revue Biblique* (1938), 508, n. 2.

3. The Role of Faith: Rom 3:27–31

> ²⁷*Where, then, is boasting? It is excluded. By what kind of law? That of works? No, but by the law of faith.* ²⁸*For we hold that a man is justified by faith without the works of the law.* ²⁹*Is God the God of the Jews only, and not of the Gentiles too? Assuredly he is God of the Gentiles too,* ³⁰*since there is only one God, who will justify the circumcised in virtue of faith and the uncircumcised in virtue of that faith.* ³¹*Does this mean that by faith we deprive law of its value? Certainly not. We confirm its value.*

This section draws the consequence of the preceding. If justification is totally the gift of God (24), there is no room for "boasting" in anything of one's own.[9] Boasting (3:27) describes the whole self-righteous and self-sufficient position of man. In the Greek Bible it is often used to describe sinners or the unjust who "glory" in their own riches (Ps 49:7) or evil deeds (Ps 51:3) even in the midst of a holy place (Ps 73:4). The devout Israelite, on the contrary, "glories in God," as is said in Ps 5:12, with the obvious meaning of putting trust in the God of Israel. This sense of trust and reliance is that which Paul evokes in using the term (Rom 2:17, 22; Phil 3:3; 2 Cor 1:12, 15; 10:7, 8), and here it means the attitude of complacency already described in 2:17–24. It is excluded not by the law of works but by the *law of faith* (3:27). Obviously here "law" is taken as a system, the divine economy or plan. To consider the law of faith as equivalent to the new law is to oversimplify the distinction, for faith was necessary under the old dispensation just as under the new.

V. 28 is of great theological moment. A man is justified by faith without the works of the law. Nowhere does Paul give us any reason to believe that the "works of the law" are only the ceremonial precepts. Man is not justified by the moral precepts either. *Nothing* can justify him except the justice of God (3:26) to which man responds by *faith*. Luther in his German translation (1521) rendered the expression, "through faith *alone*." What Luther meant by this is disputed; he was certainly heavily criticized in the Catholic camp for abusing the text (the word *alone* is not in the Greek original). However Luther was not the first to translate it this way. Ambrosiaster, the excellent Latin commentary dating from the fourth or fifth century, rendered it *"sola fide"*; one of

---

[9]The Greek *kauchēsis*, translated "boasting" or "glorying," is one of Paul's favorite and most characteristic terms. The noun in this form or in the closely related *kaukēma* occurs twenty times in Paul against once in James (4:14) and once in Hebrews (3:6); the verb thirty times in Paul against three times in James (1:9, 10; 4:16), the only other New Testament witness. It may at times be used in a good sense, as when Paul says "I may boast in Christ of my relation to God" (Rom 15:17), but often it will have a pejorative sense. Here it is more than the vice of braggadocio.

Saint Bernard's sermons has the expression "justified by *faith alone*," and Saint Thomas Aquinas, commenting on 1 Tim 3:8 and quoting our text of Romans, says: "There is no hope of justification in them (the precepts of the decalogue) but in *faith alone*." There is consequently a very orthodox sense in which the term "faith alone" can be used and one which is true to the thought of the Apostle. Faith alone here is obviously contrasted with any work which derives from merely human initiative, any work, even the observance .of the Law, which would *precede* or "merit" justification (3:23). But Paul does assume that there are works which *follow* justification by faith, primarily charity and the whole program of good works it inspires. In Gal 5:1–6, after showing the impotence of Old Law to save, he concludes: "What counts is faith that *works* through charity." The distinction between *preceding* and *consequent* works is especially clear in Eph 2:8.

The point at issue here, then, is how, in relation to the works of the Law, justification is initiated. Saint Thomas expresses this lucidly when he says:

> The act of faith is itself the first act of justice which God works in the believer. For in believing in the God who justifies, he submits himself to God's justification, and thus receives its effect (*In Rom* 4:5).

If justification were from the Law, only the Jews could possibly be justified—a principle which, however much supported by particularist rabbinic views,[10] goes against the transcendent notion of the one God (Dt 6:4), for no other real god could the nations have if not the one God, creator, and governor of the universe. And whenever a man, Gentile or Jew, makes the act of faith, God will justify him independently of the Law (3:21). Faith is an instrument in either case (as Paul will illustrate with Abraham 4:9), and the conscious use of the article before "faith" the second time it is used, shows that it is exactly the same faith in either case.

V. 31 is understood by many commentators to be a reaffirmation of the basic continuity of the Old Law with the New, thus providing the transition to the example of Abraham (4:1–25). However, in all other cases where "law" means the Old Testament, the article is used; its absence here alerts us to a broader meaning—law in a general sense. The verse thus concludes chapter 3 and announces the theme to be developed in 8:4 ff. and in the whole moral section of the epistle: "Far from unleashing a reign of anarchy, faith, communicating to man a new principle, the Spirit, alone makes it possible for any legal regime to attain its end: the justice of man."[11]

---

[10] J. Bonsirven, *Palestinian Judaism*, 45–71.
[11] S. Lyonnet, in *Rom*, Huby ed.², p. 582.

The Example of Abraham: Rom 4:1–25

In the light of the above explanations, the student may now read this passage, which has for its purpose to show that justification by faith, far from contradicting the Old Testament, fulfills it.[12] Abraham, who had good reason to boast of works, was justified by his faith (1–8), before the external observance of circumcision (9–12) and independently of the Law (13–17). Abraham's faith is thus the prototype of ours, for as he believed in the God who could bring life from the "dead" body of Sarah and thus received the promise, so we believe in the same God who brought Jesus to life from the dead. The allusion in v. 25 to the death and resurrection of Jesus announces the development to come now in chapters 5 and 6.

JUSTIFICATION: FORENSIC OR REAL?

The concept of God's justice was shown above to be identified with his salvific activity and not with his wrath. It now remains to ask: what happens to man when he is *justified* by God? The question is one that has been agitated greatly since the Reformation, and it is an important one for the ecumenical dialogue today.[13]

Justification as a Forensic Concept

The Greek verb "to justify" evokes most naturally the image of a court of law at which the judge *declares* that the crimes of which a person is accused are not to be imputed to him, that he is *not guilty*. The verb then would mean to deem, account, or judge a person righteous or just. Taken from the common practice of law among men, the word, at least in profane Greek, never has the meaning of *making* the accused man righteous but only of recognizing or declaring him so. In the Septuagint, too, where the word "to justify" occurs some forty-five times, it is nearly always used in the forensic or judicial sense. The New Testament knows and uses this forensic sense extensively (Mt 11:19; 12:37; Lk 7:29, 35; 10:29; 16:15, etc.). And above all, Saint Paul himself seems practically to define his use in the forensic sense when in Romans he writes, "To him who does not perform works but believes in him (God) who justifies the impious, his faith is credited to him as justice" (Rom 4:5).

---

[12]Joseph Cahill, "Faith in the Old Testament," *TBT* 15 (Dec. 1964), 959–967; M. M. Bourke, "Saint Paul and the Justification of Abraham," *TBT* 10 (Feb. 1964), 643–649.

[13]See the outstanding breakthrough in H. Küng's *Justification: The Doctrine of Karl Barth and a Catholic Reflection* (N.Y.: T. Nelson, 1964), especially the chapter "The Declaration of the Sinner's Justice," 208–221. Also suggested reading: "Justification" in *EDB*, 1255–1262. For a report of recent trends in Lutheranism, see "Justification Today," Supplement to *Lutheran World*, No. 1, 1965.

It would, then, be a serious mistake and a violation of the Scriptural texts to deny the forensic origin and sense to the concept of "justification" in Saint Paul. On the other hand, we may rightly ask whether the conception of a *merely* forensic justice, spelled out in human terms and transferred to God's act of judging, really corresponds to Paul's notion. Many non-Catholic interpreters from the time of the Reformation on (or at least starting with Melanchthon) have pressed the forensic concept to the conclusion that God's "justification" is *only* forensic, that it is *purely* declaratory, that it can and does represent only a fictitious justice, the man remaining essentially "impious" after his act of faith but nonetheless, because of the imputed justice of Christ, guaranteed of God's favorable judgment on the last day.

It is advisedly that we have said many (not all) non-Catholics have held this, because any generalization about Protestant positions must be qualified when we speak of specific Protestant confessions or of individual theologians. The Lutheran theologian H. Rückert in 1925 claimed that the declarations of the Council of Trent against a purely extrinsic justification applied only to Melanchthon.[14] Likewise, there is dissatisfaction among many Protestants today with the term "merely forensic (or extrinsic) justice." However, this does not mean necessarily that they would admit the conferring upon the sinner of a real, interior state of justice by the infusion of supernatural grace. The latter took place in Jesus Christ alone, and it is imputed to us as if it were ours.[15] This position is reached by the worthy concern to avoid, on the one hand, the Scylla of making God's judgment of justification an empty word (a lie) and, on the other hand, the Charibdis of giving man anything he can really possess as his own, even justification, which would form the basis of a new *kauchēsis*, a new "boasting" before God. Whence, the *real* justification takes place indeed, but it takes place in Christ, not *in* us (intrinsically). It is thus that the Pauline doctrine of justification is interpreted by N. A. Dahl in an article in *The Lutheran World* (vol. 9, 1962, 219–231):

> According to Paul the baptized person is at one and the same time righteous and a sinner, because his righteousness is and remains the "alien" righteousness of faith. The baptized person has no righteousness and wisdom of his own; he can only live righteously before God by means of the presence and support of Christ and his Spirit (p. 231).

---

[14]*Die Rechtfertigungslehre auf dem Tridentinischen Konzil* (Bonn: 1925), 105; H. Küng, *Justification*, 217.

[15]T. F. Torrance, "Justification: Its Radical Nature and Place in Reformed Doctrine and Life," in *Christianity Divided* (N.Y.: Sheed & Ward, 1961), 283–305, esp. 289–295.

In any case it should be clear that "justification" is not to be interpreted as "making righteous," in the sense that the nature and the character of the baptized person were altered by the infusion of a supernatural grace. But it is also no mere forensic judgment in heaven; the thought is not that the sinner is regarded by God as though he were morally righteous; it is much rather a question of God's judicial judgment of the world in history, on the cross and in the resurrection of Jesus Christ, through the proclamation of the gospel, and through baptism. Precisely in the sense of "declaring righteous," justification means "making righteous" insofar as the justified man is translated from the realm of sin to the realm of Christ and the church (p. 224).

But the question remains: *What happens* to the sinner when he is thus transferred from the realm of sin to the realm of Christ and the Church? Doesn't this, in the last analysis, fall back into a merely forensic, externally imputed justice, as far as the sinner is concerned? These are questions raised not only by Catholics but by a number of Protestants today, notably by Karl Barth, who, as we shall see below, gives a more positive answer.

The Reality of Justification

Let us take our problem back to Saint Paul. Granted that "justification" is a forensic concept, it will help to situate this concept properly in Paul's synthesis if we study *why* and *how* he took up the vocabulary of justice and justification in the first place. Obviously, it was the demands of polemic. He was combating the extreme Pharisaism which had a totally legalistic concept of the righteous life, reducing the "gift" and interpersonal aspect of man's religious life to an innocuous residue. By his meticulous observance of the most minor precepts, the Pharisee would merit in strict justice God's favorable judgment at death or on judgment day; he could thus *bind* God to reward him for his own efforts and thus "make" his own salvation. Against this Paul reacts violently, insisting that "justice" is not acquired by keeping the commandments of the Law (Gal 3:11; Rom 3:21; 5:1; 9:30; 10:6) but, as we have abundantly seen above, by faith. And man's justice is itself a gift of God (Rom 3:24), the "justice *from* God" of Phil 3:9. Man does not stand before God as a just man demanding that God recognize his justice, but as a helpless sinner who "needs the glory of God" (Rom 3:23).

Justification is, then, a gift of God. In the courtroom scenario this would then seem to be that the judge "acquits" the sinner despite his sin, a verdict of "not guilty" is handed down despite the sinner's guilt. To avoid making God a liar in the matter, some Catholic theologians say that God first *makes* the sinner just, and then *declares* him just, the declaration being a confirmation of the prior act. But how does this adequately do justice to Rom 4:25, where it is said, not that God declares the *just* man just but that he declares the *unjust* just? We shall return to this problem in a moment; it suffices here to observe how Paul's taking up of the forensic terminology of "justice" and "justification" raises new problems.

The point worth noting, however, is precisely that these problems are *new*. They are problems that appear almost exclusively in Gal and Rom. The verb *dikaioun*, "to justify," does not even appear in 1 and 2 Th, Phil, and 2 Cor. It appears only twice in 1 Cor; it will disappear completely again in Col, Eph, and Phm. Yet it occurs eight times in Gal and fifteen times in Rom. The other forms of the word, "just," "justice," etc., follow a similar pattern. Clearly, *"justification"* is not *the center of Pauline doctrine*. Rather it is an application of his "in Christ" theology to the question raised in forensic terms by his adversaries. Paul's frequent use of the term "accredit as justice" is also due to his frequent citation, for the benefit of the Jews, of Gen 15:6, concerning Abraham.

Before the "justification" polemic, and after it, Paul uses other themes to explain the new condition of man before God: sanctification, incorporation into Christ, union with his death and resurrection, and life in the Spirit. This is especially notable in 1 Cor 6:11, where "justification" is inseparable from a cleansing from sin and a genuine sanctification; but it also appears in the very letters which stress the justification theme (Rom 8:30; 3:4 ff.; 4:25; 8:5; Gal 3:23 ff.; Phil 3:7 ff.; cf. Tit 3:4–7). These are all very positive concepts. The Fathers of the Church considered the central and most important part of Romans to be not the chapters on justification (as they were for the Reformers) but chapter eight, which stresses the new life of the Spirit as a present certainty, the highest manifestation of God's love.

This consideration sheds some light on the fact that for Saint Paul justification is not merely the acquittal to which one looks forward on the last day (although this sense is certainly not absent, cf. Rom 2:13), but a thing already done, not only for Abraham (Rom 4) but also for Christians (5:1, 9; 8:30; 1 Cor 6:11). It is a state in which we stand, the basis for hope of glorification (5:1 f.; "the hope which justice gives," Gal 5:5).

Consequently, *justification is one facet* of the manifold mystery of life in Christ. What is proper to it, in distinction to the other facets, is the forensic sense. But then does this mean that this facet signifies merely that *from the viewpoint of God's judgment* the man who enjoys the divine life already given (shown by the other themes) is *declared* to be just?

Far from it. God's sentence of justification is *not a response to man*, not even to man's acceptance of God's own gift of life. It is the *sinner*, the impious, the unjust, *whom God* justifies (4:5). The only conclusion we can then come to is this: God does not *make* man just and *then declare* him just; *God's declaration makes him just*. God's word creates, it effects what it signifies (cf. Gen 1; Ps 29:4–9; 147:18; Jer 23:29; Ezek 12:25).

> It all comes down to this, that it is a matter of God's declaration of justice and not man's word: the utterance of the Lord, mighty in power. Unlike the word of man, the word of God *does* what it signifies. God said, "Let there be light" and there was light. He said, "Be clean" and it was clean. God commands the demons, and they get out. He speaks harshly to the wind and the waves, and there is a deep calm. He says, "This is My body." And it is His body. He says, "Stand up." And the dead man rises. The sinner's justification is exactly like this. God pronounces the verdict, "You are just." And the sinner *is* just, really and truly, outwardly and inwardly, wholly and completely. His sins *are* forgiven, and man is just in his heart. The voice of God never gets lost in the void.[16]

Saint Thomas put it this way: "God does not receive us as just but this being received makes us acceptable."[17]

It is to the great credit of Karl Barth to have reduced the justification of man to the act of God, which it is essentially, and then to have seen that any limitation of this power, even by human sinfulness, would detract from the principle of *soli Deo gloria*:

> There is no room for any fears that in the justification of man we are dealing only with a verbal action, with a kind of bracketed "as if," as though what is pronounced were not the whole truth about man. Certainly we have to do with a *declaring* righteous, but it is a declaration about man which is fulfilled and therefore effective in this event, which corresponds to actuality because it creates and therefore reveals the actuality. It is a declaring righteous which without any reserve can be called a *making* righteous. Christian faith does not believe in a sentence which is absolutely ineffective, or only partly effective. As faith in Jesus Christ who is risen from the dead it believes in a sentence which is absolutely effective, so that man is not merely *called* righteous before God, but *is* righteous before God.[18]

Barth is perhaps the most explicit of the leading Protestant theologians today on the matter of justification. Many refuse to follow him that far, but it is worth noting that the trend is toward a more interior understanding of justification among Protestant scholars. Surveying Protestant research on the theology of justification, the Lutheran H. Hofer in 1940 indicated that the contemporary trend is away from a purely juridical and imputative meaning and toward a more mystical

---

[16]H. Küng, *Justification*, 213.
[17]*De Ver.*, q. 27, a. 1.
[18]*Church Dogmatics*, T. & T. Clarke, IV, 1, 95.

interpretation consonant with the entire life of salvation. "Justification in Paul is not only the forgiveness of sin but also vocation, transformation, mobilization, a 'new' life and activity."[19]

May God soon grant us unity on this point that for four hundred years has divided us!

4. Baptism and Union with Christ in His Death and Resurrection: Rom 6:1–11

> [1]*What then shall we say? Shall we continue in sin that grace may increase?* [2]*Certainly not! How shall we who have died to sin, still live in it?* [3]*Do you not know that all of us who have been baptized into Christ Jesus, have been baptized into his death?* [4]*Yes, we were buried with him through the baptism into his death, so that just as Christ was raised from the dead by the glory of the Father, so we should also walk in newness of life.* [5]*For if we have become so entwined with his death as to bear its very likeness, so shall we be with his resurrection.* [6]*We know that our former self was crucified, so that the body of sin might be reduced to impotence, that we might no longer be the slaves of sin.* [7]*The man who dies is set free from sin.* [8]*But if we have died with Christ, we believe that we shall also live with him,* [9]*knowing that Christ having been raised from the dead, will die no more, death no longer has any dominion over him.* [10]*The death that he died was a death to sin once for all, but the life he lives is a life for God.* [11]*"Thus you too must consider yourselves dead to sin but living for God in Christ Jesus."*

Paul begins this section by replying to the libertine who, latching on to the principle, "Where sin abounded, grace abounded the more" (5:20), would excuse himself from any moral effort and continue to live as he had before his conversion and baptism. The separation from the empire of sin is as radical as that of death. In fact, the Christian has *died to sin* (v. 2). This expression, which has a curious ring to our modern ear, is easily understood by our common expression which is its opposite, "to live in sin." As one who lives in sin attaches himself to it, making it the principle or at least the atmosphere of all his actions, so he who dies to sin makes a complete and radical break with it, leaving it behind with the definitive separation a dying man experiences in quitting the world. The Christian's death to sin is not future but past. Paul never appeals to his readers to become what they are not, but only to become truly what they already are. This death to sin occurred in baptism, which was a *plunging* into Christ Jesus (v. 3). The verb here keeps its earlier sense of immersion, but the Christian consciousness has become so aware of the personal

---

[19]Quoted in H. Küng, *Justification*, 284; see the other Protestant witnesses cited by Küng, *op. cit.*, 282–284.

mystery enacted in the rite, that the object into which one is "plunged" is stated not as water but as Jesus himself. The image suggests a real incorporation into the person of Christ; but the specific power that is contacted is his *death*. It is not any action of his public life, since for Saint Paul, it was only in his dying that Christ's salvific activity began. Jesus had spoken of his own death as a baptism (Mk 10:38; Lk 12:50); Paul is probably dependent on this tradition here, but he gives it a reverse twist: The Christian's baptism is a death; it is a union with the death of Christ. Theologians ask how the present act of baptism can put us in contact with an action of Christ that is historically past. We shall discuss this below. Suffice it for the moment to point out that it is the ritual imagery that is uppermost in Paul's mind—the immersion of the neophyte is symbolic of burial with Christ, just as the emergence from the water symbolizes his rising with Christ to a new life (v. 4; Col 2:12). The latter thought is only implied. As Paul's expression goes, Christ was raised by the glory of the Father. Glory here is used in the sense of God's power in working mighty deeds in favor of his people (especially in the Exodus, Ex 15:7, 11; 16:7, 10; Ps 113:9). The Father's glory is therefore synonymous with his power (Col 1:11; 2 Th 1:10); it has been communicated to the humanity of Christ (2 Th 2:14; 2 Cor 3; 18; 4:6), constituting him "Son of God in power" (Rom 1:4). The resurrection of Christ is the principle of Christian living—*so we should also walk in newness of life* (6:4).

The profound reason for this relationship between the Christian moral life and the Paschal Mystery of Christ is now given in v. 5. It is not only that Christ has given us an example to follow, his death being an exemplar for self-denial and his resurrection a symbol of a new spiritual life. There is more than imitation involved here. Christians have become *symphytoi* with Christ in the mystery of his death. This term is a starkly realistic one taken from a frequent experience in horticulture: two branches that have grown together so as to become physically one and inseparable are *symphytoi*. Christians have thus *grown together with* Christ or with the "likeness of his death." This tells us how realistically Paul wishes us to take the being "buried with Christ" already mentioned in v. 4. Baptism effects a really *vital* union, like a graft in which the engrafted branch now is fed by the life of the tree, and grows into it to such an extent that it looks now like part of the original tree. The image at this point of course is not directly the sharing of life but the sharing of death. United with Christ in the mystery of his death, so shall we be one with him in the mystery of his resurrection, when he will make our lowly bodies perfectly conformed to his glorious body (Phil 3:21). The perspective of the life of glory here is surely the future resurrection, but Paul has already put himself on the path that will lead to the conclusion expressly stated in Col 2:12, that through baptism Christians *have risen* with Christ.

Our former self (literally, our "old man") *was crucified* (4:6). The death in baptism was a crucifixion since it was a union with the death of Christ. The "old man" is an obvious allusion to the life inherited from the first Adam, who passed on to us a *body of sin* (6:6). The *body* in Paul is virtually equivalent to the person; it expresses man's nature in its totality, especially his material dimension, his solidarity with the earth. Unlike the term "flesh" which adds the note of distance from God, or "spirit," which stresses closeness or at least pliability to God's action, "body" is a kind of neutral term—it can be "the body of sin," as here, or "the spiritual body" (1 Cor 15:44), the redeemed body (Rom 8:23). The purpose of baptism was to put to death the "body of sin," or better "to reduce it to impotence," and thus to deliver the self from the tyrannical power of sin, under which the self had been enslaved.

V. 7, *The man who dies is set free from sin*, is interpreted by some scholars as the statement of a rabbinic principle of law reflected in this saying of Rabbi Jochanan (died 279), "When a man is dead, he is free from the law and the commandments."[20] The idea would be something like the modern practice of writing in "not guilty" on the ledger when an accused man dies before he is brought to trial. Sin would thus "lose its suit"; or in another sense, death would of itself expiate a man's sins, it would "pay sin its due." The real meaning of the rabbinic text cited above, however, is that a dead man is incapable and hence dispensed of the obligation he once had during life of observing the precepts of the Law; moreover, a situation in which death itself, independent of a man's dispositions, would expiate sin before God is not in harmony with the Jewish tradition, which supposes confession and love (*Sanhedrin* 6:2; 2 Mac 7:37; 4 Mac 17:22). The context here tells us that Paul is thinking on a much deeper level than the juridical: He who is brought into a vital communion with the death of Jesus escapes, by the very fact, the empire of sin. The thought is parallel to 1 Pet 4:1: "He who has suffered in his flesh, has broken with sin." Paul is not trying to prove that the Christian is justified (this was already done in 5:1) but to show that the justified Christian must no longer sin.

V. 8 repeats the second half of v. 4. Vv. 9 and 10 insist on the definitive nature of Christ's death because Paul wants to stress that the Christian's death to sin is definitive. Christ died *to sin*. Again the curious expression already encountered in v. 2. Some exegetes have found in this expression justification for the theory, begun by Origen, which represents

---

[20]Rabbi Jochanan, *Nidda* 61b, *Chabbath* 30a, 151b; S. B., III, 232, 234.

Satan as a pitiless creditor who demands his due of man. Christ would have "died to the Law by undergoing its sentence," which was that of death, thus paying the Law its due, so that it may have no more claims on man. Aside from the fact that Paul never grants any rights to sin, the "death" which is the penalty of sin is *eternal* death, total separation from God, which Christ would have had to undergo, if it were question of his undergoing this condemnation—an obvious absurdity.

Much more illuminating is the solution suggested by Paul himself in 2 Cor 5:21. Sacred history is a return of humanity to God in the New Adam. Christ did not know sin, but he did take on our weak nature and in so doing entered into a solidarity with sinful humanity (Rom 8:3). For our sakes God "made him" to be sin, so that in him, in virtue of that same solidarity *we* might become the righteousness of God (2 Cor 5:21). The body of Christ is the place where the salvific power of God intercepts our body and begins transforming it (7:4).

Let us now try to summarize and illustrate the theological structure implicit behind these various statements. Man can be variously described as *body* or *flesh* or *spirit*, depending on what aspect of his existence is under consideration. *Body* describes man's solidarity with the created universe and other men; it is redeemed or redeemable (it becomes the body of the resurrection) but it can also be the "body of sin" (Rom 6:6). Hence, of itself *body* is static and neutral. *Flesh* refers not to what covers the bones but rather man's earthiness from the viewpoint of weakness, whether physical or moral. It does not automatically connote sinfulness but susceptibility to sin. Hence, *flesh* is dynamic and directional downward, ultimately toward death. *Spirit* does not imply immateriality but rather divine origin, destiny, character and especially movement. Because he is spirit man is movable or moved by God, who is spirit. Hence *spirit* is also dynamic and directional but upwards to life. With these concepts, Paul's understanding of the redemptive process can be viewed thus:

(1) Man without Christ is a flesh-body and a "body of sin," that is, man is a body, whose native weakness (flesh) is ruled by the tyranny of sin. Sin finds its foothold in the *flesh*.

(2) Christ in the incarnation takes on a *flesh-body totally like man's* except that it is not itself a "body of sin." Because he has in his flesh-body a

perfect solidarity with man, he can save men from within, for through *their* flesh-body (if joined to his) he also takes on *their* sins (2 Cor 5:21).

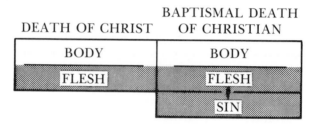

(3) When Christ dies on the cross, his flesh body disappears and in him humanity has achieved an escape from sin, for if a man is joined organically to Christ (1 Cor 12:13) in his death (Rom 6), the flesh-body will die *to sin*, sin will lose its hold, it has now nothing to cling to, it has lost its kingdom.

(4) By his resurrection, Christ's flesh-body has become a spirit-body capable of imparting life (1 Cor 15:44 ff.). Christian baptism joins us to that body, so that, simultaneously with experiencing the power of Christ's death in us, we also begin to experience the power of his resurrection (Phil 3:10), we become "one spirit with him" (1 Cor 6:17). This is a true resurrection with Christ already begun (Col 2:12). Yet just as the dying with Christ destroyed only the *root* of sin and not all its remnants (we still live a life conditioned by the flesh), so the risen life is one that grows day by day (2 Cor 4:16), Christ gradually transforming our bodies from flesh to spirit (2 Cor 3:18).

THE CHRISTIAN'S PROGRESSIVE TRANSFORMATION
INTO THE RISEN CHRIST

THE RISEN CHRIST ⟶

SPIRIT
BODY

THE BAPTIZED CHRISTIAN ⟶

BODY
FLESH

(5) At the Parousia there will be but one Christ, the whole Christ, head and members, enjoying the state of spirit-body (Phil 3:21).

THE WHOLE CHRIST GLORIFIED ⟶
SPIRIT
BODY

For the purposes of simplicity we have avoided in this tableau many nuances which a more detailed study would have to add. It is nevertheless substantially valid. It will help to understand the problem already alluded to above, as to how the past event of Christ's death can really be rendered present in the sacrament. Some theologians have proposed that the category of time is somehow abolished and that we are made contemporaries of the Paschal events of that first Good Friday and Easter Sunday. Dom Odo Casel has proposed the inverse interpretation of Paul's doctrine: "No one can die *with*, unless someone dies."[21] On Casel's view, the sacramental symbol makes the death and resurrection of Jesus actually present. The idea reflects something of the pagan mysticism by which a kind of divine drama of death and resurrection is reproduced for the benefit of the initiate. But Paul's doctrine expressly nullifies any explanation that would make Christ die *again*—the "once-for-all" of v. 10 is categoric. He never says Christ *dies* in the sacrament. His preference for the passive used of Christians dying or being raised with Christ is instructive (Gal 2:19; Rom 6:4, 5, 6; Col 2:12; 3:1). When the sinner is brought into contact with the humanity of Christ (now glorious), as happens in baptism, he inescapably experiences a transformation effected by the humanity. The life of sin is put to death (Christ's body now has this power because it once went through death) and the risen life is begun. Everything takes place *now* in the believer which once took place in Christ, and this in an ontological way. On Paul's view, then, death for a Christian once baptized is something much more of the past than of the future. For what it essentially represents, the Christian has already died with Christ. His physical death will only be the final touch of what was already done basically at his Baptism. Like the death of Christ, the Christian's baptismal death was a definitive thing. But the risen life has already begun and it too is, in the nature of things, definitive—it is merely a question of realizing it and letting it keep one "living for God in Christ Jesus our Lord" (v. 11).[22]

---

[21]*Mysteriengegenwart* in *Jahrbuch für Liturgiewissenschaft*, 1928, 123 f.; 139 f.

[22]A. Feuillet, "Fourfold Death of a Christian," *TD* 10 (1962), 31–37; S. Lyonnet, "Redemptive Value of the Resurrection," *TD* 8 (1960), 89–93; B. Vawter, "Resurrection and Redemption," *CBQ* 15 (1953), 11–23. J. M. González-Ruiz, "Redemption and Resurrection," in *Concilium* II (1966), 67–87.

5. How to Live the Risen Life: Rom 6:12–23

> [12]*Do not then let sin reign in your mortal body so as to obey its lusts.* [13]*Do not put your members at the service of sin like weapons that help the triumph of iniquity but put yourselves at the service of God as men who have come to life from the dead, and offer your members to God as weapons to help the triumph of justice.* [14]*For sin shall not have dominion over you: you are subjects not of the Law but of grace.*
>
> [15]*What then? Are we to sin because we are not under the Law but under grace? Certainly not!* [16]*Do you not realize that when you offer yourselves as slaves to obey someone, you become slaves of the master whom you obey, whether of sin which leads to death, or of obedience which leads to justice?* [17]*But thanks be to God; once the slaves of sin, you submitted wholeheartedly to the norm of doctrine to which you were entrusted.* [18]*Freed from sin, you became the slaves of justice.—*[19]*I am using these human analogies out of regard for your weak human nature.—As you offered your members to be the slaves of uncleanness and sank ever deeper into wickedness, so now offer your members to be the slaves of that justice which leads to ever greater holiness.* [20]*When you were slaves of sin, you were, indeed, "free" from justice.* [21]*But what fruit did you gather then? Things of which you are now ashamed! For the end result of those things is death.* [22]*Now, however, freed from sin and become slaves of God, you gather as fruit a growing holiness, the end result of which is life everlasting.* [23]*For the wages of sin is death, but the gift of God is life everlasting in Christ Jesus our Lord.*

This section is only the ethical application of the preceding instruction on the Christian's union with Christ. Far from excusing the Christian from moral effort, the new life challenges him to ever greater holiness—and, as chapter 8 will show, gives him the means to attain it. A popular conception among the Jews was that the inbreaking of the messianic kingdom would bring "justification" and "glorification" simultaneously. For Paul, these two moments are separated, and the interim is characterized by *sanctification.*

Worth noting is the importance given to the body in the moral struggle. Converts from paganism would normally have much to learn in this area, particularly if they had been infected by the pagan world's love for sensual indulgence. Control of the external acts first of all will help toward attaining perfect mastery of the passions. The military image introduced in v. 13 will be developed in detail in Eph 6:11–17. V. 14 reflects Paul's unbounded confidence in the power of grace aiding the Christian in his struggle.

Vv. 15–23 intend to demonstrate what the Christian's release is and what it is not. The libertine again may ask, "May we not then take advantage of our liberty as subjects of grace to sin?" The answer of Paul is: The Christian's liberation is not a freedom *to* sin, but a freedom *from* sin. As a matter of fact one is a slave of whomever he obeys. Now when a man sins, he has only the appearance of freedom, for in reality he is obeying a force to which he has deliberately subjected himself. As John will say, "Whoever commits sin is a slave of sin" (Jn 8:34; cf. 2 Pet 2:19). It is a fact of daily experience that a man cannot be freed from trivial concerns unless he gets "wrapped up" in something bigger than himself, something or some one to whom he can totally commit himself in an oblative love and service. Conversion to Christ is precisely this, and hence the condition of liberation from sin is the intensity with which one commits oneself to God in love and obedience. Only when one has experienced this change can he know really what it is; only then can he say *Thanks be to God!* (6:17) for his deliverance. This "liberating enslavement" differs from the common image of slavery in that it is embraced lucidly and freely. The new master is of course God (vv. 13, 22), but the will of God is manifest in the "norm of doctrine" which is the gospel. The unusual expression tells us that the gospel is not just "good news"; it is a rule of life to which the Christian is committed. To stress the new servitude Paul says not that the gospel was handed over to them but that they were handed over to the gospel, as a slave freed from one master enters the service of another. In saying they have become *slaves of justice* (6:19) instead of "slaves of God," Paul wishes to stress the moral demands of the new life; and, moreover, he goes on to say that the Christian life is a matter of continual growth. Slavery to sin was not just a state of imprisonment but a situation when man went from bad to worse. The new state—justice—is one that must be embraced by repeatedly renewed acts (the aorist in *offer your members* [6:19] suggests this), and it leads to "sanctification." The noun here (*hagiasmos*) stands for the process of sanctification rather than the state or quality of holiness, and, with the obvious contrast with the worsening condition prior to conversion, justifies our translating the expression *ever greater holiness* (6:19).

This is precisely the point of the sequence (20–22). Man's existential condition in either state involves both slavery and freedom. When they were the slaves of sin they were indeed not under the effective dominion of "justice," and so they were "free." But what did this freedom bring? Paul does not specify but allows the conscience of each to evoke the specter of his own dissolute life—*things of which you are now ashamed* (6:21). The immediate result of that "slavery in freedom" was moral corruption; the final result is death—not just physical death but death in its total scriptural sense of definitive separation from God. How deceptive a freedom it was!

The "freedom in slavery" to God is real freedom, for its immediate result is sanctification (growing holiness), and the end result, life everlasting. Thus the Christian life is another Exodus. The Israelites learned that to be free man must become a slave. To be liberated from tyranny, man must accept the Lordship of God. "To serve God is to reign."

The final climax (v. 23) is theologically precise. Death may be won by man as the strict due in justice for his deeds. His deeds can, of themselves, produce death. But the eternal life to which justice leads via sanctification, remains God's gift, for it is the crowning of his own previous gifts of grace and mercy.

CONCLUSION

With this last section we now get a full picture of Christian life in both its constitutive and progressive aspects, as seen in the epistle to the Romans.

(1) Man's basic predicament as Jew or Gentile is his state of *sin*, sometimes called uncleanness; in the pagan this results from a conscious turning from God as known through the universe; in the Jew it results from his native powerlessness to keep the Law, so that it results in his condemnation.

(2) Man's attitude toward his state is crucial. If he assumes the attitudes of *kauchēsis*, "boasting" or better, self-sufficiency, he takes the road to progressive wickedness, which ultimately ends in death, eternal separation from God. This inward vortex is truly man's own choosing and his own just due, but it is also a manifestation of *God's wrath* upon man who seeks to find himself in himself and refuses to find himself in God.

(3) But there is another way out. God is a saving God. He comes with his salvific justice and offers it to man. If man abandons his self-sufficiency and accepts the saving action, and this response is what we call *faith*, God's justice *justifies* him. Not only does this now set him aright with God, but it puts him on the path to the goal of eschatological salvation or eternal life.

The journey, however, is marked by a progressive sanctification, by which the remains of sin are purified and the Christian is strengthened, made worthy of final reunion with Christ in glory. The thought parallels perfectly that of 2 Cor 7:1: "Such being the promises we have, beloved, let us cleanse ourselves from all bodily and spiritual defilement, putting the finishing touches on the work of our sanctification. . . ." As God's salvific justice was manifested in his acts of justifying the sinner, so his love is the guarantee of the continuing action of sanctification which will lead the justified Christian onwards to eternal life.[23] God's justice put the Christian on the right road. God's love guarantees him everything necessary to reach his destination. As the response to God's justice was faith, so the response to God's love is hope (Rom 5:1–5; all of ch. 8). "And hope does not disappoint, for the love of God has been poured into our hearts through the Holy Spirit, who is given to us" (Rom 5:5). God's love, our companion, our Paraclete for the way, is nothing else than the person of the Holy Spirit. See the diagram below.

THE TWO WAYS

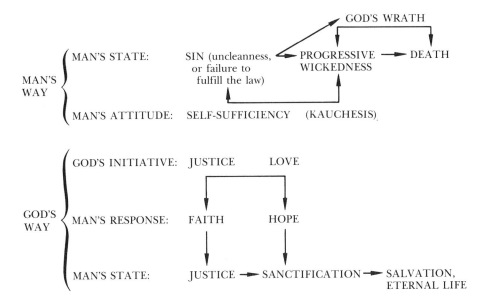

Death with Christ in baptism corresponds principally to the initial stage of justification; the risen life corresponds to the progressive stage in its positive "life for God." But the risen life communicated to the Christian, as the principle of his progress, is identifiable with the Holy Spirit. It is precisely in virtue of his resurrection that Christ communicates the Spirit to the Christian.

The magnificent role of the Holy Spirit in the dynamics of the Christian life is described in ch. 8.

---

[23]H. Küng, "Justification and Sanctification According to the New Testament," in *Christianity Divided* (New York: Sheed & Ward, 1961), 309–335.

CHAPTER SEVEN

The Captivity Epistles

COLOSSIANS

1. From Romans to Colossians

To bridge the events between the writing of Romans and the writing of Colossians, the student should read Acts 20:3 to the end, the account of Paul's return to Palestine (see map, p. 48), his imprisonment there, his appeal to Caesar and his journey to Rome (map, p. 189), giving particular attention to the following discourse sections: 20:17–35; 22:1–21; 24:10–21; 26:1–32. These passages have undergone editing by the

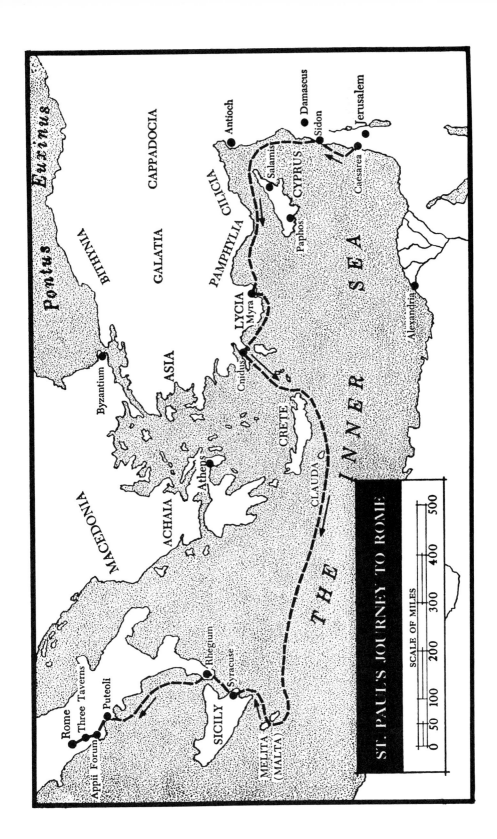

ST. PAUL'S JOURNEY TO ROME

SCALE OF MILES

0 50 100 200 300 400 500

Rome
Three Taverns
Appii Forum
Puteoli
Rhegium
Syracuse
SICILY
MELITA (MALTA)
CLAUDA
CRETE
Cnidus
Athens
ACHAIA
MACEDONIA
Byzantium
BITHYNIA
Pontus
Euxinus
CAPPADOCIA
GALATIA
ASIA
LYCIA
Myra
PAMPHYLIA
CILICIA
Antioch
Salamis
CYPRUS
Paphos
Damascus
Sidon
Jerusalem
Caesarea
Alexandria
THE INNER SEA

author of Acts, but they are helpful in understanding Paul's theology.

A classical position among the exegetes has been that Colossians, along with Ephesians and Philemon, was written during Paul's captivity in Rome. All three of the epistles refer to Paul's imprisonment. Paul was imprisoned several times (even before the writing of 2 Cor—cf. 2 Cor 6:5; 11:23), but we know the place for certain only in the case of Philippi (Acts 16:23 ff.), Jerusalem, Caesarea, and Rome. Philippi is too early and the imprisonment too brief; Ephesus is unlikely (though he probably wrote Phil from there), for both Col and Eph have greetings from Mark and Luke, but there is no evidence that they worked with Paul at Ephesus. Caesarea is the only other likely place, but against this is the indication of Acts 24:23 f., according to which Paul was kept in strict custody, the only favor allowed him being the exceptional one that his friends might serve him. But Col 4:3, 11 and Phm 24 inform us that Paul was able, in spite of his imprisonment in Rome, to carry on the work of the gospel. This squares well with the impression we get from the closing paragraphs of Acts.

A very strong argument for the later, Roman date, is the developed theology of Colossians.

2. Theology of Colossians

Colossae, a city some one hundred miles inland east of Ephesus, had not been evangelized by Paul but by one of his disciples, Epaphras (1:7). A native of Colossae (4:12), he was probably converted by Paul at Ephesus and after instruction sent to Colossae to spread the faith there, and then to Laodicea and Hierapolis (4:13). At any rate, Paul has now been informed of certain difficulties that have arisen in the churches of this area, and has felt it necessary to send Tychicus with a letter which Paul hopes will settle the difficulties (4:7–8, 16). This is the letter to the Colossians.

What these difficulties were must be gathered from the epistle itself. Obviously, the judaizing elements are at work undermining the original gospel Paul preached. They promote circumcision (2:11–13), dietary practices (2:16, 21), the observance of feasts and sabbaths (2:16). This raises for Paul the old issue about the Law (2:14) and its provisional and preparatory character (2:17). There is, however, something about the Colossian crisis distinctly different from previous clashes with judaizers; an intellectual element has been introduced (2:8). Many scholars have taken this as a reflection of a gnostic or pregnostic philosophy, but there is on reason for believing that it was necessarily divorced from the Jewish element, for in these sectors of Asia Minor, in an age of prodigious syncretism, the rise of a heterodox Judaic mysticism, with an excessive asceticism (2:23), is entirely plausible.

At any rate, the movement had, in addition to its concern for the ritual observances of the Mosaic Law, a special affection for the hierarchies of angels (2:18). We know this to be true of contemporary Judaism generally,[1] with speculation on the ministry of angels in God's governing of the world and especially in promulgating and seeing to the observance of the Mosaic Law. Paul finds that this enthusiasm at Colossae involves a special peril for the Christian faith. It stimulates him to elaborate a theology of the Lordship of Christ, his primacy over the cosmos of matter and spirit (hence, over the angles too). The basic principles are not new (cf. 1 Cor 8:6; 10:4; 2 Cor 5:19; Col 2:15; Gal 4:3, 9; Rom 8:38 f.; Phil 2:10 f.), but there is a new stress now, in three directions: (1) Christ's Lordship is not only soteriological but *cosmic* (2) The role of the Church in God's plan is clearer—it is the Body of which Christ is the "Head" (1:18), the members "filling up" what is lacking to his sufferings (1:24) and growing with the power derived from him (2:19). The realism of the image is brought out in that the bodies of Christians are by baptism united with the body of Christ and thus share the death-and-resurrection power which flows from it (2:11–13). (3) Christ and the Church are now presented above all as a *mystery* to be contemplated. Hence, the insistence on the intellectual function of faith and charity (1:9 f.; 2:2 f.).[2]

OUTLINE

---

[1] Cf. J. Bonsirven, *Palestinian Judaism in the Time of Jesus Christ* (New York: Holt, Rinehart and Winston, 1964), 33–41.

[2] G. T. Montague, "May Your Charity Abound in Knowledge," *TBT* 4 (February 1963), 240–245; *Maturing in Christ*, 143–193.

3. The Primacy of Christ: Col 1:15–20

> [15]*He is the image of the invisible God,*
> *Firstborn of all creation,*
>> [16]*for in him were created all things*
>> *in heaven and on earth,*
>> *things visible and things invisible,*
>>> *Thrones, Dominations, Principalities, Powers,*
>> *all things have been created by him and for him.*
> [17]*He exists before all things and in him all things hold together.*
> [18]*And he is the head of the body, the Church.*
> *He is the Beginning*
> *Firstborn from the dead,*
>> *in order that he might have the first place in everything*
>> [19]*For it pleased God to make all fullness dwell in him*
>> [20]*And to reconcile all beings by him and for him,*
>> *Establishing peace on earth and in heaven*
>> *through him, through the blood of his cross.*

The rhythm, parallelism, and obvious division into stanzas, which we have sought to reproduce in the translation, lead exegetes to a common agreement that this passage is a genuine hymn. Whether Paul incorporated an already well-known hymn of the baptismal or Eucharistic liturgy, or composed it for the occasion, the passage does represent a studied artistry, the analysis of which will give insight into its meaning.[3] We have here a unit of two stanzas, the first beginning with v. 15. *He is the image* . . . and the second with 18b, *He is the Beginning.* . . . Discounting for the moment vv. 17–18a, we observe that the first stanza treats of Christ's relation to creation, the second to the "New Creation," the work of redemption. The internal structure of these stanzas is similar, many expressions of the second paralleling or echoing those of the first. Vv. 17–18a provide the transition from the first stanza to the second, v. 17 by summing up the first stanza, v. 18 by giving a preview of the second.

The term *image* is one that evokes origin as well as similarity. Of itself the word does not imply equality, for man is said to be the image of God (1 Cor 11:7); but neither does it exclude equality, for already in the Old Testament the son was considered to be the image of his father (Gen 5:3), and in this epistle Christ is the Father's beloved Son (1:13), in whom dwells all the fullness of the Godhead (2:9). We cannot on this basis alone say then whether Paul by *Image of the invisible God* (1:15) is thinking of the eternally preexisting Son or of the incarnate Son (as in 2 Cor 4:4). In favor of the latter is the fact that "invisibility" here seems to be the

---

[3]Cf. B. Vawter, "The Colossians Hymn and the Principle of Reduction," *CBQ* 33 (1971), 62–81.

property of the Father alone, and, of course, both the synoptic and Johannine traditions are strong in affirming that by his incarnation and redemptive work Christ visibly manifests the Father to men (Mt 11:27; Lk 10:22; Jn 19:9). On the other hand, the context here has to do with creation; it is even said that all things have been created *by* him (v. 16), and since it is absurd to think that the humanity of Christ could have exerted an efficient causality before it existed, we would, on the second view, be reduced to interpreting the humanity of Christ as merely being in the mind and intuition of the Creator when he brought the universe into being.

More light will perhaps be shed by the next term Paul uses, literally, *the firstborn of all creation* (1:15). This too can be interpreted as a mere primacy of honor, the preeminence of the incarnate Christ over all creation even though he is not first in time; or it may mean a real antecedence, meaning "born before every creature" and in this sense it refers to his eternal generation from the Father, his transcendent origin. With the constant intention of showing the primacy of Christ over everything, Paul uses a term rich in the Old Testament theology it evokes. The firstborn son in a family had a primacy both of honor and of authority over his younger brothers; he enjoyed the right of inheritance (see the Jacob-Esau stories in Genesis), and for the king's firstborn this meant the right to accede to the throne. The term was used to describe Israel's relation as a people to Yahweh—they are his "firstborn" (Ex 4:22; Jer 31:9; cf. Hos 11:1). Later it was applied to the King who represented the people (Ps 89:28), and finally to the Messiah. It meant not only that the nation and its King-Messiah were chosen by God but also that they were raised above other nations and kings and that God would show his glorious power through men. However, there is here question of preexistence in relation to the whole created universe (firstborn of *all* creation) and consequently we are led to those Old Testament texts which speak of God's wisdom as his firstborn. "The Lord begot me, the firstborn of his ways, the forerunner of his prodigies of long ago" (Prov 8:22). Wisdom is presented in this hymn as a being which existed before all things (22–26) and worked with God as he planned and created the universe, adorning it with beauty, variety, and order (27–30). See also Wis 9:9; Sir 1:1–4; 24:9. We have here, then, a wisdom motif in hymnic form very similar to the opening lines of Saint John's prologue—so closely related in fact that some authors hold for a direct Johannine influence on this passage.[4] Consequently, although Paul affirms the personal identity between the Christ of the first stanza and that of the second, we do not hesitate to say that it is as the

---

[4] Cf. D. M. Stanley, *Christ's Resurrection in Pauline Soteriology,* 207 f.

preexisting Son, the creator of the universe in his eternal divine sonship, that Christ is contemplated in the first stanza, and not specifically as the incarnate Son.

The reason for the Son's primacy over creation is given in v. 16. All things were created *in, by* and *for* him. *In him*: Some have explained this in terms of exemplary causality—the Word was the supreme model or archetype for the created universe. Valid as this may be, it is probably closer to Paul's thought to conceive the Son as the focal point which gives order and meaning to the created universe—the "meeting-point" to which the multiple lines of creation converge, as shafts from the setting sun both proceed from the sphere and lead the eye back to it. *Were created* (1:16; aorist tense in Greek) indicates the act of creation as a single divine initiative. This act extended not only to the material universe but to the spiritual universe as well, and hence to all those hierarchies of angels on which the popular Jewish mind loved to speculate. Paul attached little importance to the names of the "choirs" of angels (the order and the names differ in Eph 1:21), and cites them only as illustrations to show that Christ is above them all. The important point is that *all* things have been created *by* him (the creator is never inferior to his creature but is the creature's Lord) and *for* him (he is their goal, their end, their "final cause"). Here Paul uses the perfect tense, *have been created*, in contrast to the aorist above, to indicate that this relationship of creation to Christ is a permanent and indissoluble one. No theology of powers, earthly or heavenly, can ever alter it.

V. 17 sums up all that has been said of Christ: he has an existence prior to all creation and eminently superior to it. And in him all things *hold together* (1:17)—he is the "key" to the universe both in the order of being and in the order of knowledge. Without him the universe would disintegrate into nothingness; without knowing him the universe remains unintelligible.

With v. 18, a new idea is introduced: *He is the head of the body, the Church*. The idea is new not so much in that we are now introduced into the order of salvation (the Bible considers the created universe itself as an epiphany of God), but because of the term *Head* used of Christ in relation to the Church. The community of believers has already frequently been presented in the Pauline letters as the body of Christ (1 Cor 6:15; 10:17; 12:12–27; Rom 12:4), but there was no occasion in these passages to stress Christ's excellence and Lordship over the other members. Now, when it becomes necessary to establish Christ's absolute primacy, even over the Church, the image of Headship comes to Paul's mind. It will become a favorite in the captivity epistles (Col 2:19; Eph 1:22, 29; 4:15; 5:23). Examination of the various texts in which Christ, cosmos and Church are related, shows that Paul puts the Church above all other created entities, the universe of matter, of men, and of angels. The reason is that the Church is Christ's own body. Hence, reasoning *a fortiori*, Paul says that if Christ is head of the Church, and the Church is above all other created entities, Christ is with all the more reason Lord of the universe.[5]

But headship means more than a mere primacy of honor. He is also the *archē*. This term means the *beginning*, not just as the first of a series, but also as the *principle* or the "originating power" of the rest. Here it is of the new creation that Paul is thinking, for the expression is used deliberately to match "He is the image of the invisible God" of v. 15, and the immediate sequence tells us in what precise sense Christ is the "principle" of the new creation: it is as risen from the dead. Paul uses the curious expression *firstborn from the dead* (1:18) to match *firstborn of all creation* in v. 15. The resurrection of Christ is of the new creation both the beginning and the principle (cf. Acts 3:15; the author [*archēgos*] of life). It was God's plan that Christ should have primacy not only in virtue of the first creation, but, passing through human existence and death, he should come forth victor even from this universal defeat of mankind. Having done so, he is now first in a wholly new sense; having entered the human predicament, he has won a triumph so glorious as to pale the pretensions of the highest angels.

What the resurrection means theologically is now explained in v. 19: it means that God has made all "fullness" to dwell in him. This curious expression can be understood only in the light of its scriptural background (Gnostic speculations of the second century provide little help here). The term *plērōma* always has primarily a passive sense—it is *something that is filled*. In the Old Testament it is the universe that is *filled* with the creative presence of God (Is 6:3; Jer 23:24; Ps 24:1; 50:12; 72:19; Wis 1:7; Sir 43:27). Paul is saying that *all* the divine fullness, i.e., the divine creative presence, has now been concentrated in the risen body of Christ. This mean, obviously, that the risen Christ is the new universe in which the incessant divine creative activity is at work, and in which alone men can be renewed. This is precisely what Paul will say a few lines later: "In him dwells the fullness of the Godhead bodily, and in him you have been filled" (Col 2:9). The concept of the *plērōma* then complements that of the primacy by stressing its dynamic aspect. See the diagram on p. 203.

The resurrection is not of course to be idealized away from the historical fact of Christ's death which preceded it as the necessary

---

[5]Cf. Rom 8:19–24; Col 1:16–20; Eph 1:10 f.; 21–23; 4:10–16; and G. T. Montague, *Maturing in Christ*, 221–230.

preamble by which peace was established in all creation (the "by him, for him" of v. 20 matches the same expression of v. 16). This does not mean that the angels were redeemed, but that the order of creation, upset by man's sins, was reestablished by the death of Christ, whose resurrection inaugurated a new order in which he stands at the head of all creation, even the angels.

EPHESIANS

If we read Ephesians carefully, we will note the great similarity of thought between it and Colossians. But we will note, too, the absence of polemic—extraordinary for Saint Paul!—and a style greatly differing from the short, choppy, explosive sentences to which we have become accustomed in the earlier epistles. This enigmatic situation has puzzled Scripture scholars and divided them on the question of the authorship of the letter. The differences have led some to deny that Paul wrote the letter; the similarities which are found are then explained as a borrowing from previous Pauline letters by someone else, even long after Paul's time. Defenders of Pauline authenticity, however, point out: (1) that a forger could hardly have mastered Paul's thought as thoroughly as to achieve the fluidity and suppleness we find in the epistle; (2) that the redundant and concatenated style has already appeared in Col and even occasionally in earlier epistles (Rom 3:21–26; 2 Cor 9:8–14); (3) that the similarity of Eph to Col may be explained in the same fashion as Romans to Galatians—in each case, a letter occasioned by a polemical or doctrinal point and written *ad hoc* is followed by a more synthetic treatise in which the theme of the earlier letter is developed in a more irenic atmosphere. The difference of style is dictated by the author's difference of purpose: the Stoic diatribe fits the argumentative purpose better; the liturgical, hymnic style is more suited to a contemplation of the mystery, such as is found in Ephesians and already, for that matter, in Colossians.[6]

Consequently, the traditional position that Paul wrote Ephesians from Rome shortly after Colossians is by no means a weak one. The doctrinal development from Col to Eph is no greater than that from Gal to Rom—though certainly it represents the incorporation of new images and concepts, perhaps even some Qumranian ones. Those who maintain that Paul himself is the authority behind this epistle try to solve the difficulties in various ways, one of which is to allow for the composition of the letter by an intimate disciple (perhaps Tychicus himself) under Paul's direction or influence.

At any rate, the letter was certainly not specifically addressed to the

---

[6]K. Sullivan, "The Mystery Revealed to Paul—Eph 3:1–13," *TBT* 4 (February 1963), 247–254; L. Cerfaux, *Christ in the Theology of Saint Paul*, 367–528.

faithful of Ephesus. Paul knew them well from his three-year stay there. But the letter indicates that he does not know his readers personally (Eph 1:15; 4:21), nor do they seem to know him (3:2–4). The letter moreover carries no information or admonition of a personal nature. And the words "in Ephesus" of 1:1 are missing from the best manuscripts. We may assume, then, that the letter is meant to be a general one to the churches of Asia Minor and was not destined for any one community in particular.

Theologically, this is the epistle of the Church.[7] In establishing the primacy of Christ in Col, Paul had already brought in the Church several times. Now he treats it specifically: the image of head and members is further developed (1:22 f.; 4:15 f.) and the new image of the bride accentuates even more the moral autonomy of the Body of Christ (5:22–32). The unity of the Church in its being (4:1–6) and its becoming (4:7–16) assumes a central importance.

OUTLINE

[7] C. F. Mooney, "Paul's Vision of the Church in Ephesians" in *Mission and Witness*, ed. P. J. Burns (Westminster: Newman, 1964), 61–78.

The Building of Christ's Body: Eph 4:7–16

> ⁷*But to each one of us grace has been given according to the measure in which Christ has bestowed it.* ⁸*Thus the Scripture says: "ascending on high, he led away captives; he gave gifts to men."* ⁹*Now what does this expression "he ascended" mean, but that he also descended into the lower parts of earth?* ¹⁰*He who descended is the same one who ascended above all the heavens that he might fill the universe.* ¹¹*And it was he who gave some men as apostles, others as prophets, others as evangelists, others as shepherds and teachers,* ¹²*so as to organize the saints for active service in building up the body of Christ,* ¹³*until we all as a whole perfectly attain to the unity of the faith and of the thorough knowledge of the Son or God, to perfect Man, to the mature age (or stature) that befits Christ's fullness—*¹⁴*so that we may no longer be children tossed about and swung round by every wind of teaching that cheating men contrive in craftiness and that leads to the trap error has laid.* ¹⁵*Rather, by embodying the truth in love, let us grow up unto him in every respect. He is the head, Christ.* ¹⁶*From him the whole body, growing more and more compact and closely knit together through every life-feeding contact (according to the measured activity each single part deploys), the whole body, I say, works out its increase for the building up of itself in love.*

To understand this passage one must read the letter from the beginning. The first part of the epistle, largely dogmatic, is devoted to the description of the mystery in God's eternal counsel (1:3–14), in its historical realization in Christ and in us (1:15–2:10), in the union it effects between Jew and Gentile (2:11–22). Paul, instructed in the mystery (3:1–6), has the mission to preach it (3:7–13) and prays that his readers reach an understanding of it and thus become filled unto the very fullness God has planned (3:14–21). The exhortatory part, to which our passage belongs, begins with 4:1, an appeal to his readers to embody in their lives the mystery of unity worked in them. He does this by showing first that the graces common to all demand this unity (4:1–6) and then that the very diversity of graces in the Church is aimed at one purpose—the very same unity (4:7–16). We thus arrive at our passage.

The *grace* of which Paul first speaks (4:7) is taken by most authorities as referring not primarily to the grace that saves, but to the *charisms*, those gifts, exceptional or ordinary, with which Christ has endowed the different members of his Church to bring it to perfection. The charisms were treated at length in 1 Cor 12–14, where the principle was established that they are not given for personal vanity nor as a measure of personal sanctity, but for building up the Church. Now in this matter order and proportion are essential. Here is one case in which Christ *has measured out* his grace. Paul never speaks of the grace that saves, nor of charity, as being measured out—it rather abounds, overflows (Rom 5:15, 17, 20; Eph 1:8; 1 Th 3:12; 2 Th 1:3; Phil 1:9)—whereas the idea of measure and proportion is associated with the social functions the members have received (1 Cor 12:18 ff.; cf. Rom 12:6). The text indicates that every Christian ("each of us") has a specific role to play. And yet, choosing the singular "grace" instead of "gifts," Paul, in preparing to discuss the diversity of the functions, wishes to stress the unity of their source. If there is diversity, it is determined not by chance nor by merit but by the grace of Christ (cf. Rom 12:6).

In line with the synoptic and apostolic tradition, the pouring forth of the Spirit in his manifold gifts was the aim and fruit of Christ's victorious ascension (Mk 16:19 f.; Acts 2:33; Jn 16:17). Paul here pictures Christ as running the circuit of the universe from base to summit and thus filling it with his presence and conquering it as his kingdom (Eph 1:20–22; Phil 2:8–10). Christ's descent-ascent, however, only traced the cosmic reaches of his "pleroma"; from the moment of his ascension, he now pursues the progressive "filling up" of the universe. Such is the sweeping perspective introduced by Ephesians 4:10. The expression *the universe* (*ta panta*) is a favorite of Paul to express all things in their unity, the *sum* of all things spiritual or material. Hence, the expression should be rendered not "all things" but "the universe."

To fill the universe was the aim of Christ's ascension—to give it meaning, to bring it to completion by giving reality and substance to all that it prepares for. The process inaugurated by Christ's ascension continues through the course of time by the ministry of the Church until the universe is effectively his.

As it is Christ who masters the evolving completion of the universe, so too it is he and no other who gave the Church its officers, that the whole body (and through it the universe) might attain his fullness (4:11). It is still the overflowing effusion that Paul has in mind when he says Christ *gave* the men; elsewhere he is satisfied with saying God *placed* them (1 Cor 12:28).

Paul's point in enumerating some of the offices is surely not to give an exhaustive list of the *each one of us* mentioned at the beginning of the passage, but rather to list some of the more important roles as representative of the diversity of graces. In view of the approaching verses on faith, knowledge, and doctrine (Eph 4:13–14), he chooses gifts which have a stable character and engage functions of authority and teaching.

The *Apostles and prophets* (4:11) are naturally mentioned first, for to them the mystery is primarily revealed (Eph 3:5); they are the foundation of the divine house (Eph 2:20). The Apostle's role is to plant (1 Cor

3:6), hence to found Christian communities, but also to build up (2 Cor 10:8) and to look to the progress of the faithful (Phil 1:25). Consequently an Apostle also may be a prophet, that is, not necessarily one who foretells the future, but he who, within the community, "speaks to men for edification, and encouragement, and consolation" (1 Cor 14:3). The prophet's position of prestige is due precisely to the fact that his speaking builds up not himself but the Church (1 Cor 14:4 f.). *Evangelists* were those whose role it was to preach the gospel to those who had not yet heard it, always, of course, in subordination to the Apostles. The office was exercised occasionally (Acts 8:4; 11:19 f.) or regularly as by Philip the deacon (Acts 21:8; 6:5; 8:5–13; 26:40). The closest modern counterpart of a prophet might be a stirring and gifted retreat master; that of an evangelist would be a "missionary."

To these offices which concerned the whole Church and were therefore exercised by itinerants, Paul adds those more stably fixed to individual churches: *shepherds* and *teachers*. The absence of the Greek article before "teachers" shows that the two functions were closely related, no doubt because the "pastor" exercised also the office of teacher. A bishop, Paul would tell Timothy, must be a teacher (1 Tim 3:2; cf. Tit 1:9).

The aim of Christ's multiform gift is now introduced in v. 12. "For the perfecting of the saints" is a gross literal equivalent of the Greek *katartismos*. But the simple translation "perfecting" is too vague and not faithful to the origin nor to the use of the word. The very root words suggest a plenitude achieved by harmonious assembling of parts, and when the verb is used of parts in relation to the whole, the idea is not only that all the parts fit together harmoniously, but also that they are ready and apt for the purpose to which the whole is destined. A papyrus of the first century tells us that when a woman, having put together the pieces of tissue to make a garment, has finished her work, the garment is *katērtismena*, it is *ready to be worn*. Thus, used on the military scale, the verb describes an admiral who *arms* a fleet or a general who *equips* an army for entering a campaign or for taking to sea.

Closely akin to the word used here is a more common one *katartisis*, which means training, education, discipline. We must then find some word which will keep as many of these nuances as possible: the nuance of bringing together disparate parts (that also fits our context well); that of "preparation," and since it is a preparation of *persons*, the nuance of "equipping" or "training." Hence a better translation would be *to organize* or *to mobilize* (4:12).

Well, then, who are the *saints* to be organized? Are they the ministers just listed? Some exegetes think so. Saint Paul then would be speaking of the "official" ministry when he discusses "service for building up the body of Christ." But this interpretation does not sit well with the theme of the whole passage, which teaches that the body works out of its own growth and every member has a share therein. "Service" (*diakonia*) does not always refer to official service, but can stand for such general "service to the saints" as the household of Stephanas showed (1 Cor 15:16). "Service" or "ministry" then is taken here in a sense as broad as the grace from which it flows—each has received his share (Eph 4:7).

Far from suffering from this interpretation, the official ministry is put in its true light. Both laity and clergy have roles that are active but not identical: *The role of the official ministers in building the Church is to release and direct the Church-building power latent by divine gift in every Christian!*

If there is diversity, it is so that the members may have care for one another (1 Cor 12:25 f.; 1 Pet 4:10). *Some* he has made apostles, prophets, etc. But their mission, be it founding, or preaching, or exhorting, or ruling, or teaching, is no other than to achieve the upbuilding by forming and directing the saints in their variously but divinely distributed powers for *building up the body of Christ* (4:12). Instead of saying that the body grows, Paul, who delights in mixing his figures, says that it is built up, thus stressing once more the saints' active role in the body's growth.

Precisely where this progress is going is now given in v. 13: *until we all attain.* . . . The expression "attaining" is used often in the Acts for travelers reaching their destination, and hence in the literal sense suggests that Christian progress is a journey (Acts 13:51; 16:1; 18:19, 24; 21:7; 25:13; 27:12; 28:13). But it is also used in the figurative sense for the full attainment of something already presently possessed in hope (Acts 26:7; Phil 3:11) or for the maturation of something already possessed in germ (cf. Gen 40:10). Those who thus attain are not simply "we," nor simply "all of us" taken individually (as in 1 Cor 10:17; Rom 11:32; Phil 2:21). The use of the article (*hoi pantes*) means that Paul is taking the whole collectively, *we all as a whole*, and thus it is specifically corporate growth that is envisaged.

The first mark of corporate growth is unity. Paul had insisted on the fact that Christians have one faith (Eph 4:5); the *unity of the faith* here (4:13) is then an evolution not in the object of the faith but in the Church's assimilation of it. The unity here is that demanded by the one faith, not merely a quality of the virtue of faith, but a definite goal or state to which they are to attain, a unity made by the one faith.

Growing unity in the faith will be marked by a greater communal penetration of the object of the faith. As all Christians come to know better and to appreciate more deeply this common object of their faith, they will find that they are not only closer to Christ but closer to one another. Unity is achieved not by ignoring the intellectual mastery of the mystery, but by universal striving ever to penetrate it more deeply.

Christians in the state of perfection will appear not as a parade of individual saints in our modern sense, but as one *perfect man* (4:13). The noun *anthrōpos*, like the Latin *homo*, is the generic term used to distinguish man from angels or lower animals. Here the term is *anēr* (the Latin *vir*), which is used to distinguish man from woman or from boy—that is, a human being grown to maturity or manhood (as in 1 Cor 13:11). The term *teleios*, too, may mean not only "perfect" but also "mature." The image of strength and virility is a favorite of Paul's to fire Christians to progress; but the stress here is upon the unity of the ideal toward which Christians progress. In Colossians 1:28, Paul had already presented as his aim "to present every man perfect in Christ Jesus," and thus the perfection of individuals is supposed. But using "perfect man" here (instead of "every man perfect" or "perfect men") contrasts sharply with the universal "we all," so as to underline the corporate unity without which individual perfection is meaningless.

Who is "the perfect man"? Surely none other than "one new man" (Eph 2:15, 4:24), namely, Christ, "perfect" being used here to stress the goal, whereas "new" stressed that he is a totally "new creation." But even the expression "new man" expresses a corporate reality primarily, not a "better self" but the *whole Christ*, with whom every Christian must strive to identify himself, to the abandonment of all individualism: "Put on the new man. . . . Wherefore, put away lying and speak truth each one with his neighbor, because we are members of one another" (Eph 4:24 f.). "Put on the new man ... where there cannot be 'Gentile and Jew,' 'circumcised and uncircumcised,' 'Barbarian and Scythian,' 'slave and freeman'; but Christ is all things and in all" (Col 3:10 f.).

Lest there remain any doubt as to what Paul means by "perfect man," he now explains that it is *the mature age (or stature) that befits Christ's fullness* (Eph 4:13). The Greek may mean "age" or "stature," but in either case the point is that Christians must "measure up" to a standard not yet attained, "the fullness of Christ." The term *plērōma* (fullness) means "that which is filled." The pleroma of Christ here, then, would mean "that which is filled by Christ" and, fortunately, Eph 1:23 tells us specifically that this "pleroma of Christ" is the Church, his body. The Church then parallels the "perfect man" and confirms what has just been said about this being the corporate ideal. For the body of Christians, perfection consists in attaining to the mature proportions that befit such a body, defined as pure capacity for Christ, made to be "filled up" by him and unto him. Surely this is an ideal that really has no limits and

THE PLEROMA

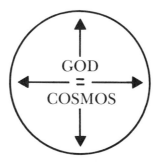

STOIC CONCEPTION

God identified with the cosmos. Thus the cosmos is "filled" with God and God is "filled" with the cosmos. A pantheistic concept.

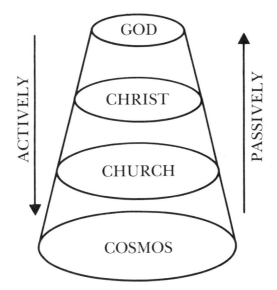

PAUL'S CONCEPTION

Pleroma a dynamic concept, meaning God's creative power and presence. God pours this "fullness" into Christ, Christ pours it into the Church, and the Church makes it present to the cosmos. Thus, the cosmos is "filled" by the Church, the Church by Christ, Christ by God. In the same way, God can be said to be "filled" by Christ, in the sense that all his revelation and grace is to be found in him, to be transmitted to the Church, which thus is in turn Christ's "fullness"; and because the whole cosmos is in solidarity with the Church and is to be incorporated into Christ, the cosmos itself is the "fullness" of the Church, of Christ, and of God.

can never be perfectly attained in this life, but Christian life is a continual progress toward it. We have tried to diagram the very complex Pauline idea of the "pleroma" in contrast to the Stoic notion on p. 203.

What is important is that Christians understand that they can no longer cling to the state of infancy (4:14), which is Paul's favorite theme to stigmatize a lack of thorough understanding and adherence to orthodox doctrine. The Pauline contrast between "infants" and "mature men" goes back to 1 Cor 1–3, to which our present passage presents many parallels: the signs of spiritual immaturity were there described as disunity and wrangling factions in the community, and capacity only for elementary instruction; whereas those who are mature are those capable of digesting the solid food of advanced spiritual doctrine and of penetrating the mystery of God. The craftiness of the pretended wise appears in 1 Cor 3:19 and here in Eph 4:14. Both passages have likewise the figure of the building with the officials who lay the foundation and supervise the construction. In Eph 4:10, Christ "fills all things"; the same cosmic sweep is expressed in 1 Cor 3:23: "All things are yours, and you are Christ's, and Christ is God's."

Here the plural "infants" contrasts with the singular "mature man." Individualism in the Christian life is immaturity; unity is maturity. As it is true doctrine that nourishes growth (1 Cor 3:2; Heb 5:11–6:1), so it is false teaching that disperses and weakens. The changing winds of doctrine have no other effect than to toss "children" about like waves or little boats and to swing them around or bear them to and fro as if they had no rudder, map, or star. The two figures combine to express the instability characteristic of a weak-minded or poorly founded faith, which lacks clarity and certitude.

It is not simply a state of adolescence which will inevitably be outgrown with time. The contrary elements are militant and cunning men, and the danger of falling into their "sleight of hand" or "trickery" is ever at hand. Such deception is attributable to "men," for, as Theophylact long ago observed, "divine things admit of no trickery or deception." These contrivers are unscrupulous ("readiness to do anything" is the original meaning of *panourgia*), but is is especially their cleverness that makes them a danger to the faith. Unlike the sincere apostle, they tamper with the word of God (2 Cor 4:2), and thus present a semblance of truth as the serpent did in seducing Eve (2 Cor 11:3). Behind their scheming and manipulating, error is at work.

It is certainly not thus that Christians grow. On the contrary, their formula for progress is *the truth in love* (4:15). The contrast of truth with error is clear, as it is in 2 Th 2:11 f., but the value to be given to the verb *alētheuein* here is disputed. The only other New Testament usage is Gal

4:16, where it means "to speak the truth." But here, where the warning is not to the false teachers but to those in danger of being misled by them, "speaking the truth" does not seem quite adequate. This particular verb form contains all that is implied by the corresponding substantive, "truth" (*alētheia*). This means much more than speaking the truth. It expresses the content of Christianity as the absolute truth, and it has a strongly practical side which expresses itself in the virtues. The Vulgate understood this by translating it as *veritatem facientes*, after Saint John's favorite expression, "doing the truth." According to John, he who is possessed by Christ knows the truth (Jn 8:32; 2 Jn 1) and does the truth (Jn 3:21; 1 Jn 1:6; Gen 32:11; 47:29; Is 26:10), stands in the truth (Jn 8:25), is of the truth (Jn 18:37), is set free by the truth (Jn 8:32). Paul's idea, like John's, is both that of living the truth and of giving it a public and practical profession. Hency, *embody*.

The truth is to be lived *in love*. The authentic Christian lives his faith in an atmosphere of love. The cryptic phrase is the epitome of Christian ethics and of spiritual progress, for it is principally in this way, by embodying the truth in love, that Christians *grow*. "Growing" is one of Paul's most technical terms for progress: the gospel grows (Col 1:6), faith grows (2 Cor 10:15; cf. Rom 1:17), and Christians grow (Col 1:10). "To make grow" is reserved for God who gives all growth and increase (1 Cor 3:6 f.; 2 Cor 9:10). In the later letters the verb is a consecrated term for the progress of the Church, whether considered as the body which grows unto the growth of God (Col 1:19), or as the building which grows into a temple holy in the Lord (Eph 2:21), or as the totality of Christians growing up unto Christ (here in Eph 4). Against the changing winds and wiles of error, Christians are not only to stand firm (Eph 6:14), but to grow, to progress. "Not to progress in the way of God," observes Saint Thomas here, "is to regress."

Christ is the goal of the Church's growth (*unto him* 4:15), but the stress falls on the expression, *in every respect*. A precious indication: "embodying the truth in love" is the key for the *universal* growth of Christians. Every phase and sector of Christian growth is commanded by this single aim, to live the truth in love. If it is faith that accepts the truth (2 Th 2:12 f.), it is love that embodies and manifests it, and this movement achieves the growth of Christians in every dimension of their spiritual life.

The mention of Christ as head focuses more clearly the goal or standard (however obscure the figure of "growing up the head"), but it especially introduces Christ as the source of growth, as in Col 2:19. *From him* (4:16) indicates that Christ is not merely the intercessory power but the power that administers the substance of growth, and that as a universal cause. If God has made all fullness to dwell in him (Col 1:19), then it can only be of his fullness that the members receive their growth (Jn 1:16).

But a long parenthesis delays the completion of the sentence, in order to give attention to the activity by which the body achieves its growth. *Growing more and more compact* (4:16) is a wordy English rendering of a single participle in the Greek, a compound word Paul himself coins for the situation, *synarmologoumenon,* which literally means something like "being co-fitted together." In the architectural language of the day, *harmos* was used for a "fitting," or for the joint or juncture where one stone was fitted to another, or for the side of the stone which was tooled so as to fit with the corresponding side of another stone. When a temple was built, no mortar was used, and hence the problem of fitting the stones snugly together was a significant one, particularly since the exact measures of the building were defined in the contract and were to be adhered to strictly.

In working the stones to achieve proper fitting, it was the custom to cut in the central part of the side so as to make it hollow, and then to smooth the margins of the stone so that they would fit perfectly with the similarly smoothed margins of the adjoining stone. After using a fine tool for the smoothing, a rubbing process was then applied. To test whether the entire surface was even, a straight bar of stone or wood (called a canon or rule) was first covered with ruddle and then passed over the surface; the presence or absence of the red material on the hewn stone would indicate where the stone was still uneven, and the smoothing process would be continued until a final use of the canon showed that the surface was uniformly red.

All this plus the further work of preparing and fixing the dowels with molten lead is evoked by the verb Paul uses here. He creates a prefix of his own (*syn-*) and applies the figure to the *body,* so as to stress in a striking way that the members of the body are becoming continually more compact in mutual adjustment, that is, continually more united, as the stones of a structure "grow together" as it is being built. To the architectural figure Paul now adds *closely knit together,* which befits living beings capable of interlacing or fusing themselves spiritually.

This process, which is going on continually, is achieved, literally *through every contact of supply* (Eph 4:16), hence, *life-feeding contact.*

What then is the theological bearing of the phrase, *growing more and more compact and knit together through every life-feeding contact* (4:16)? Is this contact with Christ or with fellow members? The context stresses the role of the members in the body's self-building. This does not diminish the role of Christ, all growth is *from* him; but it comes *through* the unification, mutual contact, interaction, and help of the members. It was this that led Saint Thomas to observe theologically:

> From Christ our head comes not only the increasing compactness of the members of the Church through faith, nor merely the connection or binding through the mutual help of charity, but certainly from him comes the members' actual operation or movement to action, according to the measure and ability of each member . . . for not only by faith is the mystical body compacted, nor merely by charity's connecting assistance does the body grow; but likewise by the *effectual composing activity springing from each member*, according to the measure of grace given him, and the actual motion to operation which God effects in us.

The body will grow, then, in the measure of each member's docility to Christ the head (1) in receiving the grace that may be ministered to him (whether sacramentally or through teaching or, broadly, through whatever other contact that offers grace); and (2) in transmitting it in service to other members and to the body as a whole.

All this will demand the sacrifice of the "rough edges" that hinder union and continuous positive effort to weave the oneness necessary to assuring the circulation of life. Mutual union is then the condition and the effect of the divine life descending from the Head to the members. "If we wish to enjoy the spirit which comes from the Head, let us cling to one another," observes St. John Chrysostom. The thought was similarly expressed by Saint John (1 Jn 4:12): "If we love one another, God abides in us and his love in us is perfected."

It is thus that the body works out its own growth, which is aimed at the building up of itself in love. Love (*agapē*) is the grand finale not only of the last verse but of the whole section (Eph 4:7–16). Since "in every respect" has already explained that *in which* the body is to grow—in everything—"in love" would seem rather to express that by means of which the body grows. It is chiefly fraternal love that is meant here, as in Ephesians 4:2, "bearing with one another in love," particularly under the aspect of union.

> But why is "in love" added? Because otherwise the Spirit could not descend. Let us suppose a hand detached from the body. The movement (*pneuma*, spirit) coming from the brain and finding the route blocked, certainly does not leave the body to enter the hand; if it does not find the member disposed, it nowise influences it. That is what happens to us when charity does not unite us (Chrysostom, *P.G.* 62:84).

To build up is the proper activity of fraternal love (1 Cor 8:1). However, our text declares that all the building power comes from Christ (*From him . . . 4:16*); moreover, "love" here bears the weight of the whole passage and echoes "embodying the truth in love" of Eph 4:15, and "growing up unto him."

Charity is thus not the goal (this is Christ) but the motive power that leads to it. Ending the passage, "love" corresponds to "grace" which opened it. Christ has so distributed his gifts that each has his own, adapting him to a special service in the building up of Mystical Body. The magnificent array which these gifts present and their organization all spring from Christ's gift. But they would be inactive, useless, even harmful for the whole, were there not a motor apt to set them in motion, to engage their interplay and thus to assure the body's corporate and unitive growth in Christ. There is such a motor, such an energy. It is the greatest of the divine gifts (1 Cor 12:31). It is love.

At the end of this at times minute analysis of the text, what are the chief significant points that we have learned? Most important, perhaps, is that it would be a great mistake to try to describe Paul's theology of progress as the ascent of an individual soul to the beatific vision, to the neglect of his essential character as member of Christ in his body, the Church. Incorporated into his body, the Christian assumes the body's conditions of growth, grows with it and in it and through it, and in turn helps it grow. It is not only the individual heart that is subject of the progressive inhabitation of the divine persons, but the whole Christian community, which progresses through mutual interaction toward a perfect temple (Eph 2:21 f.).

It is in Christ (Eph 2:2) and from Christ (Eph 4:16) and unto Christ (Eph 4:15) that the body grows. But Christ has so distributed his gifts that the body cooperates in its own growth. From Christ each member of the Church receives spiritual movement adapting him to a role of service in the Mystical Body (Eph 4:12); and this grace, proper to each, is aimed at being somehow communicated or exploited for the corporate growth of all in charity. Thus Christ diffuses his own eminent perfection in a myriad of different graces so that in and through their diversity, he may bring his members, and they may bring one another, to his own perfection.

Because this perfection of the whole consists first of all in a unity in faith and knowledge, of chief importance are those official ministers whose task it is to plant the faith, expound it, and watch over its purity and progress. But is is not they alone who build up the body. They are, as it were, only the architects or foremen (1 Cor 3:10); building is the work of all, each according to the grace given him. It follows that the Christian has the source of spiritual growth not only in God (1 Cor 3:6), not only in Christ, but likewise, in a mediate sense, in the fellow members of the Mystical Body; and he would fall far short of the divine plan of construction did he not strive to derive from this "contact" all the grace Christ wills to communicate thereby, or did he not strive to remove all the obstacles to his own "instrumentality" in communicating the divine riches. If there is asceticism in the spiritual progress of the member of

Christ, *as member*, it is certainly this: to remove all the obstacles to this unitive circulation, so as to grow as God has planned Christians to grow—together. It is in this way that, under the influence of Christ as head, "the whole Body works out its growth to the building up of itself in love."

Love is indeed the embodiment of the truth, and by continually striving to live the truth in love, Christians grow up together in all the dimensions of their spiritual being. In so doing they share actively in the glorious achievement of the divine plan for cosmic history—through them, as members of his body, Christ brings to fulfillment the universe of matter and spirit, the very aim of his ascension to the Father—"to fill the universe." Thus the Christian bears in his heart the destiny of the universe and contributes to its realization in the measure in which he lends himself to the dynamic and progressing rhythm of the divine love flowing from the head and circulating in the members, uniting them and making them grow together unto the spiritual stature of the one perfect man, Christ.

PHILEMON

The student should read this letter, which belongs to the same period as Col and Eph. Background may be found in A. Wikenhauser, *Introduction*; in the *New Testament Reading Guide #9*; in *EDB*, under "Philemon" and in commentaries. The letter is a precious witness to the gentle prudence of Paul and his mastery of a diplomacy inspired by charity.

CHAPTER EIGHT

The Pastoral Epistles

THE LAST YEARS OF SAINT PAUL

Paul's last years are obscure. The Acts of the Apostles are no help here, for they take us only to the first Roman captivity, which probably ended in his release in A.D. 63. What happened after that must be pieced together from elsewhere. We know that Paul had the intention of visiting Spain (Rom 15:24, 28); the letter of Clement (v. 5–7, A.D. 95), the Muratorian Canon (c. A.D. 170) and the Apocryphal Acts of Peter (1:3; c. A.D. 200) indicate that he actually went there. Assuming the authenticity of the pastoral epistles (the letters to Timothy and Titus), he made another journey to the Aegean area and visited Crete, Nicopolis (Tit

1:5), Ephesus (1 Tim 1:18), Macedonia (1 Tim 1:3), Troas (2 Tim 4:13) and Miletus (2 Tim 4:20). When he wrote 2 Tim, he was a prisoner in Rome (1:8, 16 f.; 2:9) with no one to help him at-his first trial (4:16). Though he managed to come through it safely (4:17), he knows that his martyrdom is now imminent (4:6–8). That Paul was, in fact, martyred in Rome is witnessed by a sound tradition going back to Saint Clement, who was bishop of Rome from A.D. 88 to 97, and supported by Caius, a priest in Rome under Pope Zephyrinus (A.D. 199–217) and by Tertullian (c. A.D. 200). The date set by Eusebius, the fourteenth year of Nero, i.e., A.D. 67, and followed by Jerome, is generally accepted as correct, in the absence of evidence to the contrary.

THE PASTORAL EPISTLES

The two letters to Timothy and that to Titus are called the pastoral epistles because, as the Muratorian Canon already indicated, their purpose was "to set in order the discipline of the church." Directed to those left in charge of communities and districts embraced by their authority, the letters differ from Paul's major ones which were addressed to the communities as such. If, from the point of view of Pauline theology, the pastorals do not reach the peaks to which Colossians and Ephesians have lifted us, it must justly be said that the author's scope here is not the same. He is concerned principally with: (1) "sound teaching," i.e., the duty of his collaborators to measure any new doctrine by the standard of its apostolic authority; (2) "good works," that is, the duty of the Christian, and especially of the cleric, to let his life bear fruit in works of piety and charity; (3) the regulation of the liturgy. The letters are of special interest for the constitution of the Church—the role of presbyters, bishops, and deacons, and the very transmission of apostolic authority to men like Timothy and Titus. Limited by space, we shall concentrate our analysis upon a passage capital for the Christian life: 1 Tim 2:1–7. But because the authenticity of the pastorals is a hotly disputed question and is denied by many scholars, a word about this is in order.

THE AUTHENTICITY OF THE PASTORALS[1]

From the second till the nineteenth century the pastorals were universally held to have as their author Paul the Apostle, whose name and title appear at the head of each letter. The German scholars

---

[1] For a more extended treatment of this question than is possible here, the student should read J. N. D. Kelly, *The Pastoral Epistles* (New York: Harper & Row, 1964), 1–36, an analysis that basically agrees with ours. For the alternative view see Feine-Behm-Kümmel, *Introduction to the New Testament* (Nashville: Abingdon, 1966), 258–272.

Schmidt, Schleiermacher and Eichorn in the early nineteenth century questioned their authenticity on linguistic and stylistic grounds—this was the era when liberal criticism sought to determine authenticity on philological grounds, i.e., through the methods of internal criticism. By the end of the nineteenth century, the German critics had largely rejected the pastorals as Pauline, and after P. N. Harrison's study in 1921, English and American scholars began to follow suit. Besides the earlier linguistic arguments (which we shall discuss), objections were raised on other grounds: (1) The type of false teaching condemned was really a second-century gnosis. This argument has lost weight today, and most scholars incline to see in the teaching a gnosticizing Judaism (1 Tim 1:7; Tit 1:10, 14 f.; 3:9) similar to that in Col (2:16 ff.). (2) The organization of the Church appeared too advanced, especially regarding the episcopacy and tradition, for the letters to have been written in 66–67. This objection too is losing ground, as more scholars are finding evidence that the Church's organization, like that of Jewish groups such as the Qumran community, was structured with considerable complexity under men who had a tradition-bearing authority, from the very beginning.[2] (3) The doctrine of the pastorals seems out of harmony with that of the other epistles. The Law now appears good (1 Tim 1:8), good works are stressed (passim), and faith is equated with orthodox doctrine; there is scarcely a mention of the cross, of the conflict between flesh and spirit, of the Body of Christ; the Parousia does not get the same attention. These arguments are stronger than the preceding, but turn out to be deceptive for neglecting to explain the many passages clearly "Pauline" and overlooking the fact that if one compares Romans or even 1 Cor with Thessalonians, one would find an equally incredible evolution of thought—for example, where is the mention of the cross in either Thessalonians or Philemon? The importance of good works, the value of the Law, the insistence on apostolic tradition and orthodoxy—all these can be found in the major epistles. The Body imagery for the Church does not appear, but the "Temple" imagery does—it is more fitting for the author's reflections on the liturgy. We must not imprison Paul in the letters critics admit he has written and exclude the possibility of his further development. He is now writing as an old man, his concern is

---

[2]The institution of overseers or superintendents in Timothy and Titus is virtually identical with the Essene institution of the *mebaqqerim*. With this discovery in the Qumran documents falls one of the major objections to the first-century dating of the pastoral epistles. Cf. R. E. Brown, "Ecumenism and New Testament Research," *New Testament Essays* (Milwaukee: Bruce, 1965). W. F. Albright, *From the Stone-Age to Christianity*, 2 ed. (N.Y.: Doubleday Anchor, 1957), 23. Actually, however, the hierarchical structure in the pastorals is much looser than what we observe in the letters of Ignatius of Antioch (c. 110 A.D.) and is an additional argument for dating the pastorals in the first rather than in the second century. Cf. Kelly, 14 f.

engaged by a distinct type of problem, heterodoxy externally and pastoral care internally. Why should a new emphasis not appear as he .directs his attention to these specific problems?

The only argument that still has some force is that of the style and vocabulary. This will not be so evident to the English reader perhaps, but it is quite noticeable in the Greek. His style is drier, it lacks the variety, the vividness, the excitability of the earlier letters. Vocabulary-wise, out of the 902 words in these three letters, 306, or one out of three, are not found elsewhere in Saint Paul. Whereas Paul's Greek in the other letters is the popular or *koinē* Greek, the pastorals have a much more literary tone.

Yet even these arguments have their limitations. Some of the new words are from root words which Paul uses elsewhere in a different form (verb instead of noun, adverb instead of adjective, etc.). Some of the new words were common and current in Paul's day and could easily be picked up and used by anyone. We have experience today of how easily new, technical terms enter our vocabulary unconsciously: automation, introversion, data-processing, updating, booster, public-image. Although Paul's world did not evolve as rapidly as ours, it is an established fact, even in the earlier letters, that whenever Paul introduced a subject hitherto untreated, the proportion of new words he uses increases accordingly. Thus in 1 Cor, of the 310 new words, 200 appear in those sections in which he treats a special subject; in Romans, of 250 proper words, 110 are found in 82 lines which treat new topics. To answer his adversaries or his questioners, Paul has to use their language. Now in the pastorals, many new problems are treated (the status of widows, the hierarchy, the virtues of a bishop, the new heretics—with their vocabularly, which evokes the Christian antonyms!). Moreover, the letters are not major treatises written to be publicly read in the Christian assembly, but personal letters addressed to the heads of these communities and treating specific topics. Account too must be taken of Paul's age. Plato's last years left a noticeable stamp on his style. Discussing new problems with disciples who already know the basic elements of his teaching, the aged Plato is more dogmatic; his style has lost its taste for eloquence, and gained more for precision, stereotyped formulas and even technical terms, with a surprising use of rare words! Students of literature come to similar conclusions when they compare the late "C" text of William Langland's *Piers Plowman* with his earlier "A" and "B" texts.

These considerations weaken the case against Pauline authenticity. If, moreover, Paul made use of a secretary, as we know he did with Galatians, many of the remaining problems vanish. Could this have been Saint Luke, companion of his last days (2 Tim 4:11)? There are several indications that make this hypothesis probable: (1) the repeated use of medical terms (besides the repeated use of "healthful teaching," see 1 Tim 4:2; 6:4; 2 Tim 2:17; 4:3); (2) a considerable number of words common to Luke and the pastorals; (3) hymn fragments not unlike those found in Lk 1–2; (4) the word *savior* applied to God the Father (Lk 1:57).

To this internal evidence comes the unanimous witness of an unbroken tradition attributing the letters to Paul. The earliest Christian literature cites the pastorals as often as the other Pauline letters. 2 Pet 3:15 seems to refer explicitly to 1 Tim 1:16. 1 and 2 Clement have numerous parallels with Paul's letters to Timothy and Titus, and so do Polycarp, the Letter of Barnabas, the Shepherd of Hermas. And the Egerton papyrus, discovered in 1934 and dating from around 150, cites explicitly 2 Tim 2:19. If these citations are given without the mention of Paul's name, we do know that the Muratorian canon classified the pastorals among the Pauline writings and Saint Irenaeus, around A.D. 185, explicitly attributes to Paul several citations from these letters (*Adv. Haer*, 2:14; 3:3, 14) and so does Tertullian (*De Praescript.*, 6).

It is impossible of course in historical matters of this kind to attain a mathematical certitude; and it should be pointed out that even conservative exegetes in studying the theology of Paul use the pastorals with a prudent reserve. Nevertheless there is, we think, sufficient weight to make the balance of probability swing in favor of the Pauline authenticity. [3]

The letters were written in the following order: 1 Tim, Tit, and then 2 Tim.

For analysis we shall limit ourselves to one text of the pastorals: 1 Tim 2:1–7. In selecting this text in preference to any other, we were motivated by the importance which the Second Vatican Council has seen in it for the liturgical renewal, as well as by the doctrine it expresses on God's universal salvific will—a point of major theological concern in our world of soaring population and increasing consciousness of human solidarity.

OUTLINE OF 1 TIMOTHY

---

[3] The Protestant E. Earle Ellis in his survey of recent Pauline scholarship, *Paul and His Recent Interpreters* (Grand Rapids: Eerdmans, 1961), 57, concludes: "It is not likely that the question of authorship of the Pastorals will find a unanimous answer in the near future. Among those favouring their genuineness are scholars representing a considerable variation of theological viewpoints.... For a minority report this roster is not unimpressive, and, if a conjecture is to be made, it may be that the future trend will lie in their direction."

PRAYER IN CHRISTIAN LITURGY: 1 Tim 2:1–7

*¹I urge, therefore, first of all, that supplications, prayers, interces-
sions, and thanksgivings be offered for all men: ²for kings and all in
stations of authority, that we may lead a quiet and tranquil life in
perfect godliness and dignity. ³This practice is good and pleasing in the
sight of God our Savior, ⁴who wishes all men to be saved and to come to
the knowledge of the truth. ⁵For there is but one God and one Mediator
between God and men, the man Jesus Christ, ⁶who gave himself a
ransom for all. This act of witnessing was done in its proper time; ⁷for it
I have been appointed herald and apostle—I am telling the truth, I am
not lying—to teach the gentiles faith and truth.*

After a brief first chapter, which was simply a recalling of the mission
of Timothy and an urging of him to be faithful to his duty as shepherd
of the flock, Paul launches into the pastoral recommendations which
obviously were his primary purpose in writing. The *therefore* of v. 1
indicates he is returning to a subject from which he has digressed, or
better, that after an introduction, he is now "getting to the point." What
he has to say is not merely a suggestion but an urging, the strong advice
which makes the Apostle's desire a command for Timothy. And it
concerns in the first place the public worship of the Church. The
expression "first of all" parallels similar epistolary formulas of Paul's
time used to introduce the body of a letter. But here it also marks an
order of excellence and primacy. The first duty of the Church is to pray,
and the first duty of the shepherd is to organize the worship of the
Church. The Second Vactican Council confirmed this principle in a
singular way. The *Constitution on the Sacred Liturgy* gave a primacy of
excellence to the Church's public worship, and, by a series of circumstances only later seen to be providential, this declaration was also
the first to issue from the council chronologically: "Every liturgical

celebration . . . is a sacred action surpassing all others; no other action of the Church can equal its efficacy by the same title or to the same degree" (#7). "The liturgy is the summit toward which the activity of the Church is directed; at the same time it is the font from which all her power flows" (#10). The apostolic college realized this very early in Jerusalem and took steps to keep the primacy of values (Acts 6:4). Here, Timothy must realize that he is more than a teacher of the truth (1:3–7); he is above all a minister of cult.

The specific aspect of this liturgical order which Paul stresses is the prayer for all men. There are only shades of difference in meaning in the four types of prayers listed. *Supplications* (*deēseis*) are prayers occasioned by some concrete circumstances or pressing need. *Prayers* (*proseuchai*), frequently associated with *supplications* (Eph 6:18; 1 Tim 5:5), is a more general term for prayer in general. It was in answer to his disciples request for a formula of prayer that Jesus taught them the "Our Father," the Lord's Prayer (Lk 11:1 f.). *Intercessions* comes from a verb used to describe the favor a subject enjoys in being admitted to the presence of his king, so as to present a petition. For the Christian this means to beseech the King of Ages, whom Paul has mentioned above (1:17). Finally, *thanksgivings* means gratitude expressed for past benefits bestowed on those for whom prayers are offered. Chrysostom has a remark here that fits the context perfectly:

> We must give thanks to God for the good that befalls others, for example that he makes the sun to shine upon the evil and the good and sends his rain both upon the just and the unjust. Observe how he would unite and bind us together, not only by prayer but by thanksgiving. For he who is urged to thank God for his neighbor's good, is also bound to love him and be kindly disposed toward him (*P.G.* 62:531).

The listing of the four types of prayer seems to have as its chief purpose to stress the intensity with which such appeals should be made, and the multiplication of them in the Church's worship. Saint Thomas notes in passing how the prayer formulas of the Roman Mass illustrate the four kinds of prayers here mentioned: "Almighty, eternal God (the lifting up of the mind, which is prayer), who have given such a benefit to the Church (thanksgiving), grant, we beseech you (supplication) . . . through our Lord (intercession). . . ."

The stress of this verse, however, like that of the whole passage, falls on the words, *for all men*. Jesus had prescribed that his disciples pray in common (Mt 18:19), and we know that the first Christians considered prayer for one another and for the Church a sacred duty (Acts 12:5; Jas 5:14 f.). This was not in itself difficult and sprang spontaneously, as it were, from the Jewish soul schooled in the value of intercessory prayer. But Jesus had also told his disciples to pray for their *enemies* (Mt 5:44), and the Church could never forget that he himself had done so as he was dying on the cross (Lk 23:34), thus fulfilling the prophecy of the suffering Servant (Is 53:12). The Christian's prayer must extend as far as his charity must extend (Mt 5:44). From such prayer, remarks Chrysostom, two advantages result:

> First, hatred toward those who are without is done away with; for no one can feel hatred toward those for whom he prays; and they again are made better by the prayers that are offered for them and by losing their ferocious disposition toward us. For nothing is so apt to draw men under teaching, as to love and be loved. Think what it was for those who persecuted, scourged, banished and slaughtered the Christians, to hear that those whom they treated so barbarously offered fervent prayers to God for them. Observe how he wishes a Christian to be superior to all ill treatment (*P.G.* 62:529).

However difficult it may be, therefore, to go beyond the limits of self and community, this prayer for *all* men, enemies included, is the touchstone of genuine Christianity. Paul himself could never forget the day he had witnessed and approved the stoning of Stephen, and heard the first Christian martyr pray for him (Acts 7:58–60).

Among the beneficiaries of these prayers, special mention is made of those constituted in authority, and first of all, of *kings* (v. 2). The use of the plural and the absence of the Greek article show that Paul is not thinking of any regent in particular but of the whole class. This would apply primarily to the emperor (*basileus* was his common title in the East), and if our letter is rightly dated, this would specifically mean Nero. But it would also apply to local monarchs to whom were delegated considerable powers in Roman times. The converted pagan would find it new to learn to pray *for* the emperor and not *to* him.

And all those in stations of authority (2:2). The Greek expression was a common one for any "dignitary" (cf. 1 Cor 2:1; Rom 13:1; 2 Mac 3:11), no matter to what branch of government he belonged, or whether he held a high station or a menial one. This text is a most interesting one because it raises the whole question of the Church's attitude toward the state. In the theocracy of ancient Israel the problem had a simple solution because, in spite of abuses, there was a basically understood unity of religion and public life. In the exile, however, new problems were raised: were the Jews to carry on an active, political resistance against their captors, or were they to promote the welfare of the community in the hopes thereby to preserve their religious freedom and one day merit repatriation? Jeremiah 29:7 answered the question thus: "Promote the welfare of the city to which I have exiled you; *pray for it to the Lord*, for upon its welfare depends your own" (cf. also Bar 1:10–12; Ezr 6:10). Inscriptions and the writings of Philo and Josephus confirm this attitude among the Jews and the practice of prayer for public authorities.

Jesus had said to render to Caesar the things that are Caesar's (Mk 12:13–17), and Paul himself, who by and large came off well at the hands of his Roman judges (Acts, *passim*), could write in his letter to the Romans a theology of obedience to legitimate authority as an obedience to God (Rom 13:1–7; cf. Jn 19:11; 1 Pet 2:13 f.). If our present text echoes something of the prophecy of Mk 13:9 and reveals a certain anxiety in the face of persecution, the principle of praying for all authorities stands as firm as ever. It is an essential element of Christian worship for all times and circumstances. This text of Saint Paul had a profound effect on the liturgy of the Church from the earliest times, and a gloss quotes the fourth-century Ambrosiaster thus: "This prescription is for the Church; *given by the Teacher of the Gentiles, it is followed by our priests*, that they should make supplications for all, praying for the rulers of this world. . . ." In later times these prayers came to be called the "common prayer" or the "prayer of the faithful." Having been kept in the prayers of the Good Friday liturgy, they are now restored and extended to the Mass throughout the year:

> Especially on Sundays and feasts of obligation, there is to be restored after the Gospel and the homily, the "common prayer" or "the prayer of the faithful." By this prayer, in which the people are to take part, intercessions will be made for holy Church, for the civil authorities, for those oppressed by various needs, for all mankind, and for the salvation of the entire world (*Constitution on the Sacred Liturgy*, #53, giving as reference our 1 Tim 2:1–2).

This prayer, if it includes persecutors, is not wholly disinterested. The great good it seeks is in the first place *peace*, the needed calm and tranquillity without war and persecution, so that the Church may lead its life without harassment (cf. Acts 24:2; Est 3:13). It is the prayer of the fourth Sunday after Pentecost: "Grant, we beseech you, O Lord, that the world's course of events be guided by your ordering in peace for our sake, that your Church may enjoy a tranquil devotedness to you."

The life the Church desires is one that is led *in perfect godliness and dignity* (2:2). The word *eusebeia*, sometimes translated "piety," is a common Greek term referring either to the fulfilling of a cultic obligations or the leading of a life pleasing to God. Saint Paul, who uses it only in the pastorals, seems to have considered it of exceptional importance in his last years. It corresponds to the Hebrew *hesed* meaning devotion to the service of God, implying gratitude, fidelity and love (Jer 2:2), and to the "fear of God," that biblical attitude of reverence and awe before the transcendent holiness of Yahweh. The Septuagint translators of Proverbs used the adjective "pious" (*eusebēs*) as an equivalent of "just" (Prov 12:12), and Sirach describes the pious man as merciful and not self-seeking (Sir 37:12), prudent in his conversations (37:11), a hater of lying (23:12), unaffected by calumny (28:22). Paul's notion of *piety* assumes all this and goes on to affirm that it is a life that is born from contemplating the Mystery of God (1 Tim 3:16). It bears fruit in good works which are like cultic offerings, pleasing to God.

Obviously, the Pauline *eusebeia* has nothing to do with the effeminate, milk-toast "edifying" religiosity which has come to be associated with the modern term "piety." Hence in the translation we have preferred "godliness" as a more virile modern equivalent.

With this notion of virile devotedness is associated a second term which we have rendered *dignity*. The term conveys a triple notion of respect, interior righteousness, and especially the external propriety which flows from the godly life. There is thought here probably of the respect for the Church that such a way of life will win from civil authorities—the faith make Christians better citizens! "In godliness and dignity" is the Hellenistic counterpart of the Hebrew "in holiness and justice" (Lk 1:75).

This practice of prayer for all men and especially authorities is good—in the strong sense of the Greek *kalos*—beautiful to behold, excellent, an outstanding work of charity. It is *pleasing* before God (2:3). The terms again evoke a cultic situation like the offering of a pleasing and acceptable sacrifice. Here, then, the faithful through their intercessory prayer for all men, fulfill their office of royal priesthood. "The priest is the common father, as it were, of all the world; it is proper therefore, that he should care for all, even as God, whom he serves" (Chrysostom, *P.G.* 62:529). Such prayer is pleasing to God because God himself is Savior (cf. 1:1) and *wishes all men to be saved* (v. 4). The "all" is meant to contrast slightly with "our Savior"—that is, if he has saved us, our gratitude should express itself by entering into his own universal salvific will. *To be saved* specifies the formal object of the divine will, *to come to the knowledge of the truth* the intermediate means. *Epignōsis*, the Greek word for knowledge here, is a technical word used by Paul frequently. It always directs attention to the object known. In the pastorals this is repeatedly "the truth" (2 Tim 2:25; 3:7; Tit 1:1), emphasizing the intellectual; or rather, the genuine and substantial nature of the Christian revelation in contrast to what is sham. At any rate, salvation, like eternal life in Saint John (Jn 17:3), is defined in terms of knowing God (1 Cor 1:21) and what he has revealed, i.e., his Son.

Very early in the history of exegesis the Fathers perceived a theological problem raised by this text: if God wills all men to be saved and not all men are saved, is this not a reflection either upon: (1) the omnipotence of his will, or (2) the universality of his will? Tertullian sought a way out by specifying *men* as "those whom he adopted" (*De Or.*, 4)—obviously contrary to the text which says God wishes *all* men to be saved. Augustine sought to render justice to the *all* by saying that the whole human race somehow exists in those who are saved (*De corr. et gratia*, 44). The Greek Fathers stood closer to the thought of Paul and understood the verb *thelei* ("wishes") of a real will-act extending to all men. This will is, however, *antecedent*. "There is a principal and antecedent will. There is also another. The first is that those who have sinned perish not; the second is that those who have become evil perish."[4] John Damascene follows with theological precision, applying to our text: "God wills by a primary and antecedent will that all be saved. . . . This primary will is called antecedent and it marks God's desire. The cause of this will is in God. The other will is called consequent; it is only a permission, and it has its roots in our acts."[5] This is the explanation ultimately adopted by Saint Thomas Aquinas. The semantics of the verb *thelō*, used here, suggest a similar sense. The verb, a favorite of Paul's (used more than sixty times) is frequently employed for a desire of the heart, a strong and sincere wish, whereas *boulomai* is used for an absolute determination, a fixed and irreversible decision (2:8; 5:14). Matthew uses *thelō*, as Paul does here, to translate our Lord's sad recognition that his own will to gather the children of Jerusalem like a hen her chicks, has not succeeded (Mt 23:37). Yet there are other divine decrees that are absolutely unconditioned by man's will (using *boulomai*, Lk 10:22; 1 Cor 12:11). The awesome reality, then, behind Paul's use of *thelei* here is this: here is a will of God *whose accomplishment depends on the cooperation of man*. If it did not, what use would there be in Paul's pleading for the prayers of the Church? The "prayer of the faithful" is not therefore mere gesture. It is a real contributing factor in God's plan for the salvation of the world!

In vv. 5 and 6 Paul seeks to establish the theological grounds for what he has just said on the universal salvific will. The basic foundation of the universality of salvation is the unicity of God. The *one God* (2:5) squares off against the *all men* of the preceding verse. Paul takes the argument, so dear to the Jews (the *Shema*: "Hear, O Israel, the Lord thy God is one God . . .") and its consequence—there *are* no other gods, no local divinities so prized by the Gentile world—and draws still another

---

[4]Chrysostom on *Eph. P.G.* 62:13; cf. on *Acts, P.G.* 61:144.
[5]*De Fide Orth.* 2:29; *P.G.* 94:969.

conclusion—then God is the God of the Gentiles as well as of the Jews (cf. Rom 3:29 f.; Eph 3:4–21; 4:6; 1 Cor 8:4–6). This religious conception in turn affects the Christian view of the race—it is one (cf. Eph 4:6; Acts 17:26). Accordingly, there can be no plurality of mediators. Obviously national priesthoods of local divinities are excluded, but now with the appearance in the flesh of God's only Son, there is no longer place for the mediatorship of Moses (Gal 3:19) or of any Jewish high priest (Heb 8:6; 9:15; 12:24) nor of any angel (Col 2:18; Heb 2:16). The single mediator is Jesus Christ, himself man. The explicit mention of the humanity of Christ is perhaps a reaction to a docetic tendency already appearing in the Church. At any rate the use of *anthrōpos* evokes the role of Christ as Second Adam, a central conception of Pauline Christology (Rom 5:15; 1 Cor 15:47; Phil 2:7 f.). Saint Irenaeus (*Adv. Haer.*, 4:20) says concisely, "he shows God to men and men to God."

The humanity of Christ is, however, never viewed statically in Paul. The *man* Jesus Christ *gave* himself a ransom for all (2:6). Here is introduced the second motive for universal prayer, Christ's self-sacrifice for all. He gave himself as a *ransom*. The idea has entered Paul's theology from Mk 10:45. "The Son of Man has not come to be served but to serve and to give his life as a ransom for many." From this text Paul has taken the term "ransom for" (*lytron anti*) and forged it into a single term, *antilytron*. By so doing, he can and does introduce before the word "all" a new preposition, *hyper*, meaning "for." This semantic detail may seem a bit of uselessly technical erudition, but it is theologically significant. For the Markan statement could be taken to mean a substitution, *anti* often having the meaning "in place of" (Mt 2:22; Lk 11:11). In this sense Christ would have substituted himself for the many, taking upon himself the punishment due to all. However, in using *hyper* Paul heads off this interpretation and gives precision as to the manner in which this "ransom" was effected: Christ offered himself *for men's sake* and not in place of them. The idea of redemption as a substitution is foreign to the text and to the overall theology of St. Paul. Even when the Apostle says Christ became sin (2 Cor 5:21) or a curse (Gal 3:13), it is always *hyper hēmōn*, "for our sake," and so it is too in those passages in which the supreme motive of the sacrifice is his love for us (Gal 2:20; Rom 5:8; Eph 5:2).

Now follows an elliptical phrase, literally, *the witnessing at the proper time* (2:6). This is best taken as meaning that the action of Christ in offering himself for men was, at a moment of time chosen by God, the supreme witness of God's will to save (as in 6:13 and Jn 18:37; 1 Pet 1:11).

But this once-for-all testimony is now transmitted to men through the apostolic testimony, the preaching of the gospel. For this Paul has been constituted a herald (2:7). The title *kēryx* (from which we get our term *kerygmatic*) is important for understanding the role of preaching in Paul's conception of the divine plan. In the Eleusinian mystery religions, the *kēryx* was a sacred officer, named for life. In Homeric times, he was an officer of the royal court, enjoying friendly relations with the king and entertaining his guests. Later the heralds were servants of the state and were recruited among the poor. All that was needed was a good voice to call a public assembly or, Paul Revere style, to announce a call to arms. In classical times he served as a diplomatic messenger, not having the rank of ambassador but simply serving as a "hot-line" for his master to whomever he might be sent. His job was to deliver the message in its integrity, nothing more, nothing less. For this reason, the *kēryx* enjoyed diplomatic immunity everywhere, and was considered to be under the protection of the god of any locality where he appeared. To dishonor him was considered an act of impiety which would bring down the wrath of the gods. The herald also had a role to play in public worship: he began the prayers before the people assembled, prayed for the common good, got everything ready for the sacrifice. Acting as speaker for the assembled community, he presented to the divinity the prayers and requests of men. At Ephesus the sacred herald was charged with reciting litanies and prayers during the sacrifice or public assemblies. Finally the herald at times is said to bring to men the message of the gods.[6] It is easy to see how fitting this image is for the role of the apostle—he is a herald of the King of Ages (1:17) charged with transmitting the good news in its integrity to those to whom it is destined, a function of faithful and totally obedient service, but also a religious function of the highest sort. Those to whom he is to transmit the message, however, are the Gentiles, all men. This witnessing, as Saint Thomas notes, completes the picture of God's salvific will:

> Above he said that God wishes all men to be saved, and he proved this on the part of God, who is the one God of all, and on the part of Christ, who is the one Mediator of all. Here he proves the same point on the part of the witnessing.

"Paul's ministry is the final argument for the universality of salvation" (C. Spicq).

There is no better text for showing the contemporary relevance of these few lines of Saint Paul than the opening paragraphs of the *Constitution on the Sacred Liturgy*. One of the four aims the Council proposed for itself was "to strengthen whatever can help to call the

---

[6]G. Friedrich, *Th. Woert.*, art. *kēryx*.

whole of mankind into the household of the Church." There follows a sentence of jolting impact: "The council *therefore* sees particularly cogent reasons for undertaking the reform and promotion of the sacred *liturgy*" (#1). The Church's conviction of the link between her mission of universal salvation and her own liturgical practice has never before been so strongly stated—if not by Saint Paul in 1 Tim 2:1–7, a text to which the Constitution refers three times, twice in the first five paragraphs. If the liturgy "is the outstanding means whereby the faithful may express in their lives, and manifest to others, the mystery of Christ and the real nature of the true Church," (#2), the common prayer for all men expresses the universality of God's love, his unicity, the value of Christ's sacrifice for all, and the awesome responsibility laid upon the contemporary Church (and that means all of us) to exercise the royal priesthood by interceding for the grace of salvation and bearing it to all men.

OUTLINE OF THE LETTER TO TITUS

OUTLINE OF 2 TIMOTHY

TO THE STUDENT:
A CONCLUDING NOTE FROM THE AUTHOR

At the end of this long and at times technical study, you will know for yourself whether the careful and detailed analysis you have made of the key Pauline texts has been worth the effort. It was obviously not possible to treat all portions of the letters of the Apostle with equal intensity, but the texts were chosen in the hope that your study of them would leave you with an appreciation of the depth of Pauline thought as well as some understanding of Paul's own doctrinal evolution. (The Epistle to the Hebrews was not considered, as the majority of modern scholars agree that it is not directly from the hand of Paul.)

If you feel at this point the need to synthesize all that you have assimilated, this book has achieved one of its purposes, and no better step could be taken now than to read one of those books on Pauline theology recommended in the bibliography. If you have written a paper developing some theme of the Apostle's thought, you will already have made an initial synthesis of your own in one area of this vast universe. The way is now open for group discussion of Paul's favorite themes and of the major steps in his doctrinal evolution. But the work of synthesis lies beyond the scope of this textbook. The present work has been an attempt, through a close study of the text, to open up to you what we might call the Pauline galaxy. It has given you a rough map with a few points of reference. The immensity that remains is there for you to explore.

BIBLIOGRAPHY

I. THE LIFE OF PAUL

(The following books vary considerably in the degree of their agreement with the conclusions of modern critical Pauline studies. Some are listed more with a view to conveying an idea of Paul's spiritual experience and also with an eye to the likelihood of their availability. In the critical questions, the student should keep in mind the observations of this text book.)

Blenkinsopp, J. *Jesus is Lord* (New York: Paulist, 1965).

Bornkamm, G. *Paul* (New York: Harper & Row, 1970). See review by C. H. Giblin, *CBQ* 34 (1972), 349–351.

Daniel-Rops, H. *Saint Paul, Apostle of Nations,* tr. Jex Martin (Chicago: Fides, 1953).

George, R. E., *Saint Paul, Envoy of Grace* (Robert Sencourt). (New York: Sheed & Ward, 1948).

Giordani, Igino. *St. Paul, Apostle and Martyr* (New York: Macmillan, 1946).

Harrington, J. *Paul of Tarsus* (Cleveland: World Publishing, 1961).

Holzner, J. *Paul of Tarsus,* tr. Rev. F. C. Eckhoff (St. Louis-London: B. Herder, 1944).

Kelso, J. L. *An Archaeologist Follows the Apostle Paul* (Waco: Word Books, 1970).

Knox, J. *Chapters in a Life of Paul* (Nashville: Abingdon, 1950).

Kinsey, R. S. *With Paul in Greece* (Nashville: Abingdon, 1957).

von Loewenich, W. *Paul, His Life and Work* (London: Oliver and Boyd, 1960).

Longenecker, R. *The Ministry and Message of Paul* (Grand Rapids: Zondervan, 1971).

Metzger, H. *St. Paul's Journeys in the Greek Orient* (New York: Philosophical Library, 1955).

Morton, H. C. V. *In the Steps of Saint Paul* (London: Rich & Cowan, 1936).

Moe, O. *The Apostle Paul* (Grand Rapids: Baker, 1950).

Macartney, C. E. *Paul the Man* (Westwood, N.J.: F. H. Revell, 1961).

Nock, A. D. *Saint Paul* (New York: Harper & Row, 1963).

Ogg, G. *The Chronology of the Life of Paul* (London: Epworth, 1968).

Penna, A. *St. Paul the Apostle* (New York: St. Paul Publications, 1960).

Perez de Urbel, J. *Saint Paul, the Apostle of the Gentiles,* tr. P. Barrett (Westminster, Md.: Newman, 1956).

Pollock, J. *The Apostle: A Life of Paul* (Garden City: Doubleday, 1969).

Prat, F. *Saint Paul* (New York: Benziger, 1928).

Ricciotti, G. *Paul the Apostle,* tr. A. Zizzamia (Milwaukee: Bruce, 1953).

Robinson, B. W. *The Life of Paul* (U. of Chicago Press, 1908).

Tresmontant, C. *St. Paul and the Mystery of Christ,* tr. D. Attwater (New York: Harper, 1957).

II. PAUL'S LETTERS AND THEOLOGY

(General introductions or specialized studies. No attempt is made to list the commentaries on the letters. * = appropriate for undergraduate level.)

*Ahern, B. *New Horizons* (Notre Dame: Fides, 1963).

*Amiot, F. *The Key Concepts of St. Paul* (New York: Herder & Herder, 1962).

*Augrain, C. *Paul, Master of the Spiritual Life* 2, vols. (Staten Island: Alba House, 1967).

*Barclay, W. *The Mind of St. Paul* (London: Collins Fontana Books, 1958).

Beardslee, W. A. *Human Achievement and Divine Vocation in the Message of Paul* (Naperville: Allenson, 1961).

*Best, E. *One Body in Christ* (London: S.P.C.K., 1955).

*Bouttier, M. *Christianity According to Paul* (Naperville: Allenson, 1966).

*Brox, N. *Understanding the Message of Paul* (U. of Notre Dame Press, 1968).

*Brunot, A. *Saint Paul and His Message* (New York: Hawthorn, 1959).

*Bullough, S. *Saint Paul and the Apostolic Writings* (Westminster, Md.: Newman, 1950).

Cerfaux, L. *Christ in the Theology of St. Paul* (New York: Herder & Herder, 1959).

——— *The Christian in the Theology of St. Paul* (New York: Herder & Herder, 1967).

——— *The Church in the Theology of St. Paul* (New York: Herder & Herder, 1959).

*——— *The Spiritual Journey of St. Paul* (New York: Sheed & Ward, 1968).

Corriveau, R. *The Liturgy of Life* (Paris: Desclee, 1970).

Dahl, M. E. *The Resurrection of the Body* (London: SCM, 1962).

Davies, W. D. *Paul and Rabbinic Judaism* (London: S.P.C.K., 1958).

*Dibelius, M. and Kümmel, W. *Paul* (Philadelphia: Westminster Press, 1953).

*Dodd, C. H. *The Meaning of Paul for Today* (Cleveland: World Publishing Co., 1957).

*Ellis, E. E. *Paul and His Recent Interpreters* (Grand Rapids: Eerdmans, 1961).

——— *Paul's Use of the Old Testament* (London: Oliver & Boyd, 1957).

*Fitzmyer, J. A. *Pauline Theology: A Brief Sketch* (Englewood Cliffs, N.J.: Prentice-Hall, 1967).

Furnish, V. P. *Theology and Ethics in Paul* (Nashville: Abingdon, 1968).

Gale, H. M. *The Use of Analogy in Paul* (Philadelphia: Westminster Press, 1964).

Gibbs, J. G. *Creation and Redemption* (Leiden: Brill, 1971).

*Giblin, C. H. *In Hope of God's Glory* (New York: Herder & Herder, 1970).

*Grassi, J. *A World to Win* (Maryknoll, 1970).

*Grossouw, W. *In Christ: A Sketch of the Theology of St. Paul* (Westminster, Md.: Newman, 1952).

*Haughton, R. *Paul and the World's Most Famous Letters* (Nashville: Abingdon, 1970).

Hester, J. D. *Paul's Concept of Inheritance* (London: Oliver & Boyd, 1968).

*Hunt, E. W. *Portrait of Paul* (London: Mowbray, 1968).

Hunter, A. M. *Paul and His Predecessors* (London: SCM, 1961).

*——— *Interpreting Paul's Gospel* (Philadelphia: Westminster Press, 1955).

*——— *The Gospel According to Paul* (Philadelphia: Westminster Press, 1967).

Jewett, R. *Paul's Anthropological Terms* (Leiden: Brill, 1971).

*Kallas, J. G. *The Story of Paul* (Minneapolis: Augsburg, 1966).

*——— *The Satan-ward View* (Philadelphia: Westminster Press, 1966).

*Knox, R. A. *St. Paul's Gospel* (New York: Sheed & Ward, 1950).

Longenecker, R. N. *Paul, Apostle of Liberty* (New York: Harper & Row, 1964).

Luccock, H. A. *Preaching Values in the Epistles of Paul* (New York: Harper & Bros., 1959).

Mitton, C. L. *The Formation of the Pauline Corpus of Letters* (London: Epworth, 1955).

Montague, G. T. *Growth in Christ* (Fribourg, Switz.: St. Paul Press, 1961).

*——— *Maturing in Christ* (Milwaukee: Bruce, 1964).

*——— *Building Christ's Body* (Chicago: Franciscan Herald Press, 1975).

*——— *The Holy Spirit: Growth of a Biblical Tradition* (New York: Paulist Press, 1976).

Munck, J. *Paul and the Salvation of Mankind* (Richmond, Va.: John Knox Press, 1959).

Murphy-O'Connor, J. *Paul on Preaching* (New York: Sheed & Ward, 1963).

Nickle, K. F. *The Collection: A Study in Paul's Strategy* (Naperville: Allenson, 1966).

Pathrapankal, J. *Metanoia, Faith, Covenant* (Bangalore: Dharmaram College, 1971).

Pfitzner, V. C. *Paul and the Agon Motif: Traditional Athletic Imagery in the Pauline Literature* (Leinden: Brill, 1967).

Prat, F. *The Theology of St. Paul*, 2 vols. (Westminster, Md.: Newman, 1950).

Rigaux, B. *The Letters of St. Paul* (Chicago: Franciscan Herald Press, 1968).

Robinson, J. A. T. *The Body* (London: SCM, 1952).

Roetzel, C. J. *Judgement in the Community: A Study of the Relationship Between Eschatology and Ecclesiology in Paul* (Leiden: Brill, 1972).

Russell, K. C. *Slavery as Reality and Metaphor in the Pauline Letters* (Rome: Catholic Book Agency, 1968).

Sandmel, S. *The Genius of Paul* (New York: Schocken, 1970). A Jewish theologian's view of Paul.

Schmitals, W. *Paul and James* (Naperville: Allenson, 1965).

——— *Paul and the Gnostics*, tr. J. E. Steely (Nashville: Abingdon, 1972).

Schnackenburg, R. *Baptism in the Thought of St. Paul* (New York: Herder & Herder, 1964).

Schoeps, H. J. *Paul: The Theology of the Apostle in the Light of Jewish Religious History* (London: Lutterworth Press, 1961).

Schweitzer, A. *The Mysticism of Paul the Apostle* (New York: Seabury, 1931).

——— *Paul and His Interpreters* (London: Adam & Charles Black, 1948).

Scroggs, R. *The Last Adam* (Philadelphia: Fortress Press, 1966).

*Selby, D.J. *Toward Understanding St. Paul* (Englewood Cliffs, N.J.: Prentice Hall, 1962).

Shedd, R. P. *Man in Community: A Study of St. Paul's Application of O.T. and Early Jewish Conceptions of Human Solidarity* (London: Epworth, 1958; Grand Rapids: Eerdmans, 1964).

Shires, H. M. *The Eschatology of Paul in the Light of Modern Scholarship* (Philadelphia: Westminster, 1966).

*Spicq, C. *The Trinity and our Moral Life According to St. Paul*, tr. Sr. M. Aquinas (Westminster, Md.: Newman, 1963).

*———— *Agape in the New Testament* (St. Louis: B. Herder, 1965).

Stanley, D. M. *Christ's Resurrection in Pauline Soteriology* (Rome: Pontifical Biblical Institute, 1961).

*———— *Boasting in the Lord: The Phenomenon of Prayer in Saint Paul* (New York: Paulist Press, 1973).

Tannehill, R. C. *Dying and Rising with Christ* (Berlin: Töpelmann, 1966).

Tresmontant, C. *Saint Paul and the Mystery of Christ* (New York: Harper, 1957).

van Unnik, W. C. *Tarsus or Jerusalem: The City of Paul's Youth* (London: Epworth, 1962).

Whiteley, D. E. H. *The Theology of St. Paul* (Philadelphia: Fortress Press, 1964).

*Wikenhauser, A. *New Testament Introduction* (New York: Herder & Herder, 1958).

*———— *Pauline Mysticism* (New York: Herder & Herder, 1960).

*Wiles, M. F. *The Divine Apostle* (Cambridge U. Press, 1967).

GLOSSARY

agraphon: a saying of Jesus unrecorded in the gospels but expressed or alluded to elsewhere (e.g., Acts 20:35).

apocalyptic: highly imaginative or visionary description of coming events, particularly of the final times. As a literary genre, it appears in later Judaism, with some of its elements borrowed from Persian motifs and tailored to the basic Jewish beliefs. In the O.T., the genre appears to a greater or lesser degree in the prophets (esp. Joel, Zechariah, Daniel); in the N.T., the gospel descriptions of the final times (Mk 13 and par) and the book of the Apocalypse.

authenticity, canonical: the quality by which a work is recognized as belonging to the canon of the inspired scriptures.

authenticity, literary: the quality by which a work is recognized as belonging to the author whose name it bears either within the text or according to tradition.

charism: a visible gift of the Holy Spirit granted to certain members of the Christian community for the upbuilding of the Church and for the sake of the rapid spread of Christianity (see esp. Rom 12 and 1 Cor 12).

crux interpretum: literally "a cross of interpreters," a particularly difficult or obscure passage.

eschatology: that which concerns the *final times*, whether this be conceived as the end of the world, the divine judgment, or the consummation of the divine plan. The Israelites were distinguished from their pagan neighbors by their eschatological hope; for Christians this hope has been fulfilled in Christ, who has ushered in "the final times in which we live" (Heb 1:2), and yet the complete consummation to which the Church looks as yet to come (return of Christ and the cosmic "regeneration") explains why there is still a strong eschatology in Christianity.

exegesis: the analysis of texts, ordinarily referring to texts of sacred Scripture. The exegete may be motivated extrinsically by faith, but his discipline itself is a human science.

genre: a literary type—as primitive history, prophecy, midrash, elegy, poetry, wisdom discourse, apocalyptic.

hapax: an expression occurring only once.

hendiadys: two coordinate terms used to express one idea, e.g., "the spirit and power" for "the Spirit's power" (1 Cor 2:4), "died and rose" for "rose from the dead" (1 Th 4:14).

kerygma: the proclamation of the "good news," demanding a conversion and commitment to Christ. Usually distinguished from *didache*, the more detailed instructions given to those already become Christians.

paradosis: tradition.

parenetic: belonging to that section of a letter in which the writer exhorts to practical action, as distinct from the more theoretical or dogmatic sections.

pericope: a given passage of Scripture, usually forming a self-contained unit.

ASSIGNMENT FOR THE SECOND
HALF OF THE SEMESTER

1. Choose one of the themes listed below, or another approved by your professor.

2. Keeping this theme in mind, read through carefully the epistles in the order given below, noting and numbering the passages which relate in some way to your chosen theme. Your professor may require you to submit these for approval or suggestions before going farther.

3. Then on each of the passages you have noted, consult the appropriate commentaries and books listed under "Bibliography—II. Paul's Letters and Theology" concerning each of the passages you have checked. For those works that do not have a line-by-line commentary, consult the list of scripture references given in the rear, and look up what the author has to say about that verse.

4. Compile your notes into an orderly essay, showing how Paul develops your chosen theme. Your principal job is to synthesize the thought. However, try as much as possible to show how Paul's thought itself develops from his earliest epistle to his last. It would thus be preferable to discuss the passages in their chronological order.

In the course of your research, some of the Pauline passages you originally selected may prove to be irrelevant, while you may discover others you had not originally noticed. Feel free to revise your choice of passages as you move ahead. Consultation of biblical dictionaries, concordances, encyclopedias, indexes to various books on St. Paul, may also prove useful.

ORDER OF THE PAULINE
EPISTLES AND TEXTS

Acts 13:16–41—Sermon at Antioch to the Jews
Acts 17:22–31—Sermon at Athens to the Greeks
1 Thessalonians
2 Thessalonians
Philippians
1 Corinthians
2 Corinthians
Galatians
Romans
Colossians
Ephesians
Philemon
1 Timothy
Titus
2 Timothy

THEMES OF THE THEOLOGY
OF SAINT PAUL

Adoption
Adoration
Angels
Antichrist
Apostolate
Ascension
Asceticism
Athletic figures
Authority
Baptism
Bishops
Blood of Christians
Body of Christ
Body of Christians
Building up
Calling
Charity
Christ (specify)
Church (specify)
Community
Confidence
Conformity
Consecration
Conscience
Consolation
Cosmos
Cross
Crucifixion
Death
Docility
Education
Eschatology
Eternal Life
Eucharist
Example
Faith
Family
Father (God as)
Fear
Fidelity
Flesh

Friendship
Fruitfulness
Fulfillment
Glorification
Glory
Grace
Heresy
Holiness
Holy Spirit (specify)
Hope
Humility
Image
Imitation
Incarnation
Individualism
Indwelling
Joy
Judgment
Justice
Justification
Knowledge
Law
Liberty
Life
Light
Liturgy
Love
Marriage
Mercy
Merit
Ministry
Mystery
Mystical Body
New Creation
Obedience
Parousia
Parents
Passion of Christ
Patience
Peace
Perfection

Perseverance
Power (of God,
  Christ)
Prayer
Praise
Preaching
Presence of God
Purity
Redemption
Resurrection
Sacraments
Sacrifice
Saints
Salvation
Sanctification
Scandal
Service
Sin
Sinner
Sonship
Spirit (specify)
Stability
Suffering
Teaching
Temple
Temptations
Thanksgiving
Time(s)
Trinity
Unity of Church
Universe
Virginity
Virtues
Vocation
Weakness
Will of God
Wisdom
Word of God
Works
Worship
Wrath of God

Subject Index

233